People before Highways

People before Highways

Boston Activists, Urban Planners, and a New Movement for City Making

Karilyn Crockett

UNIVERSITY OF MASSACHUSETTS PRESS
Amherst and Boston

ISBN 978-1-62534-297-3 (paper); 296-6 (hardcover)

Designed by Sally Nichols
Set in Minion Pro
Printed and bound by Maple Press, Inc.

Library of Congress Cataloging-in-Publication Data

Names: Crockett, Karilyn, author.
Title: People before highways / Karilyn Crockett.
Description: Amherst : University of Massachusetts Press, [2018] | Includes bibliographical
references and index.
Identifiers: LCCN 2017038236 | ISBN 9781625342973 (pbk. : alk. paper) | ISBN 9781625342966
(hardcover : alk. paper)
Subjects: LCSH: Highway planning—United States—Citizen participation. | City planning—
United States—Citizen participation | Social movements—United States.
Classification: LCC HE355.3.C58 C76 2017 | DDC 388.1/220974461—dc23
LC record available at https://lccn.loc.gov/2017038236

British Library Cataloguing-in-Publication Data
A catalogue record for this book is available from the British Library.

Contents

Preface

Toward Recovering the Intellectual (Hi)story
of an Urban Social Movement

A Note on Memory and Ethnographic Method

This is a story of land-based political struggle ultimately victorious in its key aim: the defeat of an interstate highway. Yet this book also charts how citizens mobilized their frustrations, insights, and experiences to create new forms of knowledge, authority, and policy in response to a convulsing urban landscape. This is not a traditional social history. Readers looking for a comprehensive history of the Boston antihighway movement may well be disappointed by what is offered here. It is my hope that this book points the way toward new methods for collecting and interpreting knowledge dissemination within and across activist networks.

My effort to retrieve the kaleidoscopic interplay of ideas, places, and time periods that informed and inspired the decisions of key actors within Boston's antihighway movement necessitated a discipline-blending approach. Collective memory is the scaffolding supporting this study and inviting a deeper historical encounter for readers eager to understand how lived experience travels as a type of embodied human archive. Here Boston's antihighway actors stand as conduits of multiple time periods stretching back centuries and simultaneously pointing to the future. Their memories manifest this dynamism and demand a more complex methodological framework than conventional change over time historical studies allow. I found this to be one of the most provocative and revealing findings of my study of Boston's antihighway movement and the landscapes it produced.

Within the chronicles composing this book, multiple historical moments and geographic scales are often present at once and require an expansive understanding of how varied conceptions of time and space converge and diverge in daily life. As a mode of knowing, memory, with its attendant messiness, emotional charge, and imperfection, offers a big tent for wide-ranging empirical learning and discovery. And as social vector of knowledge, memory demands reckoning with what must not be forgotten, what is emotionally significant, and what is still in the process of becoming. Cultural critic Raymond Williams offers insight on how to understand the dynamism of past time periods.

Williams argues that a reliance on "an habitual past tense" when describing culture and society obscures the ongoing processes of becoming that envelop these systems as well as our own thoughts. Williams famously described these processes of formation as "pre-emergent" and sitting within "structures of feeling" that inform individual and collective consciousness.[1] Williams identifies the struggle to effect large-scale social change as the struggle for new consciousness, new social and class relations, new modes of being.[2] Front and center in his analysis is an acknowledgment of the limitations of conceptions of time that render the *past* as fixed, known, or somehow ended as opposed to still moving.[3] Collective memory-driven social research recognizes that the past is still moving through people, within ideas, and across landscapes.

More than simply gathering old stories or sifting for "facts" to verify actors' accounts, collective memory-driven research offers a compelling pedagogy for tracing what is important to a group—its values, its fears, its mistakes, its aspirations. As a form of data, memories often telegraph the underlying ideas and values that drive our actions. And, further, memory helps trace the social and historical significance of prior events for actors themselves. In this way, *People before Highways* presents a set of narratives and ideas prioritized by antihighway activists and instructive to my own research agenda.

Antihighway activists used protests and demonstrations to conjure their own version of the future while rejecting modernism's dogmatic, technology-driven commitment to linear, forward-moving conceptions of time. For these activists, the future was tied to addressing the very present needs of local residents and sometimes past responses to those needs. The modernist version of the future presented by highway boosters was not appealing to them. The idea of progress as an uninterrupted movement away from the present to some distant time and place was deconstructed and unmasked for its not-so-subtle paternalist view that the greatest good to all was yet to come.

The antihighway leaders I interviewed are exceptional subjects not only because of their personal qualities or successes but also because of the swirl of ideas that they were successfully able to transmit to others through their organizing and public actions. They are intellectual travelers of the highest order and kindly allowed me to journey with them. In honor of these dynamic collaborations, *People before Highways* is also a story of memory retrieval, knowledge production, and the recognition that both are always derived from "collective effort (and) a series of back and forth conversations" yielding multiple meanings.[4] In this account, contemporary conversations lurch forward and back, sliding through private and public archives to tell a story that many people think they know but few actually do. The official archival sources documenting the routes of this story offer only a partial chronicle, so before you sits a collective reckoning of many. My own limited understanding and discovery process are sometimes made visible to the reader in an effort to expose not only my intellectual blind spots but also the multiple and necessary ways in which my collaborators intervened to create a narrative more representative of what their lives revealed.

My collection and analysis of more than forty ethnographic interviews (and their transcripts) completed primarily between 2010 and 2012 expose a complicated set of ideological and spatial convergences driving the behavior of the antihighway movement's key actors. I was surprised to learn that many of the movement's participants believed that fighting a highway was an exercise in futility. As one activist told me, "You don't win in highway fights. It's one of those situations where it's really a long shot at winning . . . 10–90 [odds]."[5] So how is it that this region-spanning antihighway coalition came together during the late 1960s? And how do antihighway activists and organizers now remember this successful urban social movement and its aftermath? These are major questions driving this ethnographic investigation. In addressing these concerns, I seek to advance a more robust understanding of the factors animating residents' courageous decision to protest an interstate highway system while posing a wider disciplinary question about the ways in which the built environment itself can be understood as a social change–inducing agent and holder of ideas.

This book began as two related essays for two American studies graduate seminars at Yale University. Dolores Hayden's American Cultural Landscapes and Kathryn Dudley's Ethnographic Writing and Representation provided a rigorous and creative academic forum for me to think through the cultural production of space and the variety of ways that human actors vie to define, inhabit, control, and protect the built environments they call home. These ideas lay the foundation for my study of the Boston antihighway movement and provide a useful, interdisciplinary toolkit for interpreting its larger meanings. Ethnographic method informed every aspect of my investigation and has provided an invaluable telescope for identifying key factors animating the behavior and decision making of highway actors, both pro and con.

My ethnographic interviews anchor a new archive that I have created to document Boston's antihighway protest history. This archive has been infinitely enriched by the personal memories and collected scrapbooks of several of my collaborators. Original documents, photographs, maps, flyers, meeting minutes, and other materials rescued from basements, side rooms, and even a wrecking ball have been assembled here in an effort to examine these artifacts as a formal grouping. I did not anticipate that this study would lead to the development of an independent primary source archive. However, a variety of time-based and thematic gaps between the narratives of my collaborators and available documentation within public and private archival repositories demonstrated to me the necessity of building a new collection of sources. The result is a fresh narrative account of Boston's antihighway movement backed by a paper trail linking the Massachusetts Transportation Library with archives at Roxbury Community College, the Cambridge Historical Society, Northeastern University, the University of Massachusetts–Boston, the Boston Housing Authority, the Boston Public Library, the Cambridge Historical Commission, and the private treasures of residents who opened their homes and files to me.

The collaborative assembly of these materials demonstrates the utility of ethnographic research for expanding the historical reach and relevance of formal archives, which, regrettably, tend to underdocument socially marginalized and low-income populations. Furthermore, existing archival records do not reveal how antihighway activists worked together as the movement's many goals shifted over time and especially following Governor Sargent's 1972 decision to cancel the highway. Many of the historical accounts captured here were reconstructed by moving through and between files in private homes, transcribed interviews, institutional archives, and newspaper microfiche. Marshaling these knowledge sources, this book tethers the memories of the movement's lead actors to create a more fully embodied history than the archive alone is able to produce. In so doing, the collective cultural memory of my collaborators assumes a privileged epistemological position that grounds every page.

Several of my collaborators were approaching or beyond the age of 70 and expressed not a small amount of ambivalence about where to deposit their private papers in the coming years. Part of this ambivalence was informed by the imagined labor-intensive task of separating out materials that were more private before making an institutional donation as well as various concerns about the long-term "politics" of some archival institutions, all of which was only intensified by the strong emotional attachment between these individuals and their documents. I was unprepared for this. I wrongly assumed that because many of my interview subjects were neighborhood activists, planners, and politicians who had helped propel the movement— and not residents who had lost their homes or businesses—that our conversations would be strictly tactical and ideological. I could not have predicted that a seemingly mundane meeting flyer, a map, or even a slide-based image could provoke a swell of feeling and sometimes tears among my collaborators. This suggested to me that many of the materials lent to this archive are flooded with more meaning and significance than my descriptive narrative would likely capture. Thus the intentional gathering and long-term preservation of these materials is of exceptional importance.

Acknowledgments

My deepest thanks go to the many activists and residents who said "no" to a destructive and antidemocratic urban future for the city of Boston. Thank you to everyone who granted me an interview; your names are listed in this book. Your stories, reflections, and personal archives provided me with a powerful set of resources to draw on—I can only hope that I've done them even partial justice. This project was also enriched by the steady presence of kind and patient archivists who often helped me find documents I didn't know existed. Special thanks to Autumn Haag at Roxbury Community College; Elizabeth Mock and Joanne Riley of the University of Massachusetts–Boston; Joan Krizack, Michelle Romero, and Giordana Mecagni of Northeastern University; and Lynn Matis at the State Transportation Library. I appreciate your reminding me that careful searching can be a reward unto itself. The personal archives and invaluable research support of Mel and Joyce King, Ann and Herb Hershfang, Ken Kruckemeyer, and Jack Wofford have enriched this project beyond words. Your generosity has been humbling. Thanks also to Anne Smart and Deborah Madrey of the South End Public Library for always sharing helpful research suggestions and sunny encouragement. You are true neighborhood treasures.

My scholarship has been generously supported by the League of Women for Community Service, whose housing provision made it possible for me to be a regular presence on the Southwest Corridor. Thank you for enabling me to have a wonderful place to live while being immersed in the field.

I have also benefited from the inspired teaching and warm collegiality of my many teachers at Yale University: Laura Wexler, Karen Nakamura, Hazel Carby, Emilie Townes, Jean-Christophe Agnew, Matt Jacobson, Vicki Shepard, and Birgit Brander Rasmussen. Learning with you has been a heart-racing delight.

To my dissertation committee—Mary Lui, Dolores Hayden, and Kate Dudley—thank you for your constant support and rigorous critiques. You have helped me build an ample toolkit for tackling big questions that matter. It has been a privilege to work with you to understand the cultural meanings of space making and to learn how to push toward new modes of scholarship. Your teaching and mentorship have been profound gifts to me. And to my chair, Kate, your unwavering commitment to the revelatory power of ethnographic method and oral history continues to guide my biggest adventures at home and work. Your ability to hear what is unsaid and to see beyond the seen encourages us to pay attention to what goes missing over and over.

At the London School of Economics, my former adviser, Andy Pratt, is owed great thanks for always reminding me to "cinch" the point and to challenge every geographic theory, line, map, and history every time. In Boston and beyond, my extended family has kept me grounded during numerous lengthy and exhausting explorations, including this latest one. None of this would be doable without your loving support and good cheer when I need it most: Shauna Rigaud, Tanya McClurkin, Kim Alleyne, Liz Miranda, Al Vega, Michelle Simpson, Lady Thelma James, Jamar Coakley, Bailah Thomas, Alyssa Arzola, Huong Hoang, Sherri-Ann Butterfield, Denise Thomas, Dana Byrd, David Holness, Leah Lewis, Derek Aguirre, Justin Steil, Daren Bascome, the Wrights, Danielle Youngblood, Greg Ricks, Kathy Kottaridis, Sue Goganian, Ana Valdez, Andrew Friedman, Gina Tangney, and the Fergusons. And to the larger MYTOWN diaspora and all who worked with us, thank you for making our work both necessary and possible.

For my cousins whose infinite energy, heart, and imagination stretch the boundary of what's possible for all of us—Desmond, William, LaKenya, Gennerre, Chanel, Bryant, Lauren, Deborah, and Brianna—Osheiu loves you. And to the spirit of our Nana, Mary Ann Young Crockett Williams, and her children, Beverly, Grace, Cheryl, Adrienne, Arthur, and William, for preserving her love of the written word, stories, creativity, and justice, you are my heart.

To my Boston "writing committee"—Joyce, Mel and Pamela King, Ken Kruckemeyer and Barbara Knecht, L'Merchie Frazier, Keena Banda, Alice Edwards, and James Jennings—we did this together. Many, many conversations and delicious meals have sustained me almost as much as your generous friendship. Thank you for making sure I thought hard and had some fun while doing it.

I owe many warm thanks to MIT's Department of Urban Studies and Planning and the many staff and faculty members who kindly received me during my Martin Luther King Jr. Visiting Scholar Fellowship. Bish Sanyal, Larry Vale, Anne Spirn, Phil Thompson, Ezra Haber Glenn, and Eran-Ben Joseph—thank you for a thrilling year of learning and teaching. Additional thanks to Larry and Anne for helpful dissertation feedback.

To the staff and residents of Bromley Heath Housing Development, including Jacque Furtado, Gerald Casey, David Worrell, Whitney Lewis, Walter Lewis, Maleik Tarrant, Nichlos Holley, and Bianca Terry, thank you for welcoming me to the neighborhood and reminding me why community connection is so essential. Your time and many thoughtful research contributions have taught me more than you know.

Kate Blackmer, thank you for creating a set of maps that bring detail, precision, and elegance to spatial readings of this narrative. Working with you was packed with discovery and exciting new interpretive readings.

This book would not have become a reality without the vision of Brian Halley and the publishing team at the University of Massachusetts Press. Sally Nichols and Nancy Raynor shared much needed editorial and production guidance and the balm of good humor. Thank you all for your professionalism and your patience as every possible contingency threatened this project at every step. Your steady leadership in producing scholarship that reaches inside and beyond the academy sets inspiring new standards for expanding what we truly know. My gratitude to you is infinite. Special thanks to both my manuscript readers who provided many insightful suggestions for improving this project, which I hope I have in ways you recognize. And to you, my new reader, thank you in advance for taking the journey that follows. May you be as enriched, beguiled, and energized to imagine new progressive, democratic possibilities as I have been. This story is unfinished, and I hope you will write the next chapter.

Abbreviations

BUF	Black United Front
BRA	Boston Redevelopment Authority
BTPR	Boston Transportation Planning Review
CAP	Community Action Program
CIRCLE	Centralized Investment to Revitalize Community Living Effectively
DPW	Department of Public Works
GBC	Greater Boston Committee on the Transportation Crisis
MBTA	Massachusetts Bay Transportation Authority
MHP	*The Master Highway Plan for the Boston Metropolitan Area*
NEPA	National Environmental Policy Act
NSM	Northern Student Movement
OEO	Office of Economic Opportunity
PMAC	Parkland Management Advisory Committee
RCC	Roxbury Community College
SDS	Students for a Democratic Society
SNCC	Student Nonviolent Coordinating Committee
STOP	Antihighway subcommittee of Boston BUF
SWC	Southwest Corridor
SWCC	Southwest Corridor Land Development Coalition
UPA	Urban Planning Aid

People before Highways

Introduction

On January 25, 1969, nearly two thousand residents from Cambridge, Boston, Somerville, and surrounding cities and towns stormed the Massachusetts State House to protest the state's highway expansion projects. With signs reading "People before Highways," the protesters sent a clear message of political resistance to their newly inaugurated governor, Francis W. Sargent. They issued an official statement on how the land they lived on should be developed and for whom, and they demanded that state politicians listen and respond. In this way, Boston's antihighway movement rejected the land-gobbling agenda of federal highway building and, instead, advanced a new vision for urban development based on progressive politics and the concerns of local citizens. And, seemingly, in an instant, a powerful twentieth-century social movement was born.

At stake for many of these protesting residents was not only a highway and where it should be placed or a house and whether it would be bulldozed but also a fundamental belief in democratic practice and the conviction that citizens themselves had the right to decide and control the future of their built environments. Standing at the state seat of government, Massachusetts residents delivered a forceful "no" to the type of urban development plans that local, state, and federal bureaucrats had been pushing as "progress" and the "future" since at least the 1940s and 1950s. Although it would take a lengthy timeline of activism spanning the 1960s, 1970s, and

1980s, Boston's antihighway actors restored a significant measure of citizen participation and trust within a political apparatus dangling at the far edge of democratic legitimacy. Beginning with clearance of an area known as the "New York Streets" and then the West End, Boston's urban renewal projects through the late 1950s precipitated forceful, even violent, acts of centralized local authority.

By the 1960s, Boston's citizen-led highway opposition would crash head on with an internationally scaled social movement of planning ideas traveling far across the Atlantic. In *The Transatlantic Collapse of Urban Renewal*, historian Christopher Klemek observes that official "attempts to impose a new order on cities, and specifically a modernist vision of urbanism, via urban renewal policies eventually engendered a fierce backlash, clearly discernible by the beginning of the 1960s."[1] Large-scale federal plans pledging to remake cities introduced everyday Americans to a high-octane, European urban planning movement known as "modernism." As a political movement asserting the primacy of technical knowledge and the governance of society and the built environment by elite rule, modernism rationalized itself by emphasizing the promise of a better life "through an efficient, rational and readable structuring of space."[2] As an aesthetic phenomenon of the early twentieth century, modernism dispensed new architectural and planning orthodoxies heralding a radical break with past material forms and the functional division of cities into four zones: residence, leisure, work, and transportation.[3]

Visually this ideology was often expressed through urban master plans featuring large rectilinear, horizontal, and vertical structures in every direction with little to no ornamentation. A benevolent future would unfold through multistoried, decidedly unadorned buildings of brick, concrete, and glass bound by wide city blocks all enveloped by efficient, traffic-less, multilane highways. As Klemek notes, modernism's earliest continental beginnings were rooted in a radical rejection of capitalism's class-based, hierarchical social order based on the material concentration of wealth.[4] Though this political orientation shifted over time, many of modernism's aesthetic conventions remained unchanged and were widely embraced by corporate and government leaders as heralding a new, progressive age. Well-known champions of early modernism, including Le Corbusier, Ebenezer Howard, Walter Gropius, and Ludwig Mies van der Rohe, propelled a new vision of spatial configuration that espoused a quasi-egalitarian commitment to the public function of cities. These towering figures in the fields of architecture and planning and their physically determinist ideals burst with transformative appeal. And though their urban blueprints failed to produce the changed social order they were meant to guarantee, America's fascination with modernist planning approaches remained undeterred.

In his compelling book *Manhattan Projects: The Rise and Fall of Urban Renewal in Cold War New York*, historian Samuel Zipp connects the dots between modernism as an aesthetic and ideological movement and urban renewal as a land-grabbing political project. He writes:

> If urban renewal was at root a practical, market-minded attempt to restore order and prosperity to cities, many of its proponents were also inspired and motivated by the more abstract sense that it was "modern." Confident of its appeal to contemporary visions of progress and newness, urban renewal's most idealistic supporters shared the assumption that it was modern in three senses: it advocated the economic modernization of cities, employed the arts and practices of aesthetic modernism, and stood for a new time and space of urban modernity. All three components pointed toward the creation of living and working spaces on a mass scale for an emerging mass society. This new built infrastructure of everyday life was to be, in and of itself, an emblem of that modern, mass society.[5]

Zipp's attempt to strip urban renewal to its raw operational essence offers a simplified view of the complex set of local and federal forces converging to remake U.S. cities in the postwar period, yet it is instructive for describing new ideas about spatial production and its meaning for a modern society. During the postwar period, mass production of urban space would assume priority status for urban politicians and self-interested business coalitions eager to lure suburban, white consumers and professionals back to the city. A steady pipeline of federal dollars used to hire urban planners and architects, secure contractors from all disciplines, and otherwise activate monumental construction plans for new city neighborhoods made much of this possible and at unprecedented speed.

This frenetic and diverse convergence of ideas, actors, and motives helped unleash a torrent of domestic battles stretching from neighborhood street corners to the halls of Congress. Further hastened by Title I of the 1949 Housing Act, which extended the reach of eminent domain and brought federal funding to any municipal government that could document so-called blighted areas of substandard housing, a national race to the bottom ensued and disrupted and dispersed countless vibrant U.S. urban communities.[6] The 1949 Housing Act also signaled the postwar expansion of the federal government and its increasingly hands-on role in shaping and developing U.S. cities.[7]

In Massachusetts, a road plan first launched in 1948 moved in fits and starts through the next two decades, promising a modern regional highway network and eventual integration within the federal highway system. While the state's planners proposed new highways as a means of organizing the region's intercity traffic, liberal and progressive political activists viewed these roads as catastrophic attacks on vibrant and racially diverse communities. The Department of Public Works (DPW) would later revise the state's highway plan more than once, but the original design of two circumferential (one inner, one outer) and six radial roads terminating within Greater Boston's urban core remained ostensibly unchanged (figure 1). The Inner Belt was proposed as I-95's essential connector to roads passing through Boston, Brookline, Cambridge, and Somerville (figure 2). The DPW's plan featured a north-south road that would guide Interstate 95's East Coast–hugging asphalt ribbon through the center of Boston and, according to the state's planners, bring efficient automobile transit to the entire region. Only it would never materialize in full. Citizen opposition halted this modern vision of progress and replaced it with expansive new visions for transportation planning and regional economic development authored by residents themselves.

What retrospectively appears as an inevitable success story was anything but for antihighway organizers who converged on the steps of the Massachusetts State House in January 1969. It was not clear to these actors what would happen next or if they could actually win in the face of the state's bureaucratic power. What was clear was that the state's highway plan had sparked a broad base of opposition across the entire Greater Boston region, and thousands of citizens were ready for battle. What was also apparent was that Boston's antihighway movement comprised a dumping ground for the Left's vanguard activists and the accumulated tactical knowledge of their many years of progressive agitation. And yet, despite this large-scale social mobilization, within the midcentury wave of America's citizen-led highway revolts, Boston was a latecomer. Multiple cities across the United States had

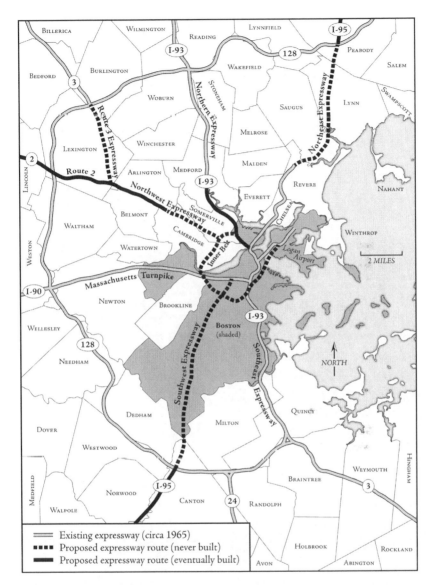

FIGURE 1. Greater Boston expressways, circa 1965, showing existing and proposed highways. Dotted lines indicate roads that were eventually scrapped but still being considered at this time. Based originally on the 1948 Master Highway Plan, this network of six radial roads was connected by an inner circumferential road called the "Inner Belt" and the outer circumferential Route 128. Interstate 95 was proposed as the north-south highway to downtown Boston and surrounding cities and towns through the Inner Belt connector. Map by Kate Blackmer, © 2017.

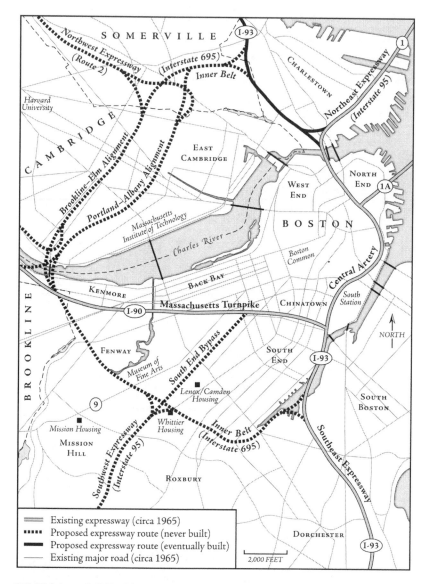

FIGURE 2. Inner Belt. The Massachusetts Department of Public Works' highway plan was anchored by the construction of a looped, multilane Inner Belt. This connector promised speedy automobile travel through Greater Boston's dense urban core. Map by Kate Blackmer, © 2017.

already fought and won or lost their highway battles. Antihighway movements in San Francisco, New York, Miami, New Orleans, and Washington, D.C., in the late 1950s and early 1960s represented unpredictable and bruising fights for local residents who found themselves fighting their own political leaders as well as special interests located far away.[8]

The Federal-Aid Highway Act of 1956 itself helped produced much of this controversy not merely because it set in motion the creation of a 41,000-mile interstate highway system but also because the Act revised where such a system could be placed. Previous legislation, notably the Federal-Aid Highway Act of 1944, had stipulated that interstate roads should be built in semirural or suburban areas and around cities to create an interregional network of highways bypassing densely populated urban areas and their frequent traffic bottlenecks. The Federal-Aid Highway Act of 1956 changed this. City politicians and state governors desperate to funnel capital investments into failing urban business districts imagined federal highway dollars as a timely antidote.[9] They successfully lobbied and won the right to direct highway funds to their urban cores. Additionally, the Federal-Aid Highway Act of 1956 created the Highway Trust Fund, a massive federal account based on revenues from taxes on gasoline, tires, and new vehicles.[10] By law, the Highway Trust Fund was used exclusively for road building and maintenance and was kept separate from the general fund of the Treasury. In practice, this meant that highway construction was backed by a near limitless source of cash and federal legitimacy. By 1968, the Highway Trust Fund had already amassed more than $4 billion.[11] Significant resource allocation coupled with a federal commitment to provide 90 percent financing for all state-led interstate highway projects only served to make the urban race for highway building all the more frenetic. The future of highway building seemed incontestable. However, much of this prohighway momentum was rising at the exact moment that city residents were demanding more participation and influence in urban planning and such federally sponsored revitalization programs as urban renewal. The result was a volatile mix of outmoded policy, plentiful federal resources, and resident-led coalitions furious over the disastrous effects of both.

On the heels of a string of urban renewal–mandated displacements and demolitions, residents of San Francisco, New York, Miami, New Orleans, and Washington, D.C., waged battle on local governments attempting new rounds of clearance for interstate highways.[12] The actions of these residents illustrate the extent to which the 1956 federal provision permitting highways to pass through, not merely around, cities provoked civic backlash. San Francisco's antihighway groups were successful in persuading California's state government to halt expressway expansion along the Embarcadero waterfront. However, New Yorkers could not stop Robert Moses's strong-arming campaign to drive the ten-lane Lower Manhattan Expressway through the city's vibrant Lower East Side. The fevered pitch of New York's highway and urban renewal battles inspired local resident and journalist Jane Jacobs to pen her classic 1961 work *The Death and Life of Great American Cities*. Jacobs's impassioned treatise critiques the role of planners and highway builders and fingers them as responsible for the destruction of cities not solely because of their commitment to physical clearance but also because of, what she considered, an ill-informed professional understanding of what constitutes a good urban neighborhood. In her assessment of 1950s-era urban planning conventions, Jacobs delivers a forceful indictment of the planning profession as a whole. Though Jacobs's comments primarily address urban renewal policies, her general discussion of the practice and values informing planners' conceptions of place-based development is instructive. In response to the redevelopment tumult surrounding her beloved Greenwich Village neighborhood, Jacobs writes:

> Unfortunately orthodox planning theory is deeply committed to the idea of supposedly cozy, inward-turned city neighborhoods. In its pure form, the ideal is a neighborhood composed of about 7,000 persons, a unit supposedly of sufficient size to populate an elementary school and to support convenience shopping and a community center . . . Although the "ideal" is seldom literally reproduced, it is the point of departure for nearly all neighborhood renewal plans, for all project building, for much modern zoning, and also for the practice work done by today's architectural-planning students.[13]

Jacobs describes planners' "ideal" urban neighborhood as a densely settled unit supported by an assortment of social and economic institutions. She contrasts this with her own notion of city neighborhoods as vehicles of self-government.

For Jacobs, cities consist of people functioning within a localized political system that is fully engaged with and immersed in the outside world. She argues that urban vitality is, in fact, largely derived from the extroverted and political nature of cities. Grounded in this analysis, Jacobs attacks planners' conception of cities as reflective of a grave misunderstanding of the essence of neighborhood life. She also moves to build a consensus on new approaches to city planning by exhorting her readers to "drop any ideal of neighborhoods as self-contained or introverted units."[14] Jacobs charges planners with a chronic inability to recognize the formal and informal political features of neighborhoods and cites these actors as guilty of producing myopic plans that destroy urban communities. By failing to identify urban neighborhoods within the political context of cities, planners, according to Jacobs, created blueprints for zoned building areas but *not* actual urban plans.

When examining automobiles' effects on the city, Jacobs repeats her assertion that planners, not cars, are what is wrong with cities.

> It is questionable how much of the destruction wrought by automobiles on cities is really a response to transportation and traffic needs, and how much of it is owing to sheer disrespect for other city needs, uses, and functions. Like city rebuilders who face a blank when they try to think of what to do instead of renewal projects, because they know of no other respectable principles for city organization, just so, highwaymen, traffic engineers, and city rebuilders, again, face a blank when they try to think what they can realistically do, day by day, except try to overcome traffic kinks as they occur and apply what foresight they can toward moving and storing more cars in the future.[15]

Jacobs blasts both "city rebuilders" and "highwaymen" as fundamentally unable to think of alternatives to their current plans, again owing to limited professional vision regarding the function of urban neighborhoods. In New York, as well as many other U.S. cities, Jacobs-like critiques were generated within citizen protests and public hearings attacking state-sponsored urban renewal and highway plans.

In *Superhighway—Superhoax*, Helen Leavitt details a particularly vocal debate surrounding the proposed construction of the North Central Freeway and its downtown-bound inner loop in Washington, D.C. This case well illustrates the types of capricious tactics that plagued postwar highway building and the legal bulldozing that typically produced only one result: highways and more highways. Angered by politicians' lack of responsiveness to their demands for formal reconsideration of the freeway system, residents of D.C.,

Maryland, and Virginia brought suit against the District of Columbia in 1967. When the District Court rejected the case, the residents appealed. In early 1968, the Federal Court of Appeals decided in favor of the residents and overturned the lower court's ruling. As Leavitt notes, this legal victory for resident opposition to highway expansion infuriated Congressman John Kluczynski, chairman of the House Subcommittee on Roads.

In a vindictive response, Kluczynski sponsored a bill ordering the local highway department to ignore the court's decision and build the roads anyway. A blistering series of resident testimonials accompanied the hearings for Kluczynski's bill. Charles Cassell, a D.C. resident and member of the Black United Front, an umbrella organization for black nationalist groups and their allies, testified first:

> I wish to remind you gentlemen that in giving aid to the forces militating against the desires and well-being of the majority of the residents of Washington, D.C., you would be confirming the findings of the President's Commission on Civil Disorders; namely, that recent unrest and frustration of poor people stem from long years of exploitation, neglect, and abuse reflected in callous and cavalier attitudes on the part of local government, in this case aided and abetted by Congress . . . Citizens in this city are also completely aware that no solution to this crisis is valid which accepts the premise that the automobile is a fixed factor around which all plans must center.[16]

Cassell warned the hearing's conveners that denying the desires of the majority of citizens would lead to a level of volatility that would best be avoided. His reference to the findings of the 1968 President's Commission on Civil Disorders (the Kerner Commission) underscores the currency of this information for residents and activists engaged in urban redevelopment issues. And, finally, Cassell's direct critique of automobile-centric planning for cities expresses the plea of D.C. residents that alternative transportation plans be studied and adopted.

According to Leavitt, Cassell's testimony prompted only terse commentary from the ranking minority member of the House Public Works Committee: "I do not intend to dignify his statement by asking any questions."[17] This response demonstrates the contentious tenor of highway hearings as well as the unwillingness of prohighway politicians to address the race-based and socioeconomic implications of highway construction. Cassell's appraisal of the "callous and cavalier attitudes on the part of local government, in this case aided and abetted by Congress," is fitting.[18] This scene depicts why citizen opposition to highways, with few exceptions, tended to proceed in one direction—defeat. Yet, despite multiple political and legal hurdles, highway-fighting citizens of San Francisco, New York, and Washington, D.C., would leave lasting national results in the form of revised statutes for highway plans and their public hearings. Massachusetts residents would benefit directly from these citizen-demanded legal revisions and would later return the favor by pressuring Congress to authorize additional amendments to federal highway law.

Both Leavitt and Jacobs authored potent critiques of professional planners and the prohighway political establishment that empowered them. Their prescient consideration of issues such as America's overreliance on automobile travel, the social and environmental danger of congested highways, and the human need for vibrant, socially connected neighborhoods could not have been more antithetical to midcentury American urban planning norms. By questioning the orthodoxy of highway building and urban planning more generally, they, especially Jacobs, brought controversy to the highest levels of the planning establishment. Needless to say, the network of universities, government agencies, and professional publications anchoring the planning establishment did not respond well to being critiqued by Jacobs or Leavitt. Notably, their political and professional status as outsiders to the planning profession as well as their gender were frequently mentioned by critics as a means of questioning the legitimacy of their arguments. This is a telling indication of the defensive posture of America's postwar planning apparatus and its intolerance of dissenting opinions of actors outside of its own male-dominated, white professional hierarchy.[19] Like Jacobs and Leavitt before them, many highway activists raised their voices to provoke a national debate that the establishment viewed as antagonistic and unwelcome.

Part of Boston's story has been documented and analyzed by legendary local journalist Alan Lupo in his critically acclaimed coauthored 1971 book *Rites of Way: The Politics of Transportation in Boston and the U.S. City.* As a streetwise and politically savvy writer for the *Boston Globe*, Lupo covered the antihighway movement's progression from worry-filled talks between young radical planners and working-class residents in kitchens and living rooms in Cambridge and Boston to a regional coalition able to exert pressure on the political establishment. Part One of *Rites of Way* presents Lupo's cogent eleven-chapter investigation of the political inner workings of the movement and a compelling argument for why opposition to federal road building was necessary. The book before you goes beyond the scope of Lupo's work by further considering how changes in Boston's physical landscape led to a new kind of grassroots politics that would hit the ground with full force in the 1970s. In assessing the antihighway movement some forty years after Lupo, I also interrogate how back-spinning memories of the movement have generated popular lore as well as valuable new insights unknown to him or his audience in 1971. Lupo references urban renewal displacements, bulldozed neighborhoods, and other ways that government-led interventions in the landscape were causing tumult, but he does not linger here. To this discussion, I bring an analysis of the national context for highway battles as well as a consideration of the ways in which nationally scaled liberation movements merged through the lived experiences of antihighway activists to create an expansive field of knowledge able to source a new movement for progressive social change.

This book also enables a fuller recovery of several notable antihighway actors and organizations not always recognized for the visionary coordinating role they played in a social movement that stretched across three decades (approximately 1965 to 1987) and more than a dozen cities and towns. Urban Planning Aid, the Boston Black United Front, and the Greater Boston Committee on the Transportation Crisis, in particular, are three organizations that provided invaluable leadership and guidance to the movement's relentless pursuit of a winning strategy. These organizations not only mobilized hundreds of neighborhood groups and thousands of individual residents to protest interstate highway growth but also served to catalyze a panoply of 1960s-era liberation ideologies into a political battering ram persuasive enough to inspire civil rights, antiwar, and Black Power activists and strong enough to wrestle government power. By 1969, Urban Planning Aid, the Black United Front, and the Greater Boston Committee were recognized as politically astute radical coalitions demanding a new kind of urban development agenda. The highway plan's promise of additional convulsions to the physical landscapes of Cambridge and Boston blasted these groups into being.

America's postwar spatial assault of urban renewal clearance and highway expansion kicked off a traumatic chain of environmental events for residents living in older cities such as Boston and Cambridge. The 1950s and 1960s were a time of rapid physical and economic change for the Boston metropolitan region overall. An emerging economy based on services, research, and technology was transforming the region's form from one based on dense urban clusters hitched to walkable downtown shopping districts to the new typography of corporate industrial parks threaded by highways and leafy suburbs. Political economist Barry Bluestone has thoughtfully chronicled the cascade of industrial changes defining this period. During the postwar era, massive downshifts in mill-based industries overlapping with rapid expansion in professional, technical, and financial services indicates that Boston was in the process of exiting one kind of industrial economic regime and entering another.[20] Boston mayor John B. Hynes and his successor Mayor John F. Collins saw the effects of this urban economic shift in the form of a declining population, declining tax revenues, and an aging urban infrastructure configured to support an old economy that was dying. Both responded with the call for a "New Boston" and an ambitious urban renewal agenda to remake the city as quickly as possible.[21]

The changing physical organization of the region fueled by the economic interests of private investors and their allied political leaders had negative consequences for longtime urban residents in need of housing and jobs. Because so many of Boston's residents did not own cars, more often than not there was literally no way for these residents to access new jobs or housing, which was exacerbated by public transportation infrastructure physically oriented to support an older economy of industrial manufacturing. And, for nonwhite residents, the pervasiveness of racially discriminatory mortgage and employment practices meant that their options were even further constrained. The overall result was a dense urban core of poor and working-class white and nonwhite workers surrounded by outward semicircles of middle-class and professional white suburbanites. Though many local and federal government leaders heralded these changes as signs of economic progress, most urban residents demanded to know at what cost to citizens were such plans permissible. This fundamental space-based conflict fermented new models of resistance politics deft at analyzing and interpreting state policy and unyielding in their demands for more economically and racially just urban development plans.

The arrival of Urban Planning Aid, the Black United Front, and the Greater Boston Committee on the Transportation Crisis signaled resident-based disillusionment with government-led planning. The words "slum," "ghetto," and "Chinatown" peppered planning documents that described which parts of the city needed to be cleared for roads, new housing, or sometimes just parking lots. Within these official documents, the language of blight assumed a pernicious urban bite capable of devouring entire communities. Although antihighway organizers employed new tactics and coalitions to battle road building in 1969, highway controversies were not a new story in Boston. Before demolition for I-95 began, large swaths of Boston's metropolitan core had already been cleared for two other roadways during the 1950s and early 1960s. Ground breakings for the Southeast Expressway, also called the "Central Artery," and the Massachusetts Turnpike began in the 1950s. Opposition from residents and politicians in suburban Newton significantly delayed the Mass Pike's urban extension, but by 1962 the road was on its way to Boston. A working-class Italian community in Brighton watched as homes were sold to the state for one dollar and demolished almost overnight. In West Newton, a long-settled African American area, known as the "Hicks Street neighborhood," was similarly uprooted and displaced by the Pike's arrival. Each of these dispossessions further enraged residents and local activists, who felt powerless in the face of a contorting landscape that was actively ejecting them.

Boston's Chinatown neighborhood had faced its own showdown with postwar highway growth. A bustling hub of residential and commercial activity, Hudson Street traveled the eastern edge of Chinatown and abutted Boston's leather and garment districts, active but fading geographic nodes of the region's historic textile manufacturing base. In the early 1950s, Massachusetts planners saw this street as obstructing interstate highway connections to downtown and decided to level it. For Chinatown's residents, the highway's threat represented only the most recent encroachment by a hostile state apparatus. Chinese exclusion laws halted the immigration flow and growth of Boston's Chinese residents through the first half of the twentieth century.[22] When Chinatown's small but stable resident population began to expand in the 1950s and 1960s with the repeal of restrictive, race-based immigration laws, government planners were busy seizing the neighborhood's land for urban renewal and highway expansion projects. These projects reduced the neighborhood's physical size by one-half and its housing stock by one-third by 1963.[23] Local and state politicians' act of claiming ground in the neighborhood at a time when the need of residents for land and housing was greater than ever would sear the political memories of a generation of Chinatown residents.

Both the development of the Central Artery and the Mass Pike taught Boston's residents key political lessons about highway building. These lessons in conjunction with residents' ongoing urban renewal battles birthed a radical grassroots political agenda intolerant of government-led efforts to reorder urban space through exclusionary, abusive, and antidemocratic means. From displaced families and acres of cleared land in the New York Streets (1956) and West End (1958–59) to each population-dispersing highway project, Greater Boston's 1960s-era topography was inscribed with warning signs about what centralized state power could exact from vulnerable residents. By 1969 and now armed with a cityscape full of cautionary tales, a fear that the worst was yet to come, and a hunger for a more just alternative, citizens in Cambridge and Boston and beyond took to the streets to see what they could do for themselves, by themselves.

Beyond a victory story about an interstate highway stopped by local citizens, the Boston antihighway movement reveals a pivotal historical moment when state and federal actors sought to centralize their bureaucratic authority within cities just as urban residents were rejecting all but devolved and democratic local governance models. The field of urban planning necessarily holds a central place within this book's discussion. In the mid-1960s, grassroots activists in Boston, and their comrades around the country, probed professional planners and their maps and unveiled a glistening web of special interests spinning urban master plans into contentious reality. By exposing the base knowledge and values embedded within urban planning as a professional discipline, Boston's antihighway activists issued a lethal attack on elite knowledge systems' perpetuation of social and economic inequalities in U.S. cities. This book takes its cue here and further analyzes twentieth-century urban planning as a cultural practice imbued with a technical language and epistemological armature designed to convey objectivity and political neutrality. The specialized semiotic coding of urban planning renders the field all but impervious to nonprofessionals and their potential critiques. In Boston the issue of who has the ability, authority, and expertise to determine plans for the city's neighborhoods erupted as a high-stakes regional battle for the democratic production of space-defining knowledge. Residents and their allies bucked professional convention by authoring new plans based on their own interests and values.

The astonishing final result was a bold and transformative new urban geography for Greater Boston fully unveiled in 1989.

For at least two generations of Greater Boston's progressive activists, the story of how citizens fought I-95 and won stands as the region's preeminent narrative of grassroots political triumph. The necessity of disciplining aberrant state authority by assertive on-the-ground activism is one of the seminal teachings of Boston's antihighway movement. Another hallmark of this movement is the collection of 343 federal highway miles that were removed from America's interstate highway system as a result of Boston's protest. Ultimately, residents' successful work to forge legitimate democratic planning practices among state and federal government actors advanced a new, spatialized expression of 1960s-era liberation politics. A dual concern about the production of urban space and transportation mobility galvanized residents in Boston and many U.S. cities to critique how the physical organization of highway-enmeshed urban landscapes compromised the civil rights and legal authority of everyday urban citizens. Boston's activists fought more than three decades to secure more democratic models of political decision making and a more just understanding of citizens' rights to use, move through, plan, and control space. In this way, Boston's activists situate themselves within the nation's long arc of civil rights history. They also demonstrate how the 1970s emerge as a rich historical period for understanding how veteran agitators of the previous decade further advanced their radical commitments.

Although America's civil rights history is often told as a growing series of citizenship claims aimed at fulfilling the Fourteenth Amendment, many of its most defining battles have been waged in the context of transportation access. From *Plessy v. Ferguson* (1896), which would federally institutionalize a policy of separate but equal based on a railroad rider's petition, to the Montgomery Bus boycott (1955), which challenged Alabama's segregationist policies and catapulted Rosa Parks and Martin Luther King Jr. to national prominence, to the Boynton Act of 1960, which outlawed separate accommodations for interstate travelers, the frontier of the U.S. civil rights movement has frequently been situated within a transportation-based legal fight. Even this cursory examination of America's transportation history recalls several definitive battlegrounds for securing constitutional protection and the rule of law for citizens continuously on the move. Transportation fights have consistently provided a legal platform for testing the constitutionality of racial separation and the constrained mobility that evidence its reach. In the end, trains, buses, and (eventually) cars as well as the interstate roads that carried them would prove essential cauldrons for expanding the meaning and relevance of American democracy.

This book is divided into six chapters that consider the progression of the Boston antihighway movement from political fringe discussion to forceful mobilizer of national transportation policy reform. Chapter 1, "People before Highways: Stopping Highways, Building a Regional Social Movement," introduces a tight circle of early actors and political organizations that mingled strategies and tactics from multiple mid-1960s liberation movements to seed a boundary-defying regional movement effective in linking cities, towns, and racial groups that did not automatically see themselves as allies. The examination of these actors continues into chapter 2, "Battling Desires: (Re)Defining Progress," which interrogates the way federal highway plans and technical mandates created a fatally flawed decision-making loop for urban areas such as Boston. Bulldozed landscapes waiting for federal highway penetration became political consciousness-raising battlefields for local residents and worrisome pressure points for elected officials anxious to complete midcentury highway plans. Chapter 3, "Groundwork: Imagining a Highwayless Future," chronicles how a physically wounded urban territory instigated a new politics propelled by novel modes of space-targeting grassroots actions. These actions coalesced on the ground and ultimately in the governor's ear.

When Governor Francis Sargent announced, "We were wrong" on statewide television, the path was laid for deep reform of regional transportation planning as well as a reconsideration of how best to revitalize Boston's aging core. Chapter 4, "Planning for Tomorrow, Not Yesterday: 'We Were Wrong,'" tackles the governor's course change while pointing nationally to a larger debate on how to name the root problems plaguing U.S. cities during the 1960s. When Governor Sargent canceled the highway plan in 1972, the movement switched focus. Activists, intent on halting highway construction, now rallied to define how land cleared for the highway should be developed. The Southwest Corridor was a dusty territory caught in a conceptual tug-of-war between multiple constituencies vying to determine its final blueprint. In chapter 5, "New Territory: City Making, Searching for Control," I investigate the 1970s fight to define the Southwest

Corridor as well as the longer historical timeline of urban development within this important connective landscape of Boston.

And, finally, chapter 6, "Making Victory Stick: New Park, New Dreams, New Plans," considers the multi-actor planning process of creating a city-wide park and transit system and activists' mission to protect the Southwest Corridor from future highway encroachment. The legacy of the Boston antihighway movement continues to assert its call for a redistribution of power within urban built environments, the field of planning, and democratic governance. The lingering question is, Will we answer?

Chapter 1

People before Highways

Stopping Highways, Building a Regional Social Movement

The common man in these groups was as interested in preserving trees as he was in preserving inner-city homes. He was as likely to be an Italian from East Boston as a WASP from Milton or a black militant from Roxbury; he was as likely to be a stoic undertaker from Jamaica Plain as a radical from Cambridge. Such heterogeneity impressed vote-conscious politicians. It said to them, "All those people are angry about the highways. Put them together and you've got damned near all of Greater Boston."

—Alan Lupo, Frank Colcord, and Edmund P. Fowler, *Rites of Way: The Politics of Transportation in Boston and the U.S. City* (1971)

People before Highways Day

On January 25, 1969, a diverse and vocal coalition of antihighway protesters rushed the steps of the Massachusetts State House to confront the state's new governor and demand his support for their position. Birthed from a handful of quiet living room meetings and loud street demonstrations, Greater Boston's antihighway protests had matured into a powerful regional coalition by 1969. People before Highways Day marked its official unveiling, with protesters from Cambridge, Boston, Somerville, Brookline, and beyond turning out strong for a historic day of progressive activism. The last few years of organizing had been difficult and frustrating, and this day was full of buoyancy and the promise of a new frontline in the highway battle. Urban and suburban

FIGURE 3. People before Highways Day. Antihighway protesters from across the region rally at the Massachusetts State House on January 25, 1969. A resolute Mary Parkman Peabody joined fellow protesters in front of the building once occupied by her son, former governor Endicott Peabody. Source: *Boston Globe.*

protesters were now united in their unwillingness to yield to federal authority or funding streams that compromised their visions of home. Their vision did not include Interstate 95 or the politicians who supported it.

Radical urban planners, seasoned antiwar protesters, and civil rights veterans converged to advance a cutting-edge planning agenda burnished in the political heat of the mid-1960s. A Cambridge resident vividly recalls the day:

> When other marchers came along from North Cambridge we cohered and marched to Central Square . . . Progressive Labor came along

Mass. Ave. in thin procession chanting: *Black Black POW-er to the . . .*
BLAACK people! Red POW-er to the . . . RED people! WOM-AN POW-er
to the . . . WOM'n people! Po-WER . . . to the peop-PLE! Central Square
was jammed with marchers. From Brookline Street on the south and
Elm Street on the north, the churches had preached their parishioners
into marching like antiwar rabble rousers. Signs bristled. All the social
agencies with their banners. One group had built a plywood black coffin
and a made a funeral cortege in black garments, mourning the neighborhood they would lose.[1]

This bustling scene of protest revelry in Cambridge moved southward to
Boston and joined an even larger contingent representing much of the
state's eastern region. A broad alliance of liberation and labor movements
led by civil rights organizers, Black Power advocates, union rank and file,
and women's liberation and Native American rights activists converged
on the streets in a dramatic display of political solidarity. For Cambridge
residents the highway's so-called Inner Belt would potentially displace a
densely populated working-class area spanning Cambridgeport and the
periphery of MIT's campus. Barbara Ackerman, who would later become
the mayor of Cambridge, remembers the highway's threat this way: "Of
the 5,000 homes to be razed for the whole new structure, 1,300 were in
Cambridge. That was about 5 percent of our city, all working class. It would
also destroy jobs. Though it would provide a ten-year spate of highly paid
jobs, it would destroy an equal number of permanent ones, most of them
at the low end of the scale. It provided no transportation for people who
didn't have cars, the very kind of people who would be losing jobs and
homes and would need transportation not just for convenience but for survival."[2] For Cambridge activists such as Ackerman, the stakes were unac-
ceptably high. A significant loss of housing and employment for residents,
with limited options for either, pushed working-class neighbors and their
middle-class allies to take to the streets. For many liberal white Cambridge
residents, racial integration was the essential social good that needed to
be protected from the highway's path. This focus gave residents a rallying
call fully aligned with Cambridge's self-image as a progressive and racially
inclusive community. The central question for Cambridge residents was
how best to preserve an important part of their city's social and physical
geography. These residents questioned both the highway's path and the
implicit racial and economic politics carried in its wake.

While liberal Cambridge activists fought for the preservation of racially and economically diverse neighborhoods, a group of Boston residents advanced a black nationalist agenda that prioritized a need for greater economic, not racial, integration. The leaders of Boston's Black United Front and Black Panther Party were emphatic in their demand for local control of land planning and use. Chuck Turner, a well-known neighborhood activist, was chairman of the Boston chapter of the Black United Front and cochair of the Greater Boston Committee on the Transportation Crisis. When I asked Turner if he had been worried about the claim that the highway would produce a more racially segregated city, he shook his head and flatly answered, "No, not at all."

As a lead organizer for People before Highways Day, Turner was instrumental in setting the political strategy for talks with Governor Sargent and his top staff. As chairman of the Black United Front, Turner had also led the effort to organize Roxbury residents living beneath the highway's proposed interchange, a clover-like twist of roads connecting I-95 to the Inner Belt. Home to several of Boston's public housing developments, the edge of Roxbury ran parallel to the elevated highway's proposed route to downtown. Turner describes this area and the highway's projected scale: "There were about five thousand units of public housing and affordable housing along that corridor. And about half the units would be on one side of the highway and the other would be on the other side. The highway was to be a sixteen-lane highway—two breakdown lanes on either side, two railroad/T [public transportation] tracks. So it'd be about six lanes of breakdown lane and rail traffic and about eight to ten lanes of highways, four going in each direction. And with the interchange . . . it was going to be about ten stories high where the Inner Belt connected with the [highway] extension."[3] According to the state's plan, I-95 would proceed into Boston along a road called the Southwest Expressway, an urban extension of the interstate. This expressway would dissect the neighborhoods of Roxbury, Jamaica Plain, Hyde Park, and parts of the South End (via a separate feeder road called the "South End Bypass") and carry an estimated load of 160,000 cars into the city's heart each day.[4] State-sponsored bulldozers began aggressive land clearance in Roxbury and Jamaica Plain in 1966 in preparation for I-95's arrival. The immediate result was demolition of five hundred units of housing and displacement of a significant number of local businesses. More than an abstract threat for residents living in this area of Boston, the highway's planned construction had already begun disfiguring the land-scape around them.

The stakes for Cambridge and Boston residents were high, though their political responses to those stakes were quite different. Cambridge residents and their elected officials began organizing against the Inner Belt almost immediately following a Department of Public Works (DPW) public hearing on the highway plan in 1960. The DPW released a slightly revised plan in 1962; however, Cambridge residents remained unsatisfied. Cambridge legislators and activists advocated for a study of alternate routes and mobilized with several other towns to pass a law to secure local veto power, enabling them to reject state highway plans the electorate deemed unacceptable. This was a significant win. For the next three years Cambridge residents remained confident that they had averted a disaster. That confidence ended abruptly in 1965 when incoming governor John Volpe repealed local veto power for highway projects. Brookline residents and their elected leaders also opposed the highway, but Boston was a different story. Boston's local and state politicians fully supported the DPW plan. By 1965, the southern portion of I-95 had been completed from Route 128 to Providence, and all that remained was the 10.2-mile extension from Route 128 to Boston.[5] Most Boston residents took this to mean there was nothing they could do to affect a project that carried the full support of local and federal authorities and was soon headed their way.

The Movement Finds a Center—The Greater Boston Committee on the Transportation Crisis

The Greater Boston Committee on the Transportation Crisis (GBC) formally began mobilizing residents in Cambridge, Boston, and surrounding cities and towns in 1968. Jim Morey, Cambridge organizer and political strategist, founded the GBC for the specific purpose of coordinating the People before Highways Day march and to start building a regional anti-highway alliance. Morey believed that a large public demonstration was needed to show Massachusetts's new Republican governor, Francis W. Sargent, that antihighway activists stood unwavering in their commitment to defeat the state's highway plan. In Morey's view, an umbrella organization was needed to execute this kind of multicity effort—the GBC or Greater Boston Committee would serve as just that. The successful orchestration of

People before Highways Day established the Greater Boston Committee as a highly visible pressure group of substantial size and reach. Furthermore, the volume and diversity of resident turnout for this day legitimized (particularly in the eyes of the media) the committee as a skilled grassroots agent able to negotiate directly with state power.

The Greater Boston Committee quickly emerged as the official communication center for a disparate set of independent neighborhood groups resisting local highway building. For the first time in the movement's history, antihighway groups in and around Boston were assembled under a single organizational banner with a unified political message. One early GBC statement read, "We oppose the concept of thrusting a ten-lane highway through the heart of the metropolitan area of Boston, destroying thousands of homes, jobs, and opportunities, and killing the spirit of community life established over many years."[6] This statement reflected the anger and exasperation of thousands of residents who had withstood the most bruising revolutionary moments of the 1960s as well as the physical disruptions wrought by multiple urban renewal and highway clearance projects. These battle-tested citizens imbued the Greater Boston Committee with authority and a brash, flame-throwing politics set to engage the many fights the 1970s already seemed to promise.

Although the Greater Boston Committee assumed a "no-highway position," many of its targeted allies did not initially share this stance. Not surprisingly, the proposed shape and orientation of the highway had a determining effect on how local residents determined their political stance on road building. In Cambridge, many early public debates questioned the placement of the Inner Belt and called for a restudy of the DPW's preferred alignment along Brookline and Elm Streets. Local activists mobilized to increase pressure on then governor John Volpe to commission a study determining the feasibility of a less controversial route but worried that the state would ignore their pleas, which it ultimately did. Father Paul McManus, a prominent Inner Belt opponent and eventual chairman of the GBC, recalls multiple organizing tactics, including closed-door meetings and public demonstrations which brought Cambridge workers, families, clergy, and academics together as a mobilized antihighway base.[7]

In Boston, residents of Jamaica Plain lobbied for a depressed versus elevated highway. Both Boston and Cambridge residents engaged in lengthy public arguments promoting changes to the highway's direction or form, but interestingly, many of their lead organizers did not question its seeming inevitability. Thus the Greater Boston Committee's seminal contribution lay not only in its ability to persuade local neighborhood groups to band together but also in its careful work to expand the spatial imagination of these communities by pinpointing how interstate highway construction would affect the region as a whole. This deliberate work to grow the political and spatial awareness of residents of Greater Boston eventually led all GBC's members to adopt a no-highway position, but this was no minor feat.[8] The challenge of persuading more than a dozen independent municipalities to see their spatial and political fates as linked and greater than boundary lines on a map took years of strenuous organizing work. The internal tension wrought by varying levels of agreement with GBC's position weakened the allegiance of some early members who would later quit the coalition.

The Greater Boston Committee accomplished much of this work through small neighborhood meetings, slideshow presentations, and the distribution of informational flyers. Using plain, direct language and neighbor-to-neighbor distribution channels, the committee's materials described for residents the impact of the planned highway system. One GBC flyer announced:

> Houses are being destroyed with no provision made for replacing the buildings, no provision for consistent rents or mortgage interest rates when the occupants are forced to move, and no compensation for being forced to move by eminent domain. All this in the context of a housing crisis in the cities.
>
> Small businesses are being disrupted and many times taken over by bigger developments with no provision for compensation or protection.
>
> Many jobs are lost since adequate relocation within the city is impossible for some employers.
>
> Whole neighborhoods will be divided or walled off by wide ribbons of concrete, noise, fumes.
>
> In the future, mobility for all will not be achieved. Those without access to cars, such as the young, the elderly, the poor, and housewives without second cars, would be isolated from employment, education, commerce, and recreation by a highway-dominated transportation system.[9]

This careful consideration of land and its uses beyond automobile-based interests highlights GBC's unique education and mobilization strategy of using clear and direct language that showed what was immediately at stake. Here the need to protect housing, businesses, and residents—especially those female, young, and old—is articulated as a shared regional goal to advance. Furthermore, mobility itself is identified as an intrinsic good to protect. For the Greater Boston Committee, mobility must be provided "for all" and not for a privileged subgroup. And in all these ways, the GBC's broad multi-issue vision established a provocative starting point for local communities to rethink their highway politics within a metropolitan framework that prioritized the needs of all citizens, not merely those of car owners.

Though the GBC's agenda would inspire many citizens to join the antihighway cause, its impact went beyond headcount. In the words of GBC leader Brad Yoneoka: "The emerging alliance went deeper than numbers. It spread out ideologically from an antihighway, pro–mass transit stance to those concerned about ecology, lack of housing, the weak financial status of the old cities, unemployment, and a host of social and economic issues related to transportation."[10] These ideological and political commitments would jointly spur more than a decade of radical planning and progressive organizing for Boston's metropolitan cities and towns.

In addition to the coordinating acumen of the GBC, the antihighway movement also benefited from the ideological and tactical leadership of seasoned 1960s-era protesters, including antiwar organizers, radical planners, antipoverty warriors, and civil rights activists. These experienced political actors brought a decisive edginess to land-based fights. They understood the limits of liberal democratic politics based on reforming and mollifying the status quo; they also understood the necessity of progressive activism and its demand for more equitable distributions of resources, including land. For this generation of activists, simple appeals to the political establishment, legal-juridical strategies, and nonviolent civil disobedience were no longer deemed sufficient means for guaranteeing America's promise of democratic equality.

Antiwar Organizers, Domestic Peace, and Route 128

Jim Morey was exceptionally well suited for the task of building a grassroots alliance focused on rethinking the development of cities. Prior to initiating the Greater Boston Committee on the Transportation Crisis, Morey had led a series of antiwar and peace-building projects. This work was largely sparked by his postcollege radicalization by antiwar organizers affiliated with Students for a Democratic Society (SDS). Morey had worked as a systems analyst managing defense and aerospace projects for the RAND Corporation. His technical training and expertise placed him comfortably inside the emerging research and technology economy of Boston's Route 128 corridor. However, around 1964, Morey began to have misgivings about the role his work played in furthering the nation's defense industry. During this same time, Students for a Democratic Society launched an initiative to convince Boston's tech and defense professionals to support the "conversion of the defense industry to peaceful uses."[11] Ostensibly, this meant lunchtime and after-hours meetings for defense workers employed along Route 128. Morey was one such worker: his expanding political awareness and the shifting focus of the peace and antiwar movements dovetailed in a way that would later prove fateful for the Boston antihighway movement.

In mid-1964, when he could not persuade the Pentagon to cancel his division's contract to develop computer-based protocols for bombing missions in Southeast Asia, Morey finally hit his ethical limit and quit his job.[12] Morey's new SDS acquaintances promptly hired him to coordinate New England–based demonstrations against the Vietnam War. A seemingly natural organizer, Morey excelled at this work. He was next hired by a group of Episcopal and Catholic priests who, like SDS members, had turned their attention to defense and high-tech workers. The group called itself the Boston Industrial Mission and believed that the moral stress exacted by advanced capitalism required a specialized ministry and the identification of new field mission sites.[13] According to its analysis, businesses along Boston's Route 128 electronics-heavy research corridor represented a site in need of clerical intervention.

Soon after the preliminary 27-mile segment of Route 128 was opened in 1951, a technology-inflected regional economy began to take root on land once home to pig farms, vegetable fields, and gravel pits.[14] Route 128 pushed Boston's urban perimeter into semirural hinterlands and provided a new frontier for postindustrial economic development. But the speed and extent of this economic transformation was a huge surprise. The road's construction as the first limited-access circumferential highway in the United States was principally intended "to provide ready access to the North and South Shore recreational and residential area and Western sections of the state."[15] State highway planners could not have anticipated that the end of World

War II would forever change the meaning and importance of this road and its surrounding territory of large, low-cost land parcels.

When WWII ended, the federal government boosted its spending on research and development and, as technology scholar AnnaLee Saxenian notes, "spurred the growth of new industries and regions by channeling resources to university labs to develop war-related technologies."[16] Firms along Route 128 were major beneficiaries of this federal largesse. Many other companies would soon opt to relocate there in hopes of taking advantage of this unexpected midcentury funding boom. In this way, Route 128's sprawling network of tech companies, university partners, and government institutions established a new, research-driven industrial geography for Boston. Yet, for priests engaged in peace-building politics, the highway represented little more than a 65-mile circumferential field site desperately in need of religious intervention.

Unlike their French counterparts, the Boston Industrial Mission's activist priests did not seek employment in processing plants or car factories. Instead, they sponsored regular on-site office discussions for industrial workers in Cambridge and along Route 128. These efforts were aided by Morey's skillful coordination of meetings and seminar-style training detailing how companies could modify defense technologies and planning to address problems in American cities.[17] Traveling parallel routes aimed at persuading middle-class tech professionals to join the antiwar movement, secular and religious activist groups incubated a potent New Left politics based on the reappropriation of technical knowledge for peaceful and domestic application. Fueled less by public protests and rallies, this politics restaged the peace movement's front line away from college campuses and within corporate cubicles. Here a highly coordinated, direct-action strategy was used to persuade defense and high-tech workers to abandon their participation in the military industrial complex and thereby destroy the nation's capacity for war technology research and development.

The priests' mission was to dismantle America's tools for international aggression before they were built and to redirect the nation's advanced technologies and industrial might to domestic problem solving.[18] Morey had a front-row seat on all of this. His professional training in systems theory, his ethical and political commitments to peace, his knowledge of corporate organizational models as well as his radical orientation as a community organizer cast him as a powerful embodiment of mid-1960s

New Left politics. Morey's work with the Boston Industrial Mission (BIM) would also enable him to build a strong professional and social network of priests across Greater Boston. Father Tom Corrigan, a Jamaica Plain–based priest and later cochair of the Greater Boston Committee on the Transportation Crisis, notes Morey's BIM-sponsored work within Route 128 as the start of their relationship as political organizers.[19] Corrigan also helped lead training and lunchtime seminars for area workers and would become increasing concerned about the region's highway controversies. While Morey deepened his political network among priests and Route 128's corporate workers, another group of citizens was also questioning the role of technical knowledge in creating a more just society.

Radical Planners: New Roads, Old Memories

In 1965 a small group of young radical planners disenchanted with old approaches to urban redevelopment began discussing an alternative highway plan for Cambridge. They named themselves the Cambridge Committee on the Inner Belt and soon authored a daring series of editorials and maps for the city's weekly newspaper. The Cambridge Committee's campaign for a new highway plan gained significant public attention and support and led to the group's eventual incorporation as an upstart planning organization called Urban Planning Aid (UPA). For early leaders of the Cambridge Committee, roads ripping through Boston's heart required a forceful and sophisticated political rebuke. Tunney Lee had been a Hudson Street resident and remembered when a large portion of it was cleared for Boston's Southeast Expressway and the state turnpike's on-ramp. "I had lived on Hudson Street, half of which was taken out by the [Massachusetts] Turnpike."[20] Lee's memory of the destruction of Chinatown's Hudson Street filled him with a foreboding sense of Cambridge's fate: demolition, displacement, and, finally, choking traffic. He knew well the impact of a multilane highway coursing through a densely populated working-class neighborhood, and most important, he understood the relationship between highway expansion and uncatalyzed neighborhood resistance.

Before the Mass Pike's extension in the 1960s, nearly half of Chinatown's residential footprint was cleared between 1953 and 1959 in preparation for the Central Artery expressway. This new, elevated, divided highway would barrel through Hudson and nearby Albany Streets and displace much of the neighborhood's mix of Chinese, Lebanese, and Syrian families. Many of these residents would later recount the groan of cranes moving down a single street, house by house, until the highway's intended path was completely cleared. According to these accounts, there was no public process for residents to participate in the planning of their neighborhood or the highway's impact on it.[21]

Local activists and artists, Jeremy Liu and Mike Blockstein, recorded several residents' memories of Hudson Street's destruction in a documentary film called *A Chinatown Banquet*.[22] The film features audio interviews of Lee and several other Chinatown residents recounting memories of Hudson Street's destruction. One unnamed resident described highway-based clearance in Chinatown as an example of downtown business interests trumping those of residents.

> One of the most important words to consider when talking about planning and construction of the Central Artery is perspective and, more specifically, *whose* perspective mattered. The perspectives that mattered were the perspectives of those suburban commuters who wanted to live outside of the city and drive into downtown and [the perspectives] of the downtown business community, specifically the employers of those suburban commuters. The perspectives of the downtown residents did not matter. Those residents, who were by and large of an immigrant population, did not work in the same places, rode mass transit to work, and did not constitute a major political constituency.

As this speaker notes, Boston's highway expansion signaled to Chinatown's residents that their neighborhood's land was being repurposed for and by people who did not live there. For many such residents, the new highways were expressions of downtown business leaders' desire to reconfigure Boston's landscape according to their own economic preferences. Furthermore, residents interpreted the demolition of their homes as a breach of political trust between themselves and government leaders who were supposed to safeguard their rights. The notion that a swirling set of nonresident perspectives and preferences was determining who could have access to Boston's core was politically and racially offensive to many of Chinatown's residents. This story provided a cautionary tale for the region's late-1960s antihighway movement as well as a lasting memory in the minds of Chinatown's neighborhood activists.[23]

When mimeographed letters were distributed to Chinatown residents to announce the state's seizure of their homes in 1963, the neighborhood faced another population-scattering eruption. Each letter proved an unforgettable messenger of government power at midcentury and the state's callous disregard for populations whose labor had enriched its coffers. Yet, beyond bearing devastating news for residents in the highway's path, these letters would ultimately serve as ammunition for subsequent activists in Chinatown and throughout Greater Boston. Lee recalls: "When the turnpike took that part of Hudson Street, people got letters. The owners got letters in the mailbox saying your property is now owned by the Massachusetts Turnpike Authority. Your rent is $50/month please pay . . . And if you want a quick settlement we'll give you the assessed value. If you don't, you go to court and we'll see you in court. I had these people come to me with these letters and say, 'What do I do with this? What should I do?'"[24] For Lee, residents' anxieties were the result of an abuse of state power and a deficient public planning process that gave the highway authority free reign. More than a textbook assessment by a skilled technocrat, Lee's analysis would later seed multiple radically participatory approaches to urban planning in Boston and beyond.[25] And when Cambridge residents learned of the state's Inner Belt proposal to slice through dense, working-class neighborhoods, Lee related the plan directly to the experiences of Chinatown's residents. His advice to Cambridge residents: Don't be the next Hudson Street.[26]

While working as a planner for the Boston Redevelopment Authority, Lee developed a friendship with fellow coworker Fred Salvucci. These two young planners watched as multiple highways reconfigured the city's landscape and dispersed poor and working-class neighborhoods farther and farther away from Boston's center. Lee recalls: "So by the time we were looking at the Inner Belt portion in Boston, nobody was contesting it. It was already sort of empty—easy to empty. People had moved out or were about to move out."[27] Despite aggressive ground clearance actions, no organization had emerged to mobilize resident opposition to the proposed highway—Lee and Salvucci shook their heads in disbelief.

Salvucci first heard about the Inner Belt as a graduate student at MIT in the early 1960s. During a professor's lecture on the importance of the road and why it should go through nearby neighborhoods, and not MIT's campus, Salvucci sat unconvinced. Salvucci's own memories of a previous

state highway project compelled him to question the planning logic behind
the Inner Belt.

> My grandmother lived near the railroad tracks in north Brighton and
> the turnpike took her house and all the houses on her side of the street
> in that neighborhood and discontinued a couple of tracks to the rail-
> road in order to create the land to put the (Massachusetts) turnpike
> on . . . they behaved atrociously. They didn't even give people an offer;
> there was no relocation assistance. They didn't even give 'em an offer on
> their land until six months after they had been relocated . . . evicted. In
> that same time period, the West End was getting knocked down with
> the urban renewal scam. So the combination of seeing this—I thought,
> ridiculous explanation in class about why the Inner Belt should go
> through the neighborhoods and not near MIT along with how my
> grandmother was getting treated led me to believe that something was
> basically awfully wrong.[28]

He cites this early story as instrumental for spurring his politics as a radical
planner and antihighway activist. Similarly, Lee traces his commitment to
grassroots, participatory planning to his absolute frustration with the state's
outmoded and undemocratic approach to neighborhood development.

For both of these young planning professionals, the approaching Inner
Belt and I-95's extension recalled earlier highway clearance projects permanently etched in their memories. Their refusals to forget the trauma of
highway expansion or the indifference of the state's planning bureaucracy
would spark the formation of the Cambridge Committee on the Inner Belt
and set the course for their professional careers. As early initiators of the
Cambridge Committee, Salvucci and Lee laid an intellectual and organizational base for radical planners and social scientists to produce cutting-
edge, research-backed plans in support of low-income residents facing
government-sponsored displacement.

Salvucci and Lee collaborated with planning colleagues Denis Blackett,
who worked with them at the Boston Redevelopment Authority; Chester
Hartman, a planner on faculty at Harvard; Robert Goodman, a planner
on faculty at MIT; Gordon Fellman, a Harvard-trained sociologist; Ira
Rosenberg, a local real estate developer with leftist leanings; and Lisa Peattie,
an urban anthropologist at MIT. This collective of scholar-practitioners
marshaled their considerable talents to create a neighborhood outreach

and engagement method that worked at the street level to build residents' awareness of the state's highway plan. The Cambridge Committee developed a signature tactic of lambasting the state's transportation development efforts via published reports, articles, and editorials. This highly visible and formal approach meant that the group had few friends within the political establishment.

In time most of the concerns raised by the Cambridge Committee would become standard elements for evaluating publicly funded transportation systems; however, in 1965, when the group was founded, this was not yet the case. Prominent government officials and public planning agencies, in fact, were typically offended by the committee's perceived attack on what remained accepted professional practice. Colonel Edward J. Ribbs, the state's Department of Public Works commissioner and overseer of road building plans had this to say: "This is all we are attempting to do—to construct the basic highway system and today there are only fragments of it . . . Our recommendations for this system are well supported and documented for the record . . . Our task, in my opinion, should be confined to a technical and professional approach to the problem leading to recommendations and whether those recommendations are implemented is the task of others and beyond our control. We have no intention, therefore, in engaging in a battle—we are only concerned with performing our professional duties for the Commonwealth."[29] For Ribbs, highway building was simply a job that his agency was legally charged to carry out. His assertion that this task "should be confined to a technical and professional approach" bypasses a broader consideration of the values and priorities informing transportation planning as a cultural practice. Thus Ribbs demonstrates the dominant political view that the technical and professional knowledge of transportation planners constituted a neutral antidote to highway opposition and not a source of controversy. Radical planners and antihighway activists would soon make plain to Ribbs and others that a larger battle was under way and the emerging highway fight was merely a symptomatic skirmish.

A growing coalition of residents in Massachusetts agreed that the state's planning practices, and especially those conducted by Ribbs and his staff, were creating uninhabitable environments via policies that were indeed part of the controversy. For these activists, democratic authority and decision making were at stake, not merely the placement of a highway. Like Ribbs, the majority of professional transportation planners remained indifferent to the ways in which their methods privileged particular segments of the public, namely white, male, suburban drivers. Radical planners brought public attention to this bias by attacking service deficits and the regressive financing underpinning the region's transportation plans. These planners' collective efforts to shift the professional norms of transportation planners away from a technocratic emphasis on traffic counts and driver destination surveys and toward meeting the needs of urban residents issued a defiant rebuttal to the state and the field of planning itself. Furthermore, these activist planners questioned the state's emphasis on automobile travel when many Boston residents did not own cars.

The Cambridge Committee and its research and advocacy agenda would later morph into Urban Planning Aid (UPA) and prevail as the uncontested leader of the Boston antihighway movement's well of data and analytics. Drawn to their progressive politics and participatory approach to planning, Jim Morey introduced himself to UPA's leaders and soon joined its ranks. Morey would eventually become UPA's leader. Early UPA president and MIT professor Robert Goodman recalls: "Jim approached us. He was working with systems analysts, some of them working for the Defense Department, and he was trying to move them in the direction of the peace movement. He saw the work that we were doing as a natural way to get these kinds of people, systems analysts and, engineers, moving in that direction so he started working with us and then at one point became UPA president. He was incredibly effective and really broadened the perspective of the organization beyond just architects and planners."[30]

Jim Morey and Fred Salvucci teamed up to cowrite UPA's blistering critique of the state's highway plan and rejected the relevance of a car-based plan for a region with a largely carless population: "In Boston about 48 percent of households are carless, in Cambridge about 40 percent . . . in the lower income areas of these cities the figures are even higher. At the same time that lower income persons without cars are becoming more and more concentrated in the central city, most new jobs are opening up in outlying areas, usually in areas very difficult to get to by public transportation. Thus one important factor in limiting job opportunities for inner-city residents is that they are unable to reach the available jobs in Route 128 firms."[31] As Morey and Salvucci note, the movement of jobs away from Boston and toward the outer suburbs of Route 128 created a spatial mismatch between low-income workers and the employment opportunities they sought. An aging public transportation infrastructure—built before many of Boston's newer suburbs existed—only exacerbated this schism.[32]

Civil Rights, Black Power, and Moving beyond Integrationism

Nine months before the Greater Boston Committee on the Transportation Crisis proclaimed People before Highways Day on the steps of the Massachusetts State House, black nationalists had occupied the very same spot for a somber expression of political and racial solidarity. They gathered in a silent vigil to mourn Martin Luther King Jr.'s death. King's assassination on April 4, 1968, provoked urban uprisings in more than 100 cities across the country. In Boston, there were no D.C.- or Chicago-like revolts requiring federal marshals. Instead, activists marched to the State House and called on their government to acknowledge and respond to the needs of local communities. With a simple sign proclaiming, "Black is Beautiful," black residents broadcast the essential meme of a burgeoning black nationalist movement.

While the nation grieved King's death, more militant black (no longer willing to be identified as "colored" or "Negro") activists read his murder as further indication of the futility of nonviolent civil disobedience. For these activists, both the tactic of nonviolence and the social ideal of racial integration represented outmoded and politically ineffectual bases for racial justice. Nationally, tempers flared among young radicals anxious to define the next steps in the movement, while older, more moderate civil rights leaders struggled to set a new agenda in King's absence. In Boston, activists, including Chuck Turner, desired immediate action that sidestepped the movement's larger ideological stalemate. Heeding the advice of Student Nonviolent Coordinating Committee (SNCC) leader Stokely Carmichael, Turner spearheaded the formation of a new black nationalist organization called the Black United Front. The Front was a direct consequence of the surge of post–civil rights politics that flourished in the wake of King's death. Many activists, like Turner, moved away from racial integrationism as a social and political goal and advanced alternative racial justice models.

In January 2010, I met with Charles "Chuck" Turner to discuss his experiences as a leader in the Boston antihighway movement. When I arrived at his office, a staff member led me past a bustling reception area and directly to Turner's desk, where he sat finishing a phone call. As I sit down, he smiles and waves at me like we know each other, which we don't. Even so,

I'm grateful for the chance to feel at ease in a room so full of activity, people, and paper files. We chat casually for a while, and then I ask him about the early years of his political activism. Turner closes his eyes. Phones are ringing in the background and several people are talking, but in this moment the room has gone completely still for just the two of us. Turner pauses and takes a breath. I can only imagine the seven-decade span of faces, conversations, and events his mind scans in this one quiet intake of air and memory. Turner starts by sketching a timeline of his young adulthood. In 1958, he left Cincinnati, Ohio, and traveled to Boston to start his freshman year at Harvard College. But it was his rumbling conscience and personal investment in civil rights organizing that would define his time in Boston more than his schoolwork. Within three years he left school and joined the Northern Student Movement (NSM), which took its direct action and voter registration cue from the SNCC, with the geographic twist of concentrating its organizing in northern cities such as Chicago, New York, Boston, and Hartford. The Northern Student Movement mobilized around students' conviction that racism and the legal obstructionism it facilitated were not phenomena confined to the southern United States.[33]

As part of their work for NSM, Turner and fellow Boston organizer Byron Rushing traveled to Selma, Alabama, in 1965 in support of SNCC's voter registration drive. Turner details the chain of events defining his early activist years:

> In '65 Byron Rushing and I went down to work with Stokely [Carmichael] when [the Student Nonviolent Coordinating Committee] was doing the organizing in Selma. In '68 when King was killed, I was working as an organizer. Stokely came back from [Guinea], I think, in January of 1968. And says, "Look, there's gonna be a crackdown. Our intelligence says that the government is going to make a move on activists so what I'm advising activists to do across the country is to form United Fronts with the more middle-class groups in the community in order to have a buffer so when they come to get you there'd be another group—another layer there, a layer that can be protective." He came to Boston because we had some connection. He talked to a group of us, and we agreed to work with him in the formation of the Boston Black United Front.[34]

During a peaceful street protest, violent mobs of white police and deputized citizens attacked the campaign's interracial assembly of volunteers and staff leaders in Selma. The attack stunned everyone and led to several deaths. In immediate response, Carmichael announced a new tactical path based on the expulsion of the organization's white members and the decision to carry arms.[35] Next, SNCC's well-known leader John Lewis was ousted, and Carmichael assumed his position as chairman. This seminal civil rights shake-up formally signaled a waning commitment to racial integration and nonviolent civil disobedience among younger and more militant black activists. For these militant activists, more hard-line actions were needed to achieve a greater sense of black self-reliance and safety in the face of intractable white racism. Turner and Rushing experienced these defining civil rights upheavals firsthand. Their time in the South would directly influence their activism in Boston. Moreover, Carmichael's deepening friendship with both men, Turner especially, would play a key role in helping to set a radical agenda for Boston's later antihighway movement.

In 1966, the year following Turner and Rushing's Selma trip, Carmichael visited Boston and led a march down Roxbury's Blue Hill Avenue with Nation of Islam's Minister Louis X (he would later replace "X" with Farrakhan). Side by side, both men trumpeted the need for unity and cooperation among the entire spectrum of America's civil rights organizations. Carmichael, then still chairman of SNCC, addressed a Roxbury crowd of thousands with this forceful directive: "It's time for the NAACP, the Urban League, CORE [Congress of Racial Equality], Exodus, the Muslims and all the black leaders in this community and in ghetto communities across the country to join hands and begin to work together regardless of their differences of approach."[36] Each of these organizations had developed distinct political ideologies for the social and economic advancement of black Americans in the twentieth century; however, at midcentury they were embroiled in increasingly contentious intergroup debates over strategy and direction. Carmichael acknowledged these divisions yet called for a stronger commitment to collective solidarity. This message set the basis for Carmichael's conception of Black United Fronts and signaled the emergence of a new, post-1960s civil rights politics.

Boston's Black United Front announced its existence mere days after King's assassination and quickly built a political coalition of activist and social service organizations supporting black constituencies. And, although the Front advanced a wider political agenda targeting housing, education, police brutality, and land development generally, a major portion of its mobilizing energy was spent on Boston's antihighway fight. The state's proposed Inner Belt and Southwest Expressway would have a devastating impact on Boston neighborhoods with significant black populations. For the Front, these highways promised yet another barrier to black constituencies' political and economic self-determination. This was unacceptable. In direct response to the state's transportation plan, the Front's founding list of twenty-one demands included a statement expressing its formal opposition to the proposed highway: "The planned construction of the Inner Belt and Southeast [*sic*] Expressway are to be halted immediately and their continued planning and construction negotiated with the Black community since both of these highway projects will radically affect the lives of people in this community."[37]

Demand 19 articulates the Front's development vision as inclusive of and responsive to a public larger than the one Massachusetts highway planners had considered. While the group would later raise a series of concerns related to the highway itself, the critique here begins as dissatisfaction with the lack of public participation in the highway's planning and construction process. To further its antihighway position, the Front set up a subcommittee—Operation STOP—to protest construction of the Inner Belt and the Southwest Expressway and to create a vehicle for black residents and their allies to assert greater leadership in the political and economic development of their neighborhoods. The formation of Operation STOP also demonstrates an increasingly self-assured and place-based politics emerging from within the civil rights movement itself. No longer was the goal simply to be in or move through space; the new goal was to determine control over space.

Under Chuck Turner's leadership, the Black United Front (BUF) marshaled groups from Roxbury, Dorchester, and the South End to share resources and strategies related to black political self-determination and unity. In this way, the Front offered a revised geography for considering Boston's physical development. Here a race-inflected and nationalist political ideology elevates blackness as a kind of organizing tent for new spatial imaginings. The local neighborhood boundary lines separating Boston's black residents were seen as subordinate to race as container for collective group membership. According to the Front and its swelling membership roster of more than fifty groups, new organizational models and maps were now required to bring greater resources and attention to communities in need.

Though the Black United Front established a new frontline of black liberation politics in Boston, some felt its politics were not radical enough.
The Boston chapter of the Black Panther Party supported the work of the
Front despite its critique of Front members as moderate "reformers." Both
organizations vied to be the ideological base camp for Boston's black residents in Roxbury and beyond, but they espoused very different organiz
ing methods and outcomes. Boston Panther Floyd Hardwick describes
the Black United Front as "having a limited view of black nationalism":
"[The Black Panthers] were talking about all people all over the world, all
colors. We were revolutionaries, and we considered them [BUF] reformers, more moderate reformers. That is not what we would have said about
them. We would have said cultural nationalists. And we thought that was
good at one point in the struggle."[38] As the captain of education for Boston
Panthers in the mid-1960s, Hardwick served as the lead local interpreter
of Panther doctrine and politics. Like their Oakland-based comrades,
Boston's Panthers clashed with reformist, integration-seeking civil rights
organizations, including but not limited to the National Association for
Advancement of Colored People (NAACP), the Congress of Racial Equality
(CORE), and the Urban League. Boston's Black United Front counted these
moderate organizations as members and thus provoked Panthers' skepti-
cism of its radicalism.

Though Boston's Black Panthers and Black United Front members
diverged in their political ideologies, they stood united in their shared
espousal of community control and opposition to local highway construction. Hardwick recounts the antihighway stance of the Panthers: "A lot of
people didn't want [the highway] to happen. We were against it. We were
concerned about what would happen to the people in those [housing]
developments down there. We had the feeling that they would be displaced
or someway harmed . . . It was a matter of community control. I wasn't
schooled in the notion of urban development beyond ideas of gentrification, ideas of the poor being moved out. It was real fundamental: white
people are going to take over—people are going to be hurt. People are not
going to have homes. People are not going to have power. People are not
going to have control of their lives."[39] For Boston Panthers, the proposed
Inner Belt and I-95/Southwest Expressway symbolized physical displacement, lost housing, and diminished local power for black residents and
their neighbors. The solution, according to the Panthers and the Black

United Front, was the adoption of a politics of community control and the progressive devolution of decision-making power to local constituents and their designated leaders.

For civil rights groups and militant black organizations alike, the anti-highway fight served as an ideological accelerator for a politics that had evolved through voter registration drives, lunch counter sit-ins, and rallies protesting police brutality. Honed in the North and the South, these tactics and their philosophical underpinnings now coalesced to yield a mature toolkit for battling state power and highways.

Alliance of Alliances: Forging One Movement

When Operation STOP, the Black United Front's antihighway action com-mittee, called a meeting three months after the successful 1969 State House rally of the Greater Boston Committee on the Transportation Crisis, an eclectic coalition of local actors gathered to articulate a new vision for the region's planning and development. Leaders from the Black United Front, Urban Planning Aid, and the Greater Boston Committee merged black nationalist demands for local decision-making control with a critique of state-sponsored planning methods and values with the goal of building a broad regional coalition. By this time, Operation STOP had established itself as an important center of gravity within the antihighway movement and reflected a multiracial, citywide assortment of organizations well beyond the Front's core membership. The attendance list of Operation STOP's March 1969 meeting lists twenty-five participants representing a wide variety of organizations and neighborhoods across Greater Boston. Brad Yoneoka, a graduate school dropout who joined the Greater Boston Committee to organize antihighway protesters full-time, chaired the meeting.

Yoneoka opened the meeting by introducing Jim Morey of Urban Planning Aid (UPA). Morey then discussed a draft of the presentations to be shared with neighborhood groups. This particular meeting focused on highway threats to the South End neighborhood and detailed the local impacts of the Inner Belt, its connecting interchange in Roxbury, and the city of Boston's proposed highway cut-through, the highly controversial South End Bypass. As Morey likely described, UPA-modeled neighborhood-based information sessions and slideshows would serve as essential out-reach tools for catalyzing antihighway activists' agenda. Yoneoka bolstered

Morey's presentation with additional commentary on STOP's objective in utilizing UPA's organizing approach: "At these meetings, the neighborhood will come up with a position towards new highways affecting the South End; the Inner Belt, the Interchange, and the South End Bypass. STOP will derive a basic position paper from the neighborhood positions."[40] Yoneoka's remarks underscore the tactical function of UPA-sourced infor mation exchange for mobilizing neighborhood-based constituencies.

Yoneoka further outlined the Greater Boston Committee's main outreach objectives: informing residents of what would be lost if highways were built, using slides and maps to illustrate the geography of highway impact, and keeping conversations open to the public and highly visible (that is, by invit- ing the press and distributing leaflets). Neighborhood informational meet- ings offered not only a tactical intersection point for the Greater Boston Committee, Urban Planning Aid, and the Black United Front/Operation STOP but also an effective outreach method for galvanizing neighborhood groups unaligned with the movement. And, interestingly, sharing political tactics enabled various antihighway groups to hone further their indepen- dent political beliefs while building the movement's larger base and goal of forging a single voice of highway opposition. For the Greater Boston Committee, this meant convincing organizations and individual residents across the region to support a no-highway position. For Urban Planning Aid, this meant producing research, analysis, maps, and images to help resident groups develop a cogent case for such a position. And for the Black United Front, this meant operationalizing its political commitment to local com- munity control and Black Power. The coordinated leadership of Yoneoka, Morey, and STOP's organizers demonstrate the early internal workings of a regional movement and how multiple organizations linked varied ideologies and tactics to create a common agenda for building more allies.

In 1969 the movement was focused yet broad enough to house the ferment of each of these tactical and political ideals. The three years that followed would test the outer limits and inner cohesion of this progressive political alliance and set in motion a regional transformation of historic proportions.

====

This chapter has introduced the Boston antihighway movement as a regional convergence of actors opposing state-sanctioned federal road building through urban neighborhoods. For these actors, the highway's

intrusion echoed multiple previous examples of government failure to protect the rights and needs of citizens. From poor and working-class Italian
residents displaced by clearance in Brighton to Chinese and Syrian families
whose housing was razed in Chinatown to African American and Puerto
Rican residents uprooted from the South End, Boston's physical and social
landscape writhed through a series of population-displacing upheavals
in the 1950s and 1960s. These dislocations would have permanent consequences for the type of grassroots politics that would immediately follow.

The cartography of highway expansion and urban renewal clearance
scratched the landscape with a raw, people-based, and memory-fueled
code for action. Furthermore, ideological cross-fertilization among multiple 1960s-era liberation movements—including fights for civil rights,
Vietnam withdrawal, and black nationalism—would spawn a forceful new
grassroots activist agenda demanding a more just development of America's
cities. Boston's late-1960s antihighway organizing well illustrates the urban
implications of all these spatial and political collisions. In the end, poor
and working-class residents' disrupted relationship with the landscape and
their political leaders would converge with the tactical strength of seasoned
liberation activists to dismantle bloated government power and restore a
badly damaged democracy.

Chapter 2

Battling Desires

(Re)Defining Progress

The system has been so located as to provide for proper connections between the various routes and the existing and planned state and federal highways as the latter approach and penetrate the Metropolitan Area.
—*The Master Highway Plan for the Boston Metropolitan Area* (1948)

Our unity as a nation is sustained by free communication of thought and by easy transportation of people and goods. The ceaseless flow of information throughout the Republic is matched by individual and commercial movement over a vast system of interconnected highways, crisscrossing the country and joining at our national borders with friendly neighbors to the north and south. Together, the united forces of our communication and transportation systems are dynamic elements in the very name we bear—United States. Without them, we would be a mere alliance of many separate parts.
—President Dwight D. Eisenhower addressing Congress (1955)

n 1948, Massachusetts planners produced a slim, 120-page document recommending the creation of a new regional highway system for the state. Filled with maps, traffic counts, and route projections, this plan catapulted the state into a local and national chase for road-building support. However, because Dwight D. Eisenhower had not yet increased federal spending on highway construction, many states, including Massachusetts, were left wishing for roads that they could not afford. President Eisenhower's signing of the Federal-Aid Highway Act in 1956 unleashed a torrent of political support and funding for national highway building. The authority of the federal government and the dreams of Massachusetts's own highway planners finally met to set new transportation policy. As the state's highway plans moved from line drawings to legislative reality, residents of Massachusetts gradually began to ask, "Who are these roads for?" This simple question would unravel the state's highway plan and launch a region-spanning debate on how to imagine transportation options not solely centered on automobiles.

The desires of numerous national and local actors converged to advance a road-building agenda whose federal decision-making armature and technocratic focus constrained the power of dissenting voices. "Desire," in this sense, implies more than the professional jargon used by transportation planners to set travel directionality but rather the constellation of intent propelling U.S. highway expansion at midcentury. Yet, a desire to determine the course of U.S. transportation planning was not limited to the nation's highway supporters. In Massachusetts, antihighway activists mobilized citizen opposition by the creation and circulation of a new transportation plan. This plan expressed activists' desire to build a radically democratic planning process informed by their deepest hopes for transforming the region's built environments.

This chapter will contextualize this set of rival desires to demonstrate how the central tension animating the Boston antihighway movement was larger than a consideration of the pros and cons of regional road building. In short, two incongruous political decision-making models were colliding. On the one hand, federal highway planners (backed by a powerful prohighway business lobby) were eager to coalesce and centralize their newly expanded authority in the wake of President Eisenhower's political and financial endorsement of the nation's interstate system.[1] And, on the other, progressive activists were broadening their approaches to strengthening the decision-making authority and political leadership of grassroots actors. Each of these moves, on the part of both federal and local actors, would set the ground for decades of highway battles across the nation.

Federal Bureau of Public Roads and the Transcontinental Convoy

It was not obvious in 1919 that the career trajectories of a little-known bureaucrat named Thomas Harris MacDonald and an undistinguished colonel named Dwight D. Eisenhower would intersect to determine America's road-building future, but so it was. The modern dream of a federal interstate system stretches back to the early twentieth century when MacDonald was appointed chief of the Bureau of Public Roads.[2] MacDonald was described

as a no-nonsense, no-frills Midwestern bureaucrat. In Iowa, he had successfully built a system of high-quality paved roads that made the state's transportation system a national model. Buoyed by success in Iowa, MacDonald
arrived in Washington in 1919 to create a federal structure to support the
development of an interstate highway system. In that same year and not very
far away, a young army colonel was unwittingly building his own highway-
focused destiny. In 1919, twenty-eight-year-old Dwight D. Eisenhower was
chosen as an official observer for the U.S. Army's highly publicized road
trip across America. MacDonald's professional career of highway building
and Eisenhower's military-based belief in the benefits of roads would propel
America's highway construction to its midcentury zenith.

When MacDonald arrived in D.C. in 1919, he was the sole staff person in
a subcabinet agency with few supporters. However, what he lacked in political resources and allies, he made up for with charismatic energy that drew
outsiders to his efforts.[3] MacDonald's experience building roads in Iowa
had taught him exactly how highway connectivity translated into regional
economic growth. He was convinced that a federal interstate system could
similarly benefit the nation as a whole. And yet, as transportation historian Tom Lewis has noted, highway building was not the only objective
fueling MacDonald's federal highway career. MacDonald, Lewis observes,
also held "a belief in the superiority of technical expertise. For the chief,
roadbuilding was a scientific enterprise. Henceforth all decisions about
matters like proper building materials and methods as well as the size and
location of the roads themselves would be made with detached scientific
objectivity."[4] MacDonald's commitment to the modern ideal of technocratic rationalism as the basis for decision making left an indelible stamp
on America's state highway departments and the roads they built. His ideological stance imbued highway administration, at both the federal and the
state levels, with a hard-driving technocratic culture. Massachusetts would
prove no exception. MacDonald presided as chief and then commissioner
of the Bureau of Public Roads for nearly four decades before his vision of a
federal interstate highway system finally yielded significant results.

While MacDonald labored to create the decision-making infrastructure
and organizational culture that would make federal highway construction
possible, Dwight D. Eisenhower was gaining war-related experiences that
would make road building a national priority. Eisenhower's military service
during both World Wars filled him with a lasting belief in the importance of

good national roads. Participation by the United States in World War I had temporarily halted the federal conversation on road building, but interestingly, the war itself dramatized the need for better surface terrain for motorized vehicles. Military dependence on trench warfare meant that soldiers often found themselves stagnated and unable to advance battle lines for long periods.[5] Thus motorized vehicles had played a key role in literally speeding up combat as well as maintaining supply lines when combatants disrupted railroad service, as they frequently did. War was slowly entering the modern age, and America's military forces led the way.

After the armistice was signed in November 1918, the U.S. War Department issued a bold plan to showcase the army's technologically advanced fleet of motor vehicles and publicize the need for better roads for the nation. In celebration of America's war triumph, a transcontinental convoy of military vehicles would travel the country in a showy display of patriotism and technological might. The selection of the Lincoln Highway, America's first nation-spanning road for automobiles, meant that much of the country would learn about an important national travel route still in its infancy. Eisenhower joined the convoy and was responsible for writing the trip's final report. But the trip did not go as expected.[6] When all designated personnel and vehicles assembled in Washington, D.C., on July 7, 1919, the chief of the Motor Transport Corps gave a sendoff speech reiterating the trip's goal:

> We hope in conducting this first transcontinental run in an army transport convoy to give an exhibition to the general public of the vast development of the motorized branch of the army and the motor vehicle for military purposes, which development is conceded to be one of the principal factors contributing to the winning of the war. It is also hoped that the trip . . . will serve the purpose of indicating the need for the immediate development of transcontinental highways and of through interstate connecting roads as military and economic assets. This trip over the Lincoln Highway is in a measure the War Department's contribution towards the good roads cause, a movement in which the Army is vitally interested.[7]

The nascent "good roads" movement—championed by Thomas MacDonald—had found an eager ally in the War Department and its armed forces. This congratulatory rhetoric was to be expected from the military's top brass; however, what was not expected was the number of breakdowns and road-related problems that would plague the army's vehicles in the coming days. During the convoy's grueling 3,251-mile journey, army repair crews mended numerous broken fan belts and tire blowouts and rescued several trucks from mud and collapsing roadways. The attempt to demonstrate the power and efficiency of the army's fleet of motorized vehicles had proved less than impressive; however, the case for building new roads was made. Eisenhower writes:

> On rough roads, sandy ones, or on steep grades the truck train would have practically no value as a cargo carrier. The train operated so slowly in such places, that in certain instances it was noted that portions of the train did not move for two hours.
>
> It was further observed that some of the good roads are too narrow. This compels many vehicles to run one side off the pavement in meeting other vehicles, snipping the tire, the edge of the pavement and causing difficulty in again mounting the pavement. This is especially true in a narrow concrete road. It causes fast deterioration of the road.
>
> It was further observed that in many places excellent roads were installed some years ago that have since received no attention whatever. Absence of any effort at maintenance has resulted in roads of such rough nature as to be very difficult of negotiating. In such cases it seems evident that a very small amount of money spent at the proper time would have kept the road in good condition.[8]

Eisenhower's candid assessment of road quality and performance highlighted the need for national road-building protocols to standardize construction materials, weight-bearing limits, lane size, and funding streams for interstate highways.

Though Henry Ford's Model T made the automobile affordable for the masses, in 1908 America still lacked the network of paved roads to make car ownership practical for the masses. America's first cars were seen as playthings for the wealthy, but something new was happening—no longer just pleasure objects for the elite or status symbols for the middle class, motor vehicles were now celebrated as essential to the nation's military defense and economic development. Motor vehicles were important, and so were roads for them to travel.

Yet, it was not just the existence of roads that Army leaders and federal highway officials emphasized as bringing financial and defense advantages for the nation. Rather it was the connectivity of roads that established their value. Thus, as the army's transcontinental convoy demonstrated, it was necessary to build strong, nation-spanning, and interconnected road systems. Prior to World War I, D.C.'s highway bureaucrats and a powerful cabal of lobbyists known as the "road gang" argued that connecting roads would enable more land-based trade across disparate geographic regions and thus promote economic growth. While equating roads with economic expansion was not a new idea, tying road building to military strength was unprecedented. The transcontinental convoy's organizers effectively added a new consideration to the pro-road-building discussion: How could America expect to protect itself during a domestic attack if military-grade vehicles could not easily traverse its landscape? This rhetorical question issued a provocative challenge to lawmakers and the general public.

Though it would take several long decades and another World War before the federal government was sufficiently galvanized to act on its road-building mission, the transcontinental convoy left a deep impression on Eisenhower. Later recalling the trip's importance and connecting it to his subsequent review of Germany's famed autobahns, he wrote:

> The trip had been difficult, tiring and fun. I think that every officer on the convoy had recommended in his report that efforts should be made to get our people interested in producing better roads. A third of a century later, after seeing the autobahns of modern Germany and knowing the asset those highways were to the Germans, I decided, as President, to put an emphasis on this kind of roadbuilding . . . This was one of the things that I felt deeply about, and I made a personal and absolute decision to see that the nation would benefit by it. The old convoy had started me thinking about good, two-lane highways, but Germany had made me see the wisdom of broader ribbons across the land.[9]

Eisenhower's participation in the transcontinental convoy and on the front lines of the Second World War showed him how an interstate highway system might benefit America. In this way, Eisenhower's military experiences served to link road building with national security and economic prosperity and formed the basis for far-reaching national transportation policy. With his signing of the 1956 Federal-Aid Highway Act, Eisenhower legislated his long-burning desire to establish an integrated road network within the United States. This desire, of course, was not Eisenhower's alone.

Thomas MacDonald, multiple prohighway lobbyists, and state highway departments across the country stood with him unequivocally.

Massachusetts Highway Planning

The Federal-Aid Highway Act of 1944 authorized designation of a 40,000-mile interstate highway system as well as the design and building standards necessary for its construction. Transportation planners in Massachusetts seized this moment to propose a new state highway network with direct connections to the federal interstate system. As their plan notes, "Four of the expressways will comprise parts of the proposed forty thousand mile network of interstate highways to serve the entire United States . . . The recommended system is designed to fulfill the needs of interstate and intercity highway transportation necessary to the future economic welfare and defense of the nation."[10] Written in response to this important yet underfunded federal highway act, Massachusetts's 1948 highway plan emphasized the region's car-based travel needs while explicitly linking itself to the nation's highway agenda. By the time Eisenhower signed the Federal-Aid Highway Act of 1956, almost a decade had passed since Massachusetts's planners had gathered the original traffic counts and population forecasts for the state's transportation master plan. While the state's transportation plan excelled at echoing federal highway criteria, by its 1948 publication, most of its base data was inaccurate.

Following World War II, Boston followed the national trend of urban population decline in the midst of suburban growth.[11] Beginning in 1950, the Greater Boston region entered a period of dramatic population shifts as suburban growth siphoned white and upwardly families out of the state's capital city. These population movements changed Boston's demographic mix significantly; however, state transportation planners looking at the city's postwar landscape saw one thing only: traffic jams.

The Department of Public Works, the State Planning Board, and the Massachusetts District Commission collaborated on the 1948 publication of *The Master Highway Plan for the Boston Metropolitan Area*. This plan proposed a single strategy for resolving the state's growing transportation needs: the construction of a regional highway system. The plan's authors write: "The traffic congestion problems of the Boston Metropolitan Area have been the subject of studies for a number of years. We recommend the

adoption of a modern high-speed expressway system as the foundation
on which highway construction should be programmed for the ultimate
solution of the problem."[12] Here highway planners in Massachusetts exhibit
America's midcentury euphoria for highway building as the primary solution to automobile-based transportation problems. In time, cities such as
Boston would learn that more roads led to more cars and more traffic and
not less, but in 1948 the state was focused on building more roads, with
little counterargument.

The Massachusetts highway plan was a joint public project of the
Department of Public Works (DPW), the State Planning Board, and the
Metropolitan District Commission—all state agencies known for patronage politics and protecting the interests of big business and unionized
labor. For these special interest groups assembled under the umbrella of
the DPW, a regional highway system meant jobs and more jobs. Thus, in
their view, there was no reason to debate or even discuss the need for new
highway construction. It was a no-brainer. Multiyear subcontracts for
unionized labor as well as lucrative vendor contracts for materials such as
gravel, asphalt, sand, and steel—all essential for road building—were not
to be denied from a regional economy rebounding from war. The financial lure of these contracts meant that expediency was the political goal
most sought and often preferred by the DPW. Moreover, a federal highway
culture of technocratic efficiency converging with a state-based cluster of
hungry special interest groups only emboldened the DPW's commitment
to top-down decision making. This approach would frame and ultimately
doom the state's highway plan. The DPW's effort to forgo a more inclusive public planning process, even with mounting citizen pressure to do
so, became a key factor in catalyzing Boston's antihighway movement.
Citizens banded together to insert their voices and needs into a planning
process they believed had largely ignored them.

A Study in Technocratic Planning

The Master Highway Plan for the Boston Metropolitan Area (MHP) recommended highway expansion as the solution to the state's growing transportation needs. A system of six to eight radial expressways linked by a central
belt was the plan's celebrated centerpiece. Although engineers would detail
these roads according to complex technical requirements, the highway

plan was based on a deceptively simple planning term called a "desire line." According to the plan's authors, "a desire line can be defined as a straight line between the point of origin and the point of destination of a trip or group of similar trips, without regard to routes traveled, in other words the line of travel if a direct highway existed."[13] In short, desire lines are imaginary routes based on the wishes of travelers moving across established roads. The MHP's authors commissioned paid researchers to survey car, taxi, and truck drivers across the state.

At various established checkpoints these researchers asked drivers where they were going and why, what routes they were traveling, and where their trip had originated. This information was plotted and coded to produce a spoke-like pattern stretching in each cardinal direction. This pattern would directly inform the proposed design for a state highway system (figure 4). The plan's authors reference desire lines as the "backbone" of the state's proposed highway network: "The traffic analysis has shown that a number of well-defined major desire lines of travel exist in the Boston Metropolitan area. To serve the present and the future traffic along these travel lines a system of expressways has been developed to form the backbone of the highway transportation network."[14] Alongside text, maps, and schematic drawings, plan authors displayed desire lines to illustrate what they saw as the current necessity and future purpose of regional highways. In this way, desire lines were used to produce an authoritative symbol of the state's public planning process. For antihighway activists, the essential question hinged on who exactly made up the DPW's conception of public and whose desires should determine the shape, placement, and direction of the state's highways.

For the plan's authors, steadfast in their commitment to a rational, technically precise planning process, the answers to these questions seemed obvious: "The logical shape for an expressway to serve the heavy volumes of traffic indicated by the desire lines takes the form of a Belt route circling the downtown area."[15] The "logical shape" identified by the state's planners formally established the cartographic outline of the Massachusetts expressway system. In this way the state's highway system was modeled to reflect the "desires" of a select subset of drivers. With the production of more technical maps, the language of desire lines was replaced with official highway route numbers linking Massachusetts to the nation's interstate highway system. And, thus, a map starkly illustrating the personal preferences and desires of

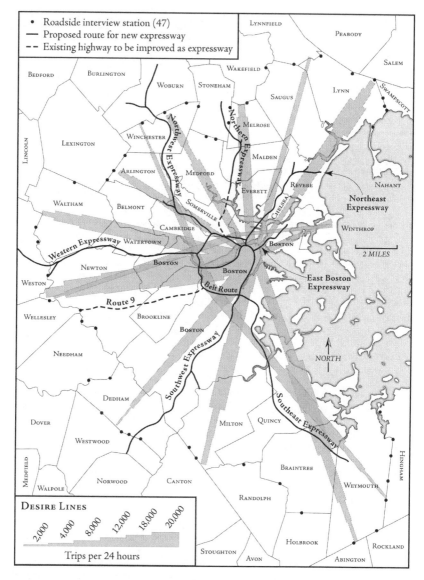

FIGURE 4. Highway "desire lines." This map shows proposed road construction as drawn in the 1948 *Master Highway Plan for the Boston Metropolitan Area*. Map by Kate Blackmer, © 2017.

drivers was transformed into the official highway plan for the state. As the abstract expression of the needs of a supposed "everyman," highway maps generated by the state would become deeply contested battlegrounds for residents not persuaded by the state's claim of democratic planning.

In their act of adopting federal road-building standards and bypassing the needs of a broader electorate, the state's highway planners initiated a highly technocratic planning process. The long hand of Washington and its revered highway champion Thomas Harris MacDonald had finally reached Massachusetts. MacDonald's Interregional Highway Committee mandated adherence to its design standards and protocols as a precondition to state participation in the federal highway programs. In this way, MacDonald's own commitment to technocratic planning and expertise stretched across the decades and into state-led highway programs. For Massachusetts this would mean a highway plan initiating major changes to the state's built environment without a local process for citizens to authorize it. In fact, the state's highway planners looked outside the state and to Washington for the authority and justification of their blueprint: "Basic standards utilized in the location and design of the expressway system are in conformity with those proposed and adopted by Federal and State Governments for use on the interstate highway system."[16] Federal highway standards, which had been devised under MacDonald's watchful eye and in cooperation with his handpicked collection of state government leaders, dictated the design, scale, and alignment of new highways in Massachusetts. Lane sizes (12 feet), width of rights-of-way (300 feet), shoulder span (12 feet), and even grade height were all federally specified in exacting detail. "A maximum 3 percent grade has been established as one of the governing conditions in this study. Both vertical and horizontal clearances at all railroad and highway separation structures should conform to the minimum requirements for interstate highways."[17] Based on the federal government's criteria, planners in Massachusetts proposed a complete multilane, limited-access expressway system connecting several cities and suburbs surrounding Boston. In this way, Washington policymakers' technocratic specificity established the "governing conditions" of the state's 1948 highway plan.

However, the essential question of *where* to locate this system was only partially addressed by federal guidelines or the radial pattern of desire lines set by the state's origin and destination surveys. Land acquisition costs played a determinative role in guiding state planners' road placement decisions.

Beyond issues related to the limitations of local topography, population density, and land use, this one variable preoccupied state highway planners the most. "In general the expressways will require rights-of-way from two hundred to three hundred feet wide. Locations have been selected therefore where such takings of real estate will not entail prohibitive cost. Long sections of sparsely developed property have been found for this purpose. Where populated areas must be traversed, the routes have generally been located in neighborhoods where real estate values are low and where they are still declining. The new service provided by the expressways should arrest the deterioration of such neighborhoods and aid in their rehabilitations."[18] The decision to privilege locations of low real estate value for the highway's path meant that both low-income and economically declining areas were exceedingly vulnerable to population displacement. Despite the planners' optimistic claim that the advent of highway travel "should arrest the deterioration of such neighborhoods and aid in their rehabilitations," highway planning itself offered anything but a positive gain for populations within these neighborhoods.

Federal design and construction mandates set in motion a set of development conditions and values that rationalized large-scale land clearance and residential displacement. This was all the more so for urban communities along the highway's intended path. Urban expressways required more rigorous standards, higher levels of materials, and (so the hope was) greater allocations of government funding. By proposing highway travel near and through these communities, Massachusetts planners sought to maximize the full range of benefits tied to federal interstate recognition. These planners argued that the region's current urban highways were inadequate and should be developed first. Furthermore, they argued, "Because almost the entire Metropolitan Area is rapidly developing urban characteristics, it is recommended that all expressways included herein be designed to urban standards."[19] And thus, with these sweeping gestures, planners would put the state on track for political battle with its electorate. Development biased toward technocratic planning and real estate of lower value may have worked in MacDonald's District of Columbia–based Public Roads Bureau, protesters seemed to say, but in Massachusetts, democratic politics still mattered, or so they hoped. A series of 1950s road-building projects, including the Massachusetts Turnpike and Central Artery, pushed highways farther into Boston's urban core and angered residents who lost homes and businesses in the process. More roads seemed to mean more of the same. The state's highway planners had attempted to divorce the commonwealth's built environment from more than half its users. In so doing, they set the stage for bristling public debates as highway clearance officially began in 1966.

While the state's 1948 highway plan sat on a shelf collecting dust and awaiting funding for nearly a decade, urban renewal programs pushed the federal government and its commitment to centralized planning farther into cities. This would prove disastrous for relations between planning authorities and the populations they claimed to represent. The drama unleashed during urban renewal's pattern of neighborhood clearance, resident displacement, and political stonewalling did not produce revitalized cities but rather increasingly large groups of politicized and angry citizens. These citizens were impatient with planning processes indifferent to their needs and input. This foment provided fertile ground for new approaches to urban planning. When President Eisenhower signed legislation enacting the Federal-Aid Highway Act of 1956, the federal government pledged 90 percent reimbursement funding for states willing to join their regional highways to the national interstate system. This single act mobilized state-led road-building efforts like nothing before or since. A highway planning and building race had officially begun, and within a decade in Massachusetts, a new organization called Urban Planning Aid would rise to contest it.

In the mid-1960s, Urban Planning Aid (UPA) harnessed its base of planning expertise to translate the meaning of the Massachusetts highway plan into simple, nontechnical terms for grassroots audiences. By interpreting the state's official maps and plans for the general public, UPA unmasked a special interest–led road-building agenda doubling as a transportation plan for the commonwealth as a whole. In this way, the group's analysis destabilized the authority of the state's maps as legitimate reflections of the travel needs of the entire region. This critique sparked an impassioned public battle that would last more than two decades.

From State-Led Planning to Advocacy Planning

Despite its pioneering role in grassroots politics in Massachusetts, the organization that would come to be known as Urban Planning Aid began informally in 1965 as a set of disgruntled comments lobbed over lunch. Fred Salvucci, Tunney Lee, and Denis Blackett were three Boston Redevelopment Authority (BRA) employees already thinking about alternatives to the state's highway plan. Each of them had been lured to the city's planning agency by its director, Ed Logue, and his promise of a new approach to rehabilitation of the city of Boston. But what was commanding their attention most was happening across the river in Cambridge.

> A group of us used to go have lunch on the Boston Common. A large number of people who worked at the BRA lived in Cambridge; I didn't, I lived in Brighton. But we began talking about how Cambridge was going to get screwed by what the state was planning because they still were going to go through the Brookline Elm Corridor and wasn't it too bad that no one seemed to be doing anything about it. And particularly, there were no planners involved in proposing alternatives. So who knows how long we just bullshitted at lunch—I'm sure a long time. But eventually an ad hoc group formed . . . The real leader of the group, in my view, is Denis [Blackett] because he was organized and structured and he developed a very simple but ultimately effective strategy . . . Denis just started writing articles—getting them printed in the *Cambridge Chronicle* saying, "Shouldn't there at least be a discussion about alternatives?"[20]

And within just a few minutes the Cambridge Committee on the Inner Belt was founded. This first meeting established its communication plan.

From lunchtime conversations to meeting in Blackett's living room, the group would quickly add members and start writing a series of articles in the *Cambridge Chronicle,* a local weekly. The trio was joined by Lisa Peattie, an urban anthropologist at MIT; Robert Goodman, an MIT architect and planner; Chester Hartman, a planning professor at Harvard;[21] Ira Rosenberg, a progressive-minded real estate developer; and Gordon Fellman, a professor of sociology at Brandeis. In Salvucci's view, Blackett "was the real spark plug, he was the one that was taking action."[22] Blackett wrote several articles critiquing the state's highway plan and demanding a public review process. By timing the completion of these articles with the Cambridge City Council's weekly meeting cycle, Blackett established a public platform and tactical communications loop that could not be ignored. In this way a small team of BRA employees grousing on Boston Common seeded a politically potent pressure group that would soon grow strong enough to bring city and state government road building to a grinding halt.

Blackett's articles caught the attention of a young Catholic priest named Father Paul McManus, who was concerned about the highway's potential displacement of members of his Cambridge parish. Father McManus contacted Blackett and suggested that they meet. Salvucci cites this connection as the "most important thing that happened because it tied technical observations—which would have just been letters to the editor that ultimately meant nothing—to a group that actually represented some voters and had some clout but didn't know how to use their clout."[23] Father McManus's parishioners were concerned about how the road would change the neighborhood. He hoped that Blackett's committee of engineers and architects could help them.[24] But in addition to his concern for his flock, it was McManus's own emotional memory of clearance in the West End that spurred him to action. "I was very conscious of the West End and the way that it had been destroyed—that was dreadful. That was a great community. That was a unified community, and it was a diverse community. You had Polish people, you had Jewish people, you had black people, you had Irish people, the whole thing, and they held together—that was devastating to some many of those people."[25] Like, many antihighway protesters, McManus desperately wanted to avoid a repeat of the West End. To him, Blackett and Salvucci and the Cambridge Committee offered a way to fight back.

Under the headline, "Three Alternate Routes Urged for Inner Belt: Committee Urges State, City Study," the newly formed Cambridge Committee on the Inner Belt launched a hand-drawn counteroffensive to the MHP. The committee's three-part map was featured on the *Cambridge Chronicle*'s community events page. Here, nestled above an announcement for a benefit for the Norwegian Old Peoples Charitable Association and Home, a dinner dance and costume party for the VFW, and a community program promising "beautiful slides of Hawaii," a new vision for defeating interstate highway expansion entered the public record. A large black-and-white image of three overlaid street maps lined with hatch marks simultaneously offered a visual understanding of the state's plan, a subtle critique of that plan, and a few alternatives. This was achieved without incendiary rhetoric or sophisticated, technical graphics. Instead, a drawing that looks like it could have been sketched on the back of the proverbial cocktail napkin tells the entire story. Because most residents had not seen a map of the

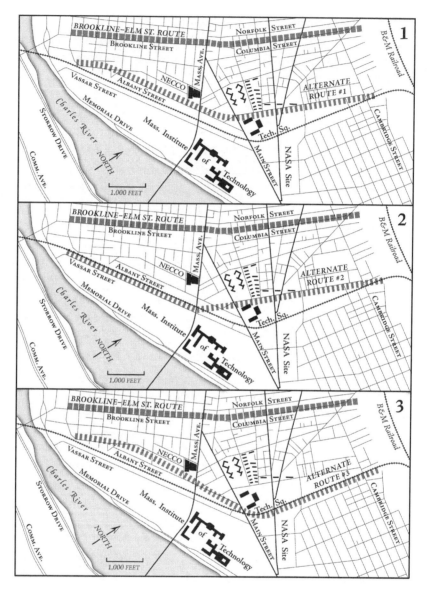

FIGURE 5. "Three Alternate Routes Urged for Inner Belt." The Cambridge Committee on the Inner Belt published three possible route alternatives to the state's proposed highway alignment along Brookline and Elm Streets, home to a vibrant multiracial, working-class residential community, which was threatened with significant displacement of area residents and businesses. The alternatives moved the highway's right-of-way away from these communities and closer toward existing railroad tracks along Albany Street and MIT's property line. Map by Kate Blackmer, © 2017; *Cambridge Chronicle,* Thursday, October 21, 1965.

state's proposed highway plan, the Cambridge Committee's crude, street-level drawing provided a lightning bolt of public information (figure 5).

Circulation of the committee's drawings allowed residents and local politicians to visualize the highway's path of demolition and displacement. What had been a dormant public discussion quickly became a surging political argument. The committee's maps were deft in their ability to focus debate at the scale of resident-occupied streets and blocks. Topped by a dashed line along Brookline Street, each map indicates what was known as the Brookline–Elm Street route. This route was the Massachusetts Department of Public Works' preferred Inner Belt path through Cambridge. Slicing straight through a working-class community of longtime residents, this route threatened high levels of social dislocation.

Marked with the numbers 1, 2, and 3, each map also features an alternative route proposed by the Cambridge Committee. Tracing Albany Street in map 1, Vassar Street and the railroad tracks in map 2, and just north of Albany Street in map 3, the bottom set of dotted lines proposes alternate highway routes. The DPW's Brookline–Elm Street route laid next to three alternative routes provoked new questions about the state's highway plan and the community's ability to influence it. The committee's act of specifying the highway's intended route made obvious much of what was at stake for Cambridge neighborhoods. What had previously been a hazy and obscure technical discussion about road building and the importance of the interstate highway system now crystallized into a place-based struggle for power.

Three weeks prior to publishing its alternative route map, the Cambridge Committee had announced that it would issue a series of reports on the state's Inner Belt proposal, which it did. The series ran weekly in the *Cambridge Chronicle* and used simple and highly readable maps to spatialize key findings, such as "5,200 individuals or about 6 per cent of the total population of Cambridge will be displaced" and the "loss of 1,000 jobs."[26] The consequences of the highway's planned path framed the committee's critique as well as its outreach approach for area neighborhoods.

The first map released by the Committee used a wide-angle view to show the highway's proposed route as it crossed the Charles River and entered Cambridge and Somerville. A large shaded "V" casts two shadowy legs across a partial street grid. It's a primer: one map, a few lines, a river, and three cities.[27] It allows viewers to orient themselves quickly and then wonder, "What do these lines mean?" And, perhaps, to ask: "Where is my house?" Blackett most likely followed this map with a few more meetings in his living room, then a few more group discussions, more analysis, and more maps. The decision to guide the public through a step-by-step examination of the DPW's highway plan was prescient not only because it afforded greater exposure for the committee's ideas but also, most important, because it created an informed base of residents ready to mobilize.

The committee published maps for public review while also making its political position, formal demands, and identity known:

> 1) Complete opposition to the Brookline-Elm St. Route; 2) Support for the additional and combined DPW and city of Cambridge studies in Albany-Portland St. and railroad area.
>
>
>
> [signed]
> The Cambridge Committee on the Inner Belt—
> Denis Blackett, City Planner
> Gordon Fellman, Sociologist
> Robert Goodman, Urban Designer
> Chester Hartman, City Planner
> Tunney Lee, City Planner
> Ira Rosenberg, Real Estate Developer
>
>

In an accompanying article the committee sketches its story: "Set up as an independent citizens group, the committee lacks both the funds and the time to undertake the detailed engineering analyses of the three routes. It has, however, analyzed such problems as ramp access, road curvature, and service roads to the extent that it believes the three proposed routes to be sufficiently realistic and feasible to warrant further study."[28] This is not the inflammatory rhetoric or histrionic debate indicative of many urban land use battles of the time. However, the committee's measured and exacting tone does not mask its radical political agenda.

Salvucci remembers the flash of inspiration that directly informed the Cambridge Committee's growing sense of identity and mission.

> We were meeting in Denis Blackett's living room as we usually did to plot the next step. Bob Goodman came in very excited, carrying I think in his hand a magazine article called "Advocacy and Planning" by a city planner who invented the term "advocacy planning." Goodman said, "Look at this guy, he's got this theory that the traditional view of

planning is—there's God and the planner talks to God, God tells the
planner the plan then the planner draws the plan. And there's like one
plan and that's what we do. This guy's saying that's not the way it works
at all, plans represent interests. The planners tend to represent the powerful interests, that's why we get screwed-up cities, that there really are
different interests involved and it should be the role of planners to work
as advocates, just as lawyers do, for low-income communities so that
they have at least some voice in this discussion." And Goodman said,
"That's us! *We're advocacy planning*. He's given us a name! We've been
doing it for the past year." So it was kind of a very exciting moment.[29]

Salvucci identifies this "aha" moment as the group's formal turning point.
Bob Goodman's discovery of Paul Davidoff's field-busting 1965 article
"Advocacy and Pluralism and Planning" gave the committee's founders
an expanded framework for articulating their work. Davidoff's attack on
traditional planning approaches laid bare the field's professional practice
of reproducing the interests of the powerful at the expense of the needs of
local citizens. Goodman and Salvucci adopted Davidoff's idea of planning
advocacy as a corrective for a field that needed one. This was a radical planning agenda in the making. And yet, for many Cambridge residents, the
committee's plan was not radical enough.

Then a graduate student in urban planning at MIT, Robert Goodman
recalls the committee's early days debating the highway's alignment.
Goodman and everyone else would soon find out that such was not what
the community wanted at all:

> Interesting thing about the project is finding out how did we come up
> with the idea of getting rid of all these highways? That wasn't our ini-
> tial idea. What we originally came up with was an alternative plan. We
> had no notion that you could get rid of these highways. And really that
> impetus came from the community itself. So here we were planners say-
> ing, "If we just gave them a more rational plan instead of destroying
> all these businesses and housing through Central Square, Somerville,
> and Brookline then we would be able to convince them that there were
> alternatives." And it wasn't until the community said, "Look, we don't
> want any alternatives. We don't want anything coming through here."[30]

The committee had its political mettle publicly tested almost immediately,
first by local residents and then by MIT. For Goodman, still enrolled as an

MIT grad student, this was particularly problematic. "One of the things that happened with the alternatives is that MIT felt threatened especially by the ones that came close to MIT. I believe there was one along the railroad tracks. And there was a meeting where they had their lawyer. He was arguing how we were going to destroy part of the nation's defense policies by affecting these buildings that were doing Defense Department work like the instrumentation lab at MIT. So this thing ballooned into stuff that we had never anticipated. We just thought, look, we'll come up with an alternative [or three] and if we have a good enough alternative one of them could have been picked."[31] The committee's three alternative maps had set off multiple unexpected controversies among local families and seniors and elite leaders of national defense research. And the worst was yet to come. The resulting scramble for community support and legal cover threw the committee into a productive spiral of agenda refinement and base building that would soon stretch itself across the river to include Boston.

The Cambridge Committee on the Inner Belt laid the operational bones for what would become Urban Planning Aid (UPA). Without the skill and tactical imagination of organizers such as Blackett, Salvucci, Goodman, and Lee, it is unclear whether the Cambridge antihighway fight would have gained its historic force, momentum, or victory. The early legwork and research of the committee would also prove decisive for the city of Boston's antihighway fight just a few years later.

The transition from an ad hoc committee of local renegades to a fully staffed, federally tax-exempt nonprofit organization did not happen overnight, but close to it. When the Massachusetts Legislature rescinded the municipal veto power of cities and towns in 1965, Cambridge residents lost their formal means of contesting highway development. The mayors of Boston and Somerville had already endorsed the state's highway plan, and until that point, Cambridge had been the only holdout. With the loss of veto power, Cambridge's antihighway protesters had no choice but to look outside of governmental structures to build their political agenda. Enter stage left: Blackett, Salvucci, and Lee and the Cambridge Committee on the Inner Belt. The committee's formal emergence could not have been timelier. More than an organizational response to planning issues in Cambridge, the group delivered a broader grassroots assessment of what was at stake for working-class neighborhoods facing urban development–related battles across the region.

According to its incorporation papers, UPA was established to "combat physical and social deterioration of low-income urban communities by providing technical aid to such communities to improve their housing, educational facilities and social welfare, and by making and publishing broad studies concerning the physical and social welfare of low-income urban communities."[32] Its organizers used maps, drawings, and statistics to communicate to residents how their democratic rights were being compromised by the state's transportation plan and why their direct participation in the highway fight was necessary. Jerry Riordan was a suburban resident radicalized by UPA's message and approach: "I don't know how they [UPA] did it but they'd take a map, a street map of the town. Not a Rand McNally map but something you could get down at the planning department in the town that showed streets and houses on the lot. A high-detail map showing this intersection, and then they'd either draw on the map or draw on the slide—I'm not too sure—a Magic Marker to show where the [highway] corridor was gonna go. That was very effective . . . And the neighbors would see and say, 'What, that damn thing is going to be close to me!' It was very effective in getting people [involved]."[33] UPA's use of Magic Marker–annotated maps crystallized the highway's threat for Riordan and many suburban residents like him.[34] Interstate 95 would pass between the northern suburbs of Peabody and Salem heading south through Lynn and toward Boston's downtown. By showing the highway's pathway in street-level detail, these maps were effective in both educating and galvanizing residents, most of whom typically did not know the highway's proposed alignment. Riordan himself had no idea of the road's right-of-way until he attended one of UPA's neighborhood information sessions. Soon thereafter he joined the group as lead organizer for Boston's North Shore suburbs.

Organizers of UPA led slideshow-backed information sessions for suburban towns as well as urban neighborhoods along the highway's right-of-way. Boston resident Ann Hershfang recounts the first time she attended one such meeting in her South End neighborhood: "They didn't lobby—I don't know if that was part of their deal that they weren't supposed to organize or lobby or anything. They just presented what was going to happen . . . Just presented them. And those of us there had no idea it [the highway] was going to happen."[35] A straightforward discussion of the state's highway plan coupled with detailed analysis of the impact of road building offered residents an opportunity to decide for themselves what course of action they wanted to take. As Hershfang observes, the group did not lobby residents. Public discussion of the highway's arrival enabled residents to consider its meaning and effects on their own. And, as Hershfang's comment reveals, UPA's audience members often sat in a state of shock while listening because they "had no idea" a highway was coming their way. Part of the effectiveness of UPA's work to increase highway awareness among neighborhood residents can be traced to the forthrightness of its message. However, this should not be confused with having a politically unsophisticated approach—in fact, just the opposite.

Reflecting on the development of what would become UPA's signature organizing approach, Goodman, too, expresses surprise: "It was always surprising to me how little people knew and how little information they were given by the official agencies, a lot of times very simple maps showing what the plan was, how many people were going to be displaced by it, how many businesses, who those people were in the businesses. All of those things people had very scant knowledge of—it was surprising to us how little they knew and how important it was for them to understand it."[36] This flow of place-based details created an important exchange circuit of information and trust between UPA and its partners. The immediate goal was to get residents, activists, planning advocates, and public agencies on the same page. This would prove no small feat. As Goodman notes, public agencies and their unwillingness to share relevant and timely data with residents constituted a key flame for igniting the highway battles.

> One of the things I remember saying on a number of occasions was that these public agencies, whether it was the Bureau of Public Roads, the Massachusetts Highway Agency, or the Boston Redevelopment Authority, were the most effective organizers we had because of how recalcitrant they were in terms of changing the plan or being responsive to the community. Had they been more [collaborative] in getting the community involved with these projects and actually listened to people they might have been more effective, but they were so adamant and felt that they had the only answers to the problems. They did very effective organizing for us because people recognized that they were up against a formidable problem.[37]

Goodman's paradoxical observation that the actions of state agencies helped fuel the antihighway movement indicates the deep brokenness of technocratic approaches that refused to be responsive to the needs of constituencies on the receiving end of their plans. This dynamic was producing a political powder keg that UPA would take on full force.

In his 1971 book *After the Planners*, Goodman later reflected on UPA's auspicious beginning: "It seemed we had found an important way for professional planners to be relevant to some very important social problems. Expertise at the disposal of the poor was going to counter the arguments and programs of the government's bureaucrats. In the process, the injustice of these government programs would become apparent, and plans would have to change."[38] Urban Planning Aid's commitment to public advocacy with social justice results meant that its work demanded more than rhetoric. Professional urban planners and designers, like Goodman, moved beyond the familiar world of architectural drawing boards and lecture halls and took their plans to the street. The group's premise was simple: assemble professional planners, architects, transportation experts, and social scientists to aid grassroots, low-income communities to create livable urban alternatives made possible not by displacement but by better and shared public decision making.

The early leaders of UPA—Blackett, Lee, and Salvucci—eventually went their separate ways. Blackett became a housing developer active in community organizing in Roxbury and the South End. Lee took a job in Washington. Salvucci continued his work at the BRA and assumed a position on UPA's board. Salvucci later joined the staff of Boston mayor Kevin White as his transportation adviser. Despite these personnel changes, the group continued to gain steam. At its peak in 1973, UPA employed a full-time staff of two dozen professionals with an annual operating budget of more than a quarter million dollars.[39] Though the group's funding was primarily based on private and federal grants, there was also an effort to solicit contributions from sympathetic allies. In one fundraising letter addressed to an academic colleague, Gordon Feldman offered a partial history describing UPA as "offer[ing] free research, planning and technical assistance to low-income community groups in the Greater Boston area . . . Started with a small grant from the American Friends Service Committee, UPA began with a half-time staff person and six volunteers all employed full-time in planning, architecture, urban anthropology, engineering, systems planning and sociology who wanted to use their professional skills outside the classrooms and offices where they worked."[40] UPA's public advocacy role meant meetings—lots of them. While the group was highly effective in building allies among Greater Boston residents, it was also good at making political enemies, especially among state and local government leaders. One such enemy was Ed Logue, chief of Boston's planning and development agency, the Boston Redevelopment Authority.

Opposing Desires Meet: UPA and Ed Logue

> [It's] not so much right or wrong. They just weren't used to dealing with regular peo-
> ple. It was the Ed Logue thing: "We'll speak for the people of Boston." I suppose Ed
> Logue was right; he was speaking for some people in Boston, but he wasn't speaking
> for a lot of other people. There were a lot of people that were disenfranchised, not
> disenfranchised, never were franchised at all! They just didn't have a say. And this
> thing [UPA] gave it to them. He [Logue] was probably a great planner, but he didn't
> have too much patience for people's needs, for regular people's needs.[41]
>
> —Jerry Riordan, UPA organizer

The Boston Redevelopment Authority (BRA), Boston's formal, but unelected, body responsible for planning and development, was an early institutional antagonist of UPA's vision of democratic, resident-driven planning. On a Tuesday morning in October 1966, UPA's leaders had their first face-to-face meeting with Ed Logue, the BRA's director. Logue had arrived in Boston in 1960 to much fanfare based on his successful execution of the urban renewal program in New Haven, Connecticut. Logue was a World War II veteran and Yale Law School graduate. He joined New Haven's mayor Dick Lee for a six-year (1954–60) experiment to transform that city's aging center in what would be known as the most extensive and expensive urban renewal plan of its era.[42]

By redefining the development authority of local government and drawing enormous levels of federal highway and urban renewal funding to New Haven, Logue built a nationally recognized professional profile as well as his own unique brand of planning management. According to political scientist Doug Rae, it was in New Haven that Logue cultivated the idea that his work as a planner was above the realm of politics and, furthermore, that "the small doings of regular politics were impediments to be overcome, or to be ignored if possible. In a sense, therefore, the effective element of city government itself became detached from local issues and local potentates."[43] By the end of his first year on Mayor Lee's payroll, Logue had already established a solid reputation as a brash, "testosterone-powered" hardliner unwilling to mince words or take orders from others. Just what New Haven's mayor wanted. When Boston's newly elected mayor John Collins decided that his city also needed a bold, large-scale urban renewal plan, he tapped Ed Logue without reservation. In Boston, Logue set his sights on redevelopment of the city's downtown business district and a nearby area that he would name Government Center. He promised a new approach to urban renewal in Boston, based less on bulldozing and more on rehabilitation. However, his autocratic planning style won him few fans among Boston's neighborhood activists.[44]

Urban Planning Aid leaders, Chester Hartman, Denis Blackett, Bob Goodman, and Lisa Peattie, and two other members met with Logue in 1966 for roughly thirty-five minutes. The meeting did not focus specifically on antihighway organizing but on the city's planning approach and UPA's role as a planning advocacy organization. As Goodman describes, UPA's members had arranged the meeting "to explain why our group was helping a neighborhood organization oppose the city's official plan."[45] For the BRA, UPA was a nuisance. For UPA, the BRA was a bully. The core issue centered on responsibility and authority.

The fateful first meeting of these two organizations was captured not by audiotape but by the detailed notes of an unnamed UPA member present. Six UPA members assembled to meet Logue at his office; the surviving notes suggest that they were very nervous about his potential reception of them. This collective anxiety was not likely helped by the fact that Logue kept them waiting for almost half an hour. Logue (signified as "L" in the notes) eventually appears. He sits down and asks, "Where should we begin?" In response, Bob Goodman opened the discussion with an overview of advocacy planning and its merits. The notetaker duly recorded this exchange: "After perhaps three or four minutes of Bob's presentation, L interrupted, with something to the effect that advocacy planning could not be recognized unless it was responsible. Some organizations, he said, get 'satisfaction' from 'conflict.' The point was that they like conflict for its own sake . . . Several people asked what he meant by this. As seemed to be his manner, he repeated the charge several times. When pressed at least three or four times for detail, he said that the map of a plan presented at the July hearing at the Timilty School, was never 'returned' to the BRA."[46] His inability to cite a more substantive example of UPA's supposed lack of public responsibility suggests the possibility of a wider ideological battle at play in the meeting. Logue's comments shift the tone of the discussion to something less conversational and more combative. "We said neighborhoods should be able to choose their own planners and explained that such a process would make planning more democratic. He listened with a patient smile, asking only a few questions as he sat facing us from the end of his large conference table. When we finished, his smile vanished."[47]

When UPA members insisted that the needs of low-income residents should be considered and incorporated into plans that represent their interests, Logue countered: "There is and has been an organization which does indeed serve the interests of low-income people and that organization is the BRA."[48] For Logue, the group's efforts represented an irresponsible redundancy. He argued that his agency planned with citizens and that he likely was "the first planner in the nation to do this." While highlighting his own reputation as a nationally renowned urban planning leader, Logue cast doubt on UPA's professional legitimacy. He further argued that the BRA accomplishes what UPA claimed to do and therefore charged that the group's true aim was to "stir up trouble, that must be its genuine purpose." In Logue's estimation, UPA's work was illegitimate and possibly reckless.[49]

As might be expected, his audience did not appreciate this assessment. It is hard to imagine the full range of emotions experienced by UPA's leaders as they listened to the city's most powerful planning official discredit their work; however, the notetaker's parenthetical comment offers some insight: "(I found, unlike most meetings I have attended and later taken notes on, this one aroused much emotion in me, to the extent that even while it happened, I was aware of remembering very little actual conversation, indeed, and recognizing the conflict between observing and participating, in an unusually highly charged setting.)"[50]

Although most of the planning examples discussed during this meeting referred to urban renewal's local execution, Logue lobbed one critique directly at the highway fight itself. Citing a previous Cambridge-led antihighway rally in 1966, Logue charged the state's Department of Public Works with caving to public pressure from antihighway activists. "[A] crowd of people march up to the gate of the State House, and [Governor] Volpe delays the schedule for the Belt. That's ridiculous. The trouble with the DPW is that it doesn't have an efficient way of making decisions."[51] Logue does not question the highway plan, nor does he address the concerns of protesters. Instead, he slams the DPW, the state's road-building agency, and its decision-making structure as the source of the highway conflict. Here Logue shows not only his contempt for this particular state agency but also his preference for tightly managed, agency-centered public processes. In contrast, UPA conceived of centralized planning as largely fed and directed by vocal grassroots actors flanked by skilled technicians and social scientists; its version of planning sought to reconceive government authority through a more robust expression of citizens' demands and decision making. Logue clashed directly with UPA on this point. He chafed at what he viewed as the group's willful attempt to undermine the authority of his office and city government itself.

Despite contentious sparring with Logue, UPA's commitment to providing the public with a radical alternative to government-led planning produced transformative results for the people of Massachusetts. From authoring the lead analysis for dismantling the state's highway plan to later battling the real estate lobby's campaign against rent control, UPA distinguished itself as an organization unafraid to take on powerful public and private interests.

In many ways, UPA's activism embodied an unbridled rebuke of powerful and self-serving political interests: "In trying to achieve a more pluralist society through advocacy planning there is an attempt to balance off the interests of those with financial power, who can buy planning expertise and the material goods they want, such as better housing and better schools, against those who can only ask for what they want. If those who already control the economy and the government were *willing* to share power, then of course the problem would be one of *articulating* and arguing the needs of different interest groups."[52] By identifying economic and political actors' unwillingness to share power as the core problematic sabotaging pluralist political expression, Goodman unmasks the structural inequity within state-sponsored planning processes. As a twentieth-century outgrowth of technocratic rationalism, highway planning concealed a nested set of political prejudices favoring white, male, middle-class suburban car owners and residential neighborhoods located far outside the city. By advancing the preferences of an elite group in place of broad public desire, federal and state highway planners were complicit in legalizing discriminatory planning practices. Highway plans themselves thus perpetuated a kind of racial and economic segregation that many 1960s protest and liberation movements vowed to dismantle. And while advocacy planning provided a means for working-class and low-income communities to articulate their own needs and visions, Goodman and others conceded that this approach by itself was insufficient for affecting large-scale social change. More actors, more approaches, and more political resistance to oppressive systems would be needed to achieve true social and economic equality.

Urban Planning Aids's critique of structural power as well as its uncomplicated approach to citizen education fueled the organization's many successes. Chief among these was the group's ability to galvanize local residents across the Greater Boston region. By addressing the transportation needs of a wide array of suburban and urban residents, UPA's analysis showed how highways raised new problems for Boston's entire metropolitan region. Interstate highway systems displaced urban populations, destroyed existing housing stock and small business networks, yet even greater costs were exacted. Alan Lupo, Frank Colcord, and Edmund P. Fowler's seminal book on the Boston antihighway movement describes the impact of highways this way: "Highways do not simply remove housing from the market, they destroy something far more difficult to replace: established neighborhoods that enjoy a deep sense of community. The casual motorist driving down the proposed Inner Belt route in Cambridge might not see anything that he would identify in a physical sense as a community, but the residents of Brookline and Elm Streets have an enviable history of shared experience and mutual assistance."[53] Here the collateral damage of highway construction is cast in terms of lost social attachments. Highways disrupt the connections between residents sharing a neighborhood, often permanently. For Urban Planning Aid's members, these kinds of losses were undemocratic and unacceptable.

As the historic basis of America's democratic contract, associative networks based in place are vital to the political efficacy of cities and towns. More than quaint markers of a bygone era, functioning communities steeped in mutuality constitute the nation's fundamental political unit and, as UPA frequently argued, deserved to be recognized as such and not merely as obstructions to the right-of-way of a federal highway. Neighborhoods, like the one occupying Brookline and Elm Streets in Cambridge, were the bedrock of America's political and economic power, and UPA made sure that anyone reading its publications or listening to its live presentations understood this point loud and clear.

UPA's progressive platform expanded the claim-making agenda of 1960s social movements by foregrounding citizens' rights to define, plan, and use physical space according to their own needs and desires. Its work amplified the rousing missions of the both the antiwar and civil rights movements. More than fights for military withdrawal abroad and racial integration at home, these social movements called for a new democratic order recommitted to the fulfillment of citizen-defined needs. Urban Planning Aid contributed to this activist agenda by bringing grassroots attention and leadership to the democratic use, development, and control of physical space.

====

This chapter has sketched how U.S. highway expansion in the mid-twentieth century was not a natural or inevitable development but rather an extension of the desires and preferences of powerful political and business leaders. These actors produced a vision of a physical landscape molded according to their own nation-spanning interests. As a result, much of America's highway infrastructure was being configured according to the values and interests of a tiny but highly influential minority. The gradual recognition of this fact among grassroots actors set in motion a raging conflict that spilled into streets, town halls, government offices, and neighborhood meetings. In each location, citizens demanded to know exactly whom new highways were for and who had the political right to displace one group of citizens for the convenience of another.

This battle had profound material and psychological consequences homes, business, and entire neighborhoods were lost in the process of road building. And, of these losses, none was arguably more devastating than citizens' loss of trust in the efficacy of liberal democratic government. In Greater Boston, a fight erupted over not just roads but also the right to think about and respond to the totality of needs of metropolitan residents and not solely to the preferences of suburban drivers. This conflict unmasked a fatally flawed and inadequate state transportation plan and spawned a new set of grassroots organizations calling for more responsive government, better transportation plans, and more authentic democratic practice for the region. Residents no longer willing to let someone else speak or plan on their behalf made this possible.

Chapter 3

Groundwork

Imagining a Highwayless Future

A group of harried travelers pour out of the train station's heavy aluminum doors. We are all rushing—across the street toward the bus stop, down the block to the bank. Racing home or to work or to errands. The train has dumped us here, and we are now dispersing in every direction. This is Roxbury Crossing, bustling at 1:00 p.m. on a weekday afternoon. A guy is standing outside selling incense, African black soap, and essential oils. Behind him, Domino's Pizza is doing a brisk midday business of pepperoni pizza, twisty bread, and large Cokes. The woman next to me eyes her watch. A teenager talks into her cell phone. We all know where we are supposed to be and when. But I wonder, Is anyone else thinking about how we got here and why?[1]

The story of this train and its bustling station is rooted in Boston's 1960s-era highway fights. The landscape here tells the story of a forced halt orchestrated by a diverse spread of activist groups intent on attaining more local control of the policy decisions transforming the built environment around them. Roxbury Crossing is not the site of a multilane elevated highway connecting suburban motorists to downtown Boston. Instead it is a busy stop along the city's central rapid transit line, the Orange Line. Where I-95's medusa-like interchange would have roared above Boston's streets, a glossy plaque commemorates what did not happen. It reads:

> You are standing in the middle of the Southwest Corridor. It was origi-
> nally planned as the twelve-lane highway shown in the drawing below.
> The efforts of thousands of citizens banding together to save their homes,
> neighborhoods and open spaces created the orange line rapid transit, the
> railroad, and the Southwest Corridor Park you are enjoying today.

Antihighway protesters stopped a highway from slicing through the center
of Boston and pressured the state to establish new uses for land intended
for the highway's path.

What would have been an extension of I-95 called the Southwest
Expressway and its Inner Belt connector was transformed into public
transportation and a new park bearing the highway's old name in 1989.
But before any of this was built, a large swath of city land lay dormant for
more than twenty years. The plaque at Roxbury Crossing tells the story
of citizen activism that produced permanent social, physical, and, arguably, political change in the city of Boston. A timeline of the antihighway
movement's history, a drawing of the proposed highway, and a photograph
of a grassy lot where businesses and homes once stood document what
preceded the train line. The top edge of the plaque features more than one
hundred names described as "a few of the many people who gave their time
and energy to the success of the Southwest Corridor." Chuck Turner's name
appears first.

While Cambridge residents had debated road placement, Boston residents were already confronting its effects. Clearance for I-95 began in
Boston in 1966. Homes and businesses anchoring a multiracial, working-
class population were leveled and replaced with a near empty smear of
dirt. Even as citizen opposition to the highway grew across the region
and prompted the governor's call for a transportation restudy, the state's
Department of Public Works continued its demolition and acquisition of
land in Roxbury and Jamaica Plain. Like much of the clearance that accompanied federal urban renewal plans, highway development projects produced yawning chasms of blight. Emptiness. For the state's transportation
planners, this emptiness represented progress and the promise of revitalization through federally funded highway investment. For residents, this
emptiness was a visual reminder of who and what were gone and that the
government was responsible. The promise of the highway, coupled with

the reality of vast stretches of cleared land, situated residents of Roxbury and Jamaica Plain upon an ever-shrinking urban archipelago. An organic strategy to reclaim empty land by identifying new, local land uses began as a symbolic gesture and evolved into a complex series of resident-sponsored urban redevelopment plans.

Claiming Ground

In Roxbury in 1969, members of the Black United Front (BUF) denounced the state's land clearance and erected a wooden structure on the Corridor in protest. The BUF issued a formal press release to publicize this action across the city: "We of Operation STOP, a committee of the Boston Black United Front, are here today to dedicate the first community building project on the land that was to be used for the [highway]. This community information house stands as a symbol that there will not be a highway system built through our community. It symbolizes the commitment of the Black community to use its land for its own development . . . A question for all to consider is why isn't the alternative of a rapid transit system being considered since it is cheaper, takes less space, and benefits both the rich and the poor."[2] A reporter on the scene described BUF's community information house as a "small wooden building recently constructed by community members on a triangle of land in the middle of the intersection of [Columbus Avenue and Tremont Street]."[3] The house was intended to serve as both a symbol of local resistance to highway development as well as a center for information about the highway, its effects, and how to fight both.

The media-covered dedication of this modest building brought public drama and urgency to a cause that had garnered minimal attention among Boston residents. Chuck Turner, BUF's leader, and his fellow organizers invited press to the event to expand the circulation of their public message. Their actions were intended to educate residents along the Corridor as well as further politicize the issue of Boston's redevelopment. Turner would later explain: "As a committee [STOP] we decided to focus on a closed gas station that was in the middle of the spot where there would be an extension of the I-95, the new highway into downtown Boston . . . So what we thought was that we ought to put a symbol there of the fight against the highway. So initially we built a building there on this cleared land that said 'People before Highways' because there also was a sign that had been painted by people in Jamaica Plain on the railroad embankment that was there. So it was just designed to keep a focus—to remind people that there was a struggle going on as to what would happen on this piece of land."[4] Under Turner's leadership, BUF's antihighway subcommittee known as "Operation STOP" would become a forceful and vocal source of highway resistance organizing in Boston.

Operation STOP mobilized residents within and beyond the predominately African American neighborhood of Roxbury to understand the full impact of a twelve-lane highway and to try to imagine what might be built instead. Operation STOP's 1969 decision to construct a building on cleared land as a "symbol" of its highway opposition furthered a grassroots wave of sign making along the Southwest Corridor. Several months before, residents in the nearby neighborhood of Jamaica Plain had transformed the granite wall beneath a nineteenth-century elevated railroad track into an eye-catching antihighway billboard (figure 6). With white spray-painted letters declaring "People before Highways," this visual

FIGURE 6. Stop I-95 People before Highways, circa 1970. One of the antihighway movement's most frequently referenced slogans is seen here painted on the elevated train's stone embankment wall bordering Roxbury and Jamaica Plain along the Southwest Corridor. Source: Janet Hunkel Personal Archives.

cue along the highway's intended right-of-way reminded neighbors and passersby that the antihighway battle was alive and kicking. Antihighway activists had not yet succeeded in persuading the state to abandon its road building plans and could not afford to lose the public's attention. As Turner recounts, "There was a struggle going on," and members of local activist groups did not want anyone to forget this.[5]

As Boston's antihighway sentiment began to spread from neighborhood to neighborhood, activists and residents expressed their fears to one another, the press, and politicians. Chuck Turner once again used his commanding oratory to detail what was at stake for residents along the Southwest Corridor: "We are here as representatives of organizations in Boston's black community to tell Mayor White, Gov. Sargent and Secy of Transportation Volpe that their game is over—that just as David slew Goliath to protect his people, we are ready to fight the federal government to protect our community from the five story, eight lane monster designed to destroy it . . . We stand united with the Greater Boston Committee on the Transportation Crisis, whose members are also fighting the destructive effects of the highway on their communities."[6]

Turner faced the crowd and reporters assembled before him but directed his message to local, state, and federal politicians governing the highway project. The allusion to David and Goliath foregrounds the territorial nature of the antihighway debate while suggesting that, yes, a threatening giant can be conquered. Here the magnitude of the highway battle is conceived in epic, even biblical, terms and linked directly to the Greater Boston Committee on the Transportation Crisis's (GBC) growing coalition base.

Standing in solidarity with local residents and the GBC's regional coalition, Turner was a crucial unifying force. Turner served as cochair of the GBC with Father Tom Corrigan, the young priest serving a parish in the Egleston area of Jamaica Plain. As Turner mobilized black residents in Roxbury, Corrigan tapped his network of activist priests within the Association of Boston Urban Priests to provide additional communication and outreach channels for GBC. Reflecting on his work with Turner, Corrigan describes how their personal relationship and disparate organizational bases helped fuel the coalition: "We were friends. It was cooperative. We each brought in our own constituencies and our own point of view. I had tremendous respect for him. He was an extremely effective neighborhood leader . . . The two organizations were separate organizations. The importance of the coalition was to show that a project like this had impacts that were as important to middle-class and working-class white people as they were to African American people in Roxbury and the South End."[7]

Like antihighway activists in Cambridge, Turner and his allies chose a resistance strategy that critiqued highway building and called for alternative solutions to the region's transportation issues. With Turner's roles as chair of both the Black United Front and the GBC, Operation STOP would play a lead role in GBC's development as an umbrella organization for highway-fighting groups across Massachusetts.

Roxbury's residents were prepared to defend themselves, no matter what the odds, against a government perceived as indifferent to their needs. Although their forceful and condemning language set a confident tone, these actors were anything but. Turner himself questioned the odds: "So we said you don't win in highway fights; it's one of those situations where it's a long shot of winning. We felt we didn't have any alternative but to fight against it."[8] Previous highway and urban renewal battles in Boston and elsewhere had convinced Turner and others that government-ordered bulldozers could not be stopped. Many low-income residents, in particular, had learned from previous unsuccessful battles that government leaders were not responsive to their demands. By refusing to accept highway construction as inevitable and drawing public attention to the issue, Turner and his activist allies in Boston were successful in provoking neighborhood engagement in a battle that many residents had already considered lost. Residents mobilized themselves and began warning state, municipal, and federal leaders that "their game is over"—meaning that the city's residents were no longer willing to allow others to assume control of land that belonged to the public.

Chuck Turner and Operation STOP birthed a local planning agenda that condemned the state's prohighway plan while advocating for community-generated development alternatives. The dedication of "the first community building project" on land cleared for the highway dramatized the dual nature of STOP's agenda while underscoring deep uncertainty surrounding the Corridor's fate. When Roxbury residents and their allies erected a symbolic structure to reject the state's highway plan and demanded public consideration of an "alternative of a rapid transit system," they did not know that they were creating a working blueprint for Boston's future urban development—though they hoped they might be. They did not know that

less than twenty years later, in 1989, a new rapid transit line and 52-acre
park would serve to connect neighborhoods that the proposed highway
would have permanently severed.

Looking around this stretch of land today, it is hard to imagine that this
was once a blighted landscape or remember that its development is the
result of collective resistance to local and federal highway plans. It is also
hard to imagine that the story of Chuck Turner's decisive leadership for
the Boston antihighway movement is relatively unknown. When the Black
United Front ceased operation in the late 1970s, its records were transferred
to an office in the Dudley train station for storage.[9] These records, including meeting minutes, financial information, incorporation filings, photographs, news clippings, and internal memos, sat dormant for more than a
decade. Variously exposed to the train station's extremes of heat, cold, and
moisture, the records were damaged but not destroyed. When I learned the
survival story surrounding these records, I was struck by yet another type
of antihighway activism: the efforts of antihighway actors themselves to
save materials documenting their story. Their attics, basements, personal
address books, and photo albums introduced me to actions and actors that
would have otherwise been virtually unknowable.

In the mid-1980s, a last-minute effort by historian and Massachusetts
state representative Byron Rushing (Democrat, 9th Suffolk) saved the
Black United Front's records from the wrecking ball when the train station
housing them faced demolition. While the razing of Boston's elevated train
signified a victory for the antihighway movement's fight to expand public
transportation for the city, this event itself nearly erased the paper trail
describing how such a victory was made possible. The records were moved
to a storage room in Cambridge, where they remained for nearly ten years.
When Lenny Durant, the Front's office manager and first paid staff member, realized the records were neither in the city of Boston nor accessible
to the public, he gathered the collection and maintained it in his house for
the next few years. Durant reorganized the records according to memory
and donated the entire collection to Roxbury Community College in 1999.
Today the Front's records are housed in the college's archives directly across
the street from Roxbury Crossing Station.

The story of the retrieval of the Black United Front's records is the kind of
cautionary tale that haunts archivists, librarians, and historians. It demonstrates the inherent fragility of collecting and preserving documents among

activist organizations as well as how essential these organizations are for shaping and recording local responses to state and federal policies. The Black United Front's strategy to erect a series of community-built structures on land cleared for the highway predated several groups that would do the same with increasingly large media attention. But beyond a simple documentation of who did what first, the Black United Front's early records invite a con sideration of how the idea of "community control," first articulated within the political context of black nationalist organizations, became a widely accepted organizing principle for Greater Boston's antihighway movement.

Black Power and Political Self-Reliance

Black nationalist leaders had abandoned faith in integrationist and liberal pursuits of social reform and now advanced a race-based agenda of local self-help. Although these leaders and their agenda were frequently dismissed by liberal politicians and the national press as racist, growing numbers of urban residents of all races conceded that self-help and community control were the only viable strategies for pursuing their collective interests in the face of an unresponsive political establishment. Historian Peniel Joseph has argued persuasively for a more nuanced understanding of black nationalist ideologies and Black Power politics more generally. In his edited work *The Black Power Movement: Rethinking the Civil Rights–Black Power Era*, Joseph reframes the civil rights and Black Power movements as interconnected and not indicative of "two fundamentally dichotomous eras."[10] With this interpretive move, Joseph extends the historical timeline for considering black liberation organizing beyond the tight chronology of the 1960s alone, describing earlier decades of the twentieth century and later, especially, the 1970s and 1980s as crucial time periods for analyzing new modes of black political expression.[11]

Rooted within the core of Black Power politics, the notion of "community control" offered a grassroots antidote to top-down public policy. Instead of waiting for elected officials or government administrators to determine how to help local communities and risk more urban renewal or worse, proponents of Black Power opted to defer only to themselves. As an emerging ideological edge of the civil rights movement in the late 1960s, community control challenged local communities to bypass traditional channels of institutional and political authority and instead adopt participatory models of direct democracy. Komozi Woodard has noted how America's 1960s urban uprisings largely in response to "the collapse of basic government and commercial services in the postindustrial ghettoes" helped produce a new generation of black activist organizations committed to Black Power as the suggested remedy for America's political and economic failures.[12] These organizations were further unified by a shared belief in the primacy of black self-reliance and self-determination and a nationalist view that conceptualized black Americans as living as an "internal colony of the United States."[13] In these ways, Black Power stretched the political, social, and geographic boundaries for reforming American democracy in the twentieth century.

When Stokely Carmichael first brandished the term "Black Power" during a Mississippi rally in 1966, a new kind of civil rights agenda was emphatically called into being. Black Power in its simplest form argued for a conservative, and controversial, notion of race-based self-help in the Black Belt South and in northern cities.[14] Instead of seeking multiracial coalitions engaged to reform the nation's legal system, Carmichael and his allies sought a new kind of politics expressly focused on blacks addressing the needs of blacks, neighborhood by neighborhood. He writes: "We must begin to think of the black community as a base of organization to control institutions in that community. Control of the ghetto schools must be taken out of the hands of 'professionals,' most of whom have long since demonstrated their insensitivity to the needs and problems of the black child."[15] By advocating a mode of political organization based on race and self-help, Carmichael advanced a provocative counterargument to the civil rights movement's integration-focused mission. The idea that black citizens must "control" schools and other institutions that govern its daily life generated critics and detractors both within and outside black communities. Accusations of reverse racism and separatism fueled a public backlash against Carmichael's ideas, overshadowing the merits of his trenchant analysis of urbanization's production of new kinds of political, economic, and spatial problems for American citizens.

In his book *The Black Demand for Participation in Large American Cities*, political scientist Alan Altshuler offers an overview of Black Power and community control as modes of articulating black citizens' collective efforts to increase their "participation in the political and economic lives of their cities."[16] Altshuler's analysis broadens the discussion of community control to consider the political, economic, and material conditions inspiring its currency. While he questions the full application and efficacy of community control as a black mobilization strategy, he does not, in his words, dismiss it as "nonsense" as numerous whites had.[17] As a white MIT professor critical to the next wave of mobilization within the Boston anti-highway movement, Altshuler brought a useful understanding of both the benefits and limitations of black liberation politics. He summarizes his view this way:

> Here is the crux of the problem. Whites (especially those who live in homogenous jurisdictions) take the basic values of local government for granted. Blacks do not. Whites disagree on precise spending priorities, and they grouse about tax increases; but they do not question the system itself. Blacks do. Whites chuckle over bureaucratic inefficiency, but they assume that the objectives being sought are proper. Blacks do not. Whites are fundamentally satisfied because they sense that the institutions of American government have been shaped by men like them, for men like them. Blacks are not, because they do not. As Stokely Carmichael has observed, no one talks about white power because it goes without saying that power in America is white. For Negroes, the issue is indeed justice—not abstract justice for others, but justice for themselves.[18]

In *Black Power: The Politics of Liberation in America*, Stokely Carmichael and Charles Hamilton present an incisive critique of twentieth-century urbanization and call attention to the social conditions that they identify as making the notion of local control a necessary political ideal. Metropolitan development in the postwar period was typified by increased public and private investment in suburban areas. Thus the aging transportation infrastructure and housing stock of older city centers typically were not upgraded. And, when they were, through government-led highway or urban renewal projects, low-income and black residents often bore the brunt of the impact brought by displacement. Carmichael and Hamilton write: "Urban Renewal and highway clearance programs have forced black people more and more into congested pockets of the inner city. Since suburban zoning laws have kept out low-income housing, and the Federal Government has failed to pass open-occupancy laws, black people are forced to stay in the deteriorating ghettos."[19] For Carmichael and Hamilton, the web of institutional and governance failures surrounding black communities required the creation of new and more responsive organizational forms: "Black people have seen city planning commissions, the urban renewal commissions, the boards of education and the police departments fail to speak to their needs in a meaningful way. We must devise new structures, new institutions to replace those forms ... There is nothing sacred or inevitable about old institutions; the focus must be on people, not on forms. Existing structures and established ways of doing things have a way of perpetuating themselves and for this reason, the modernizing process will be difficult ... Essential to the modernization of structures is a broadened base of political participation. More and more people must become politically sensitive and active."[20] Here Carmichael and Hamilton offer Black Power as a response to the need for greater citizen participation at the grassroots level to offset an overreliance on technocratic experts and professional administrators. In this way they offer a nuanced view of modernization dependent not on elite professional knowledge systems but on expanded opportunities for citizens' political participation. They argue that Black Power offers "the last reasonable opportunity for this society to work out its racial problems short of prolonged destructive guerrilla warfare."[21] Thus Black Power stands as an ideological alternative to a politics of violence by advocating for the self-determination of black communities in place of race-based warfare. In the context of the wider civil rights movement, Black Power politics represent a provocative politics of final resort.

In Boston, local residents' decision to ignore a state-sponsored highway plan and erect new construction in its place, however modest, exemplified community control at its most literal. Operation STOP's structure denouncing the state's highway agenda and proposing new uses for Southwest Corridor land joined a series of public construction projects inspired by the burgeoning idea of community control. Operation STOP members would describe its actions, including the later creation of a functioning street hockey rink, as "intended to serve present community needs and to show the community the value and potential of the land."[22] In many ways the hurdle of pushing residents to rethink the meaning and value of cleared and abandoned land defined the most formidable early challenge to Boston's antihighway activists. This step would prove essential to enabling Boston's residents to advocate convincingly that the land could be used for purposes more productive than the transport of suburban commuters.

When I discussed these neighborhood efforts to redefine land use with Mel King, lifelong political activist and director of the Urban League in the 1960s, he described a meeting he convened in the South End neighborhood during the antihighway movement's height. King led a Black Power–based agenda for the Boston Urban League despite its more moderate national civil rights mission to increase black employment. Thus when King called public meetings, a broad political spectrum of civil rights and social service agencies typically attended.

He recounted one such meeting in the South End as brief but defining: "There was a decision that one way to stop this [highway] was to show what alternative use could be. So we got a trailer and used it for job recruitment—the Panthers, they [also] got a trailer. So it was very interesting to see these trailers staffed on this land."[23] These two trailers—one for job recruitment by the Urban League and the other for health services provided by Boston's Black Panther chapter—were not merely symbolic visual gestures. As King explained, both projects sought to fulfill as well as dramatize the needs of residents living along the Southwest Corridor. For the Urban League, this meant providing job information to the Corridor's nearby public housing residents. For Black Panthers, this meant staffing a health center that would become a lasting feature of the landscape.

King's mention of the Black Panthers' trailer sends me on a search for related stories and images. Subsequent conversations with area residents would surface additional references to the Panthers' modest health trailer. Memory-laden flashbacks of residents made me wonder, What did the trailer look like, and what was the scope of the Panthers' daily activity on the Corridor? A scan of local newspapers from the period turned up nothing. King gave me former Panther Floyd Hardwick's phone number, and the story of the Panthers' trailer began to unfold. Hardwick directed the Panthers' education initiatives, including its hot-breakfast programs for area school children, as well as its health program based inside a white trailer on the Corridor. "I was sorta in charge of the health clinic, raising money. The doctors we were involved with would bring us supplies. It all kind of just showed up." Hardwick's first recollection of the trailer is of it being sprayed with bullets. "I remember it being shot up; I wasn't there." No one was hurt.[24]

Fifty-four years old at the time of our interview, Ronald Perry was just a young boy living in the Mission Extension Housing Development when the Panthers first set up their trailer on the Corridor. He, too, remembers this incident: "One time the police had shot it up. When it happened, the Black Panthers wanted to make sure the media knew what was going on so somebody came outside and circled all the bullet holes." This memory underscores the aggressive antagonism that the Panthers' presence inspired as well as their dangerous clashes with police. Yet, Perry's memory also demonstrates the Panthers' nationally renowned reputation of fearlessness. "As I look back on it now, it was like being impressed. They stood up to the police. They stood up against the government. What they believed in they were ready to die for." For the thirteen-year-old Perry, recently migrated from North Carolina, the perceived fearlessness of the Panthers earned his respect. "Being from North Carolina, I had no idea about prejudice and racism. It was segregation that I grew up in. It's like going to Woolworth's and you have to sit down the other end. Culture shock coming here . . . growing up in North Carolina it was definitely segregation. You didn't have the signs up, but you knew your place. It was something."[25]

Perry's reflection that he "had no idea about prejudice and racism" highlights the ways in which segregation governed his childhood as a little questioned daily reality. Perry's family left North Carolina before the famed 1960 Woolworth counter sit-in in Greensboro catapulted the state's civil rights activists to the vanguard of segregationist resistance. Invoking an oft-used phrase to describe the geography of racial domination, he concludes simply, "You knew your place."

When Perry's family arrived in Boston, little had prepared them for life in a city with few job prospects for unemployed blacks or for the dramatic land transformation occurring right outside their living room window. Perry details the landscape he observed as a kid: "Lots of vacant land, gas stations, hamburger places. There was a place called Kemp's of America; it was like a McDonald's, that kind of format. The government had a food program—they would give out cheese and powdered eggs. This was outside Mission [Housing Development], on Tremont Street. Right where the new police station is . . . that used to be a food distribution center. Also in that same area the Black Panthers used to have a set-up."[26] Perry's description suggests a barren terrain offering just a few essentials: gas, cheese, hamburgers, and powdered eggs. Here, emptiness marks ground zero for the state's dream of economic revitalization via the development of an interstate highway system. As the investment of federal capital reorganized Boston's physical and social landscape, emptiness became an increasingly pronounced feature of the city's material transformation. Accordingly, when Ronald Perry and his family settled near Roxbury Crossing in 1969, what was most evident to them were the many things missing from the neighborhood, namely, private homes, businesses, daily conveniences, and, especially, jobs. The presence of a federal surplus food center disseminating cheese and powdered eggs further illustrates the wide variety of the area's missing resources, nutritional and otherwise.[27]

Formerly a booming zone of industrial activity in the nineteenth century, Roxbury Crossing no longer boasted the assortment of tanneries, shoe factories, and trade importers once powering Boston's economic status as the region's industrial anchor. Multiple railroad lines once crossed this strip of land at street level until a sharp increase in the number of inbound and outbound freight and passenger trains prompted the city to raise the tracks along a stone embankment. However, this elevated track configuration, the height of efficiency and elegance during the nineteenth century, had become a noisy eyesore by the mid-twentieth century.

The area's industrial-era mix of Irish, German, and English laborers and families was further disrupted by a series of federally funded, large-scale development plans requiring land clearance. Clearance for the construction of public housing developments, including Heath Street, Bromley Park, Mission Main, and Mission Extension, reconfigured the Corridor's immigrant population. These developments, followed by demolition for the interstate highway system, meant that this part of the city was dramatically, and repeatedly, reorganized during the twentieth century. Eminent domain–driven dispersals of large portions of Boston's working-class white population also altered Boston's racial composition. The final result was a sharp set of spatial divisions between the city's working-class white ethnic and black and Latino residents. By the 1960s the elevated train embankment between Jamaica Plain and Roxbury served as a physical marker of the social boundaries of at least two racialized territories as well as a hulking reminder of the region's industrial golden age.

Within this new economic and spatial vacuum being created in the city's heart, the need for a robust political agenda offering change was greater than perhaps it had ever been. Boston's Black Panthers entered this moment as forceful seekers of change eager to recruit black youth living in public housing. As Perry recalls, "With the I-95 [fight] in that time, there was a lot going on." He remembers Panthers marching through his housing projects with "their berets and leather coats."[28] He shakes his head trying to remember a Panther chant, then in a snap the tune comes rushing back. He leans forward and sings:

> "No more brothers in jail.
> Off the pigs!
> Pigs are gonna catch hell.
> Off the pigs!
> No more pigs in our community.
> Off the pigs!"

So it was that kind of chant and they would march through the projects. They were pretty pronounced around there.

They had a trailer right on the same land where the police headquarters are . . . The trailer was like their headquarters. They would do distribution of leaflets. They had a Ten-Point program of what they believed in as far as what the black man should do.[29]

The presence of Panthers and black nationalists mobilizing along the Corridor meant that a radical form of antiracist, pro-black politics was spreading a message of community control to new audiences. Not only did the trailer offer an alternative land use for the Corridor, the Panthers themselves offered an ideological alternative for resetting the limits of white social authority. Panther occupation of the Corridor signified yet another creative demonstration of alternative land use strategies as well as the ongoing presence of Black Power politics of self-determination within the antihighway movement's strategizing.

Today, a state-funded police headquarters sits on land that the Panthers' outreach trailer once occupied. The presence of the Panthers on this land, as well as their deep distrust of police and state authority, has not been totally forgotten, despite the Corridor's contemporary redevelopment. For such Boston residents as Mel King, Floyd Hardwick, and Ronald Perry, the corner of Columbus Avenue and Ruggles Street is at once a vacant lot, a Black Panther call for local control, and a steel and granite box containing 180,000 square feet of office space for Boston's police force. Residents' multiple memory overlays for the Roxbury Crossing landscape suggest more than irony; their collective ability to envision various possibilities for this land was instrumental to the antihighway movement's political success.

In the spring of 1970, the executive committee of the Greater Boston Committee on the Transportation Crisis (GBC) noted, "The Panther Health Clinic is now on site at the Interchange. The DPW wants to throw them off. The next few days, a series of very crucial negotiations will go on to keep the trailer there, and set up procedures for interim land use of the S.W. Corridor."[30] This comment illustrates that Panther activity held an important political position not just for local Roxbury residents but also within the antihighway movement itself. The exact content of the "very crucial negotiations" regarding Panther presence on the Corridor is not evident based on existing GBC records; however, it is clear that grassroots-led building efforts, such as the Panthers' creation of a local health clinic, assumed regional significance within antihighway activists' strategizing. Like the Black United Front with its wooden information house and the Urban League with its job recruitment center, the Black Panthers' health trailer communicated a clear message of local highway resistance while pressuring the public to consider a host of alternative land uses and political organizing approaches. Similarly, the GBC was eager to identify additional means of communicating its highway opposition across the state.

The Greater Boston Committee on the Transportation Crisis Creates Policy—Building a Legislative Agenda

In 1970 the GBC filed seven legislative bills to further its aim of establishing an integrated and balanced transportation system. Like the neighborhood activists who erected physical structures to increase visibility for the antihighway cause while addressing current social needs, GBC's multipronged legislative agenda built a legal structure for advancing the antihighway debate on the floor of the Massachusetts House of Representatives. The proposed bills were drafted to achieve the following objectives: 1) to amend the state constitution to allow money collected from the gasoline tax to be used for mass transit (House 2693); 2) to revise the timetable for determining fair market value of property so "as to prevent a loss due to diminution in value following announcement of location" of a highway (House 2696); 3) to require the Department of Public Works to pay the difference in interest costs if a relocated person purchases a new house with a higher mortgage (House 2699); 4) to set acceptable levels of jet aircraft noise with the stipulation that citizens can sue and collect damages to ensure compliance

(House 2800); 5) require the Department of Public Works to reimburse city or town governments for lost property taxes that result from land takings; 6) to give cities and towns "veto power on where a road is to be located if at all" (House 2823); and 7) to mandate "one to one replacement housing prior to any demolition" (House 2907).[31]

While the GBC's larger organizing vision imagined stopping the region's interstate highway plan, its legislative agenda reflected a more reformist tactic at play. The set of bills filed by the committee delineated a more just distribution of resources tied to highway expansion and the establishment of a participatory citizen planning process. None of these bills explicitly denounce highway building; instead, they focus on redressing the process by which highways are built. At this time, the fate of the state's highway plan was still unknown. What was known was that Governor Sargent was formally reviewing the plan itself.

A young public interest lawyer named Steve Teichner convinced the committee's leadership that creating a legislative package to raise visibility and awareness of the transportation crisis was a worthwhile effort. With Teichner's guidance, the GBC attempted to win converts to its cause. In public, Governor Sargent maintained a prohighway position even as he was gradually reconsidering his stance. The majority of state legislators were also prohighway. This political calculus kept Teichner and GBC's leaders sober minded in projecting the outcome of a legislative push. He recalls: "We never thought any of our legislation would pass. We thought at times we couldn't even get it drafted. We had so many diverse groups that getting them to agree on any single thing would be impossible . . . Then I set the ground rules. I would submit no more than ten bills, and every community had to support every bill. It was the first time I saw GBC really work as an alliance. I saw the North Shore suburbanites volunteer to withdraw bills that wouldn't help the black community."[32] Indeed the process of drafting legislation, rallying citizen support, and lobbying state lawmakers had a catalytic effect on the committee's membership base. Despite large public rallies, local demonstrations, letter-writing campaigns, and a few sympathetic newspaper reporters, the highway seemed unstoppable.

The GBC's authoring of state legislation created another formal opportunity for urban and suburban protesters crossing geographic, racial, and class lines to imagine themselves as a cohesive opposition block. And, significantly, as Teichner himself later quipped, "A community group, to live, must provide its members with something to do."[33] That something "to do" was to reach out to neighbors and legislators and spread the antihighway message in as many formats as possible. Similar to its previous coordination of the People before Highways Day march to the steps of the State House, the committee's legislative organizing provided a new opportunity to strengthen its functional identity as an alliance. For Teichner, this was noteworthy and necessary even if it did not guarantee legislative success.

Despite an invigorating blast of energy for its neighborhood-based organizing, GBC's legislative agenda required a measured approach to information sharing with state legislators. On the one hand, GBC needed to make its position known while being careful not to alienate the Department of Public Works' many allies and collaborators. Yet, on the other hand, the group was eager to expose the ways in which this agency had used its authority to advance a planning process that failed to consider broad public opinion on highway expansion. As the state agency charged with executing the highway plan as well as its land acquisition and clearance, the Department of Public Works (DPW) was a formidable political giant of extraordinary influence and power. When reflecting on this political dilemma and what it meant for the GBC's legislative work and his attempts to lobby for the group, Teichner remarked:

> The problem was getting the legislature to take me seriously. They didn't know me. They never heard of the group [GBC], and we were touching the single strongest interest in the state. There are guys who have perpetuated themselves in office for years by the DPW. Bite the hand that feeds them? The agency that gives them small projects or gives their constituents thirty- or sixty-day summer jobs on road crews? Also, many legislators see highways as progress.[34]

DPW's reputation as an agency steeped in patronage politics meant that its loyalists formed a kind of ad hoc prohighway lobbying block whenever the legislature was in session.

The fact that Governor Francis Sargent himself had been the head of the DPW before assuming elected office only added to the precariousness of the GBC's political maneuvering at the state level. Another challenge, as Teichner identifies, was how to craft an antihighway message that legislators and prohighway bureaucrats would not equate with being antiprogress. For the majority of the state, highways continued to signify modernization, economic growth, and progress. Furthermore, federal investment in Massachusetts's road building promised nearly $1 billion in contracts for unionized labor trades. To appear to stand in opposition to these goals during a time of social and political upheaval was a fatal risk to one's credibility. The GBC knew this all too well.

When the GBC completed its legislative filings, a summary flyer was distributed to its members to explain what was needed next. The flyer's text is straightforward and hopeful: "GBC cannot lobby in the traditional sense of the word for it lacked the favors, the money and all those other trappings that usually go along with the lobbying for a private interest. The only asset that GBC has at its disposal is the validity of its cause. Therefore it is extremely necessary that all people who subscribe to the GBC philosophy do their utmost in contacting their legislators either by phone, by telegram or by letter urging them to support GBC legislation. Only is [sic] this is done on a statewide basis can we be assured of ultimate legislative success."[35] The Greater Boston Committee's admission of its weakness as a lobbying body is framed here as a call to action. As the flyer announces, the group's message must be spread through citizen-led communications and outreach. In this way, the committee encouraged citizens across the region to take greater ownership of the antihighway movement and to activate their own planning and advocacy agendas, arguably a version of community control. Ken Kruckemeyer was one resident who heeded the call.

A resident of the South End and an MIT-trained architect, Kruckemeyer first became involved in the antihighway fight when he learned that an auxiliary feeder road for I-95 called the South End Bypass was planned to bisect the end of his street.

> BRA [Boston Redevelopment Authority] was tearing down the buildings at the end of the streets here—or getting ready to tear down the buildings to make way for the South End Bypass. People had pretty much thought, "Oh, that road's gonna get built. I won't buy a house there. Won't buy a house anywhere near there and life will go on." They sorta abandoned life at the end of the street, if you will, in their minds. And, as somebody would get moved out of the house and it would become vacant, that was further proof that that's what was going to happen at the end of the street. So those of us who were involved in lobbying against the expressways were trying to get people to be invested in what was going on at the end of the street so we tried to keep families in

the houses that were being bought up or not get them so that they would get vandalized and ready to be torn down. So we tried to be protective of the houses, the empty houses or the about-to-be-empty houses.[36]

In the South End, announcement of the highway's arrival produced a nihilistic flurry of avoidance among home buyers. As Kruckemeyer observes, the Boston Redevelopment Authority's demolition of homes along the neighborhood's northern edge was regarded as physical proof that the highway could not be stopped. Fearful homeowners as well as potential buyers began fleeing the South End. As this pattern intensified, the neighborhood's physical form changed. The growth of vacant and abandoned homes adjacent to empty lots, where other homes once stood, now created a checkerboard-like territory where blocks of residents faced desolate squares of cleared land. In response, Kruckemeyer and his neighbors mobilized to prevent and protect empty houses.

> We tried to get little things to happen in the vacant lots that were already at the ends of the street. One summer, and it must have been around 1970, we built an amphitheater in Braddock Park on a vacant lot. It was a lot that had a shape that was almost a natural amphitheater. It sloped down in two directions toward the alley back there. This must have been after the house fell down. So we got the city to grade the lot and put down a bunch of wood chips. We may have even had some railroad ties as sorta benches or something and we got a bunch of lumber. We had two donations of some money to put into the wood. Some of it was salvaged wood and some of it was brand new and we built a triangular shed with a roof on it. The kids spent the whole summer building this amphitheater and then they had rock concerts in the amphitheater at night . . . All these things were part of our method of getting people to say this land is precious to us in our neighborhoods.[37]

The organic, resident-led construction of a wooden outdoor amphitheater communicated not only that neighbors were concerned about the condition of empty land but also that they were willing and able to repurpose the land themselves according to their own planning decisions. In many ways Kruckemeyer and his neighbors' attempts to reclaim empty land in the South End echo those of the Panthers, the Urban League, and the Black United Front in Roxbury. Each of these interventions marked the landscape with a physical symbol of political resistance, participatory planning, and protest.

When I asked Kruckemeyer how his efforts to build an amphitheater might relate to the idea of local control, he answered as if already anticipating my question: "Local control, local involvement. I think that Black Power, to my mind, in the late 60s, early 70s was not all whitey and the power structure is bad—I think it was some of that but it was also, 'We've got to do our own work. We can't expect somebody else to do it for us. We've gotta raise our kids well. We've gotta make sure they get to school. We've gotta make sure to find ways of believing in ourselves'—that I think is powerful and good and constructive."[38] Kruckemeyer notes Black Power and local control as contributory to urban residents' belief in their ability to create better political and environmental conditions for themselves. While he acknowledges that these ideas became equated with "whitey and the power structure is bad," he counters such easy, racialized reductions by concluding that a place-specific, resident-driven politics is at once "powerful and good and constructive." To other white residents living in the city during the late 1960s, Kruckemeyer's comments would no doubt seem curious, even misguided. His was a rare opinion. Yet, Kruckemeyer's wariness of segregationist politics as well as the increasing centralization and professionalization of government decision making aligned him with activist agendas, excoriating both: "In the case of Black Power, was it being misused? Yeah, it probably was too because it was an exclusive club. But the positive things that were there which were, I think, contributory to other neighborhoods thinking about having good control of their responsibilities as well as needs. We're saying we can't let the big-scale planners do it all for us, we can't let the folks who are making all the decisions in Washington do it."[39]

Kruckemeyer's work as an architect exposed him firsthand to the ways in which professional experts were creating an exclusionary built environment based on an appeal to white, middle-class, and suburban populations and not the needs of the city's current residents. For Kruckemeyer and his fellow neighborhood activists, it was no longer prudent to leave local decisions to "big-scale planners" in Washington, D.C., or the "highway boys" in Massachusetts: "Leaving the public employees, the 'highway boys' to plan the interstate was not what would work from the standpoint of our belief in urban neighborhoods, in walking to school, or any number of those homey types of things that people were into, whether it was with respect to Black Power, whether it was respect to take back your streets, any of those sorts of things. We were [reacting] to the government policies and the big corporations and the others who were trying to convince us we should live in the suburbs and abandon the cities and that folks who were poor didn't count."[40]Kruckemeyer and his activist neighbors rejected the government's adoption of values that bypassed democratic authority of the full electorate in favor of market-driven and class-inflected goals. The impact of such a political shift at the federal and municipal level would have grave consequences for the physical and social organization of older multiethnic communities such as Kruckemeyer's South End neighborhood. Thus neighborhood-based decisions to seize political power by asserting independent and local acts of self-determination define a critical aspect of late twentieth-century resistance to expert-led transformations of land and polity.

From 1969 and forward, resident-led efforts to identify abandoned land as valuable and "precious" sparked several waves of grassroots activism across the city and formed a veritable urban planning campaign within the larger antihighway movement itself. In the years that followed, this "campaign" would prove more effective in creating a posthighway blueprint for Boston than antihighway activists in the South End, Roxbury, or Jamaica Plain could have dreamed.

My first meeting with Ken Kruckemeyer occurred as a scheduled interview in his kitchen over breakfast. Toast, oatmeal, tea, juice, and a gaggle of my questions filled one hour and then a second. He invited me back for a second meeting, promising to "show you the boxes." I came for the second meeting, but he said he had "one more thing to tell" me before we explored *the boxes*. I arrived for the third meeting and he told me the same thing, only this time he asks, "So where did I leave off last time?" And so it went. I agreed to this multipart interview series partly because I was eager to hear his eyewitness accounts and reflections and partly because I held the secret hope that I would find photographic evidence of the Black Panthers' health clinic trailer or a few of the slides used by Urban Planning Aid and the GBC in their efforts to raise resident awareness of the highway. These mythical carrots never materialized.

However, one morning Kruckemeyer did show me his personal slide collection chronicling the many physical changes to his neighborhood over the last several decades. His collection is spectacular. From the railroad tracks at the end of his street, which were to be replaced by the new highway, to a daytime shot of the vacant swath of land stretching through Roxbury to the now well-known drawing of the interstate itself, Kruckemeyer's photographs succinctly capture a sprawling narrative of forty years of neighborhood change. Although I never found an image of the Black Panthers' health clinic or an official slide used by Urban Planning Aid within Kruckemeyer's exhaustive historical archive, I did unearth a wealth of new stories and documents made possible only because of his dedicated collecting.

At our next meeting, Kruckemeyer tells me that it is finally time to explore his collection of basement boxes. Throughout our conversations, he had referenced this subterranean collection of papers, reports, photographs, and files related to stopping the highway and the aftermath. The chance to explore Kruckemeyer's personal archive of antihighway and Southwest Corridor memorabilia seemed too good to miss except for one thing: its existence in a dank basement. Eyeing my slow descent on the basement's steep, ladder-like steps, Kruckemeyer reaches his hand to me: "Watch your step." A row of white boxes stretches out along the wall, on the floor, on tabletops, and into my imagination. And with that, I enter a greatly anticipated historical frontier waiting for my eyes, hands, and questions.

Kruckemeyer thumbs through a thick row of papers. "What is this?" He laughs to himself and then flashes me the front page of his daughter's middle school math quiz. She did well on it. I smile. Based on the fact that Kruckemeyer's daughter, Kate, currently has two small children who make him a very proud grandfather, it is safe to say this particular box is at least twenty-five years old. We've now established an archival dating method. Then, as if on cue, Kruckemeyer begins describing the world events swirling around him and his neighborhood in the late 1960s. I'm curious to know what propelled him to act, to protest a highway, and later to become one of the state officials charged with implementing the resident-planned alternative. Kruckemeyer is formally trained as an architect. When I ask him about what informed his community-based approach to planning and design, he thinks for a moment and then puts the question in historical context: "I think that a lot of that came out of the antihighway movement and the moment of time when we were doing this. It was after the major efforts in the civil rights movement—during or contemporaneous with the demonstrations against the Vietnam [War] . . . about the same time as the first Earth Days. People had come to sense that it was time to stand up and be counted. People were actually standing up and saying this stuff is wrong, we've got to do it differently. The highway stuff is wrong, we've got to do it differently. The Vietnam War is wrong, we've got to do things differently."[41] Kruckemeyer's coming-of-age story is both persuasive and provocative. As a twenty-something graduate student, he forged his leftist politics during the social upheavals of the 1960s. He cites the Vietnam War, the civil rights movement, and America's burgeoning environmental activism as drivers of a popular ethos of "we've got to do it differently." This ethos would spur Kruckemeyer's activism as a student, professional architect, neighborhood resident, and government administrator.

Kruckemeyer sifts through box after box, fingering various newspaper clippings, meeting minutes, and creased photographs. He comments on an old image of Columbus Avenue, one of the main through streets in his neighborhood. I marvel aloud over the old cars parked on the streets, but he instead looks intently at the curbs and talks about traffic patterns, the city's water table, and grade levels. This is another one of those winding conversations where Kruckemeyer's technical knowledge and ability to decode jargon for the uninitiated are on full display. Just as he launches into a probing analysis of storm drains, his hand grazes a file labeled "Highways/STOP." Silence. He holds up the file. Could it be? Could it actually be the main file he's been alluding to for weeks? He hands it over to me. Considering its potential importance, I'm surprised it is not heavier. Carefully, I fold back the manila sleeve to a first page that looks like handwritten notes. Kruckemeyer hovers expectantly over my shoulder. More pages. A meeting flyer. I'm eager to find evidence of how the antihighway movement's activists spread their message and built momentum. We find two more folders—one labeled "STOP current" and another simply "GBC." We've now been in the basement for more than three hours. It's time for lunch.

I left Kruckemeyer's basement that afternoon and spent the next two months attempting to reconstruct the files we retrieved. What I found out was that the antihighway movement was busily recruiting residents from Boston and Cambridge to its cause, not primarily because it was winning its early battles but because it was losing them.

By 1970 Kruckemeyer was spearheading a series of local meeting and actions related to the highway's threat to his neighborhood, but the Greater Boston Committee's legislative efforts pushed his gaze farther afield. Committee organizers asked Kruckemeyer to offer public testimony in support of House Bill No. 2823. This bill reached beyond geographically specific grievances to enable cities and towns across the state to have a greater role in local planning as well as "a voice through veto power." A form letter circulated to "GBC testifiers" explains the group's assessment of the bill: "We think it is a good bill because it allows local community participation in planning, instead of having an outside authority make plans that have no relation to the local area, and that often disrupt the area, and upset places for local improvement."[42] The letter was intended to tell its legislative testifiers what to expect during House proceedings and to tailor each individual testimony to echo the group's broader political agenda. The letter offers specific speaking instructions, including a parenthetical reminder that "you don't have to repeat the above summary in your testimony, because it will be given in the introduction to all the people to testify for GBC." Yet, each speaker was encouraged to reference GBC's "fact sheet of specific damage the proposed highway would have done" and to add "to the testimony from your own knowledge and experiences."[43]

Kruckemeyer was asked by GBC's leadership to discuss the concerns of residents of the South End and Roxbury. His statement would supplement a chorus of resident speakers from East Boston, Cambridge, Jamaica Plain, Somerville, Lynn, Brookline, and Peabody. In this way the Greater Boston Committee orchestrated the construction of a series of public testimonials emphasizing the potential physical damage wrought by the interstate highway as well as the social effects of its impact. These testimonials collectively produced a dramatic and damning regional statement against highway expansion in the state of Massachusetts. The committee's careful shepherding of each resident-authored narrative enabled the coalition to fortify its identity as a geographically representative body of concerned citizens. Furthermore, GBC's effort to legalize a more participatory planning process called for a devolution of decision-making authority from the state government to local municipalities.

As with its neighborhood organizing work, GBC's legislative work sought to debunk the premise that "outside authority" meant superior plans for cities and towns. The idea that local communities might possess the ability to conceive and approve large-scale land and transportation improvements remained dangerously unorthodox. The dominant view in Massachusetts, as within state legislatures around the country, upheld the primacy of state-commissioned experts' determination of what was best for local residents. In response, the committee leaders offered Bill No. 2823 and placed a controversial intellectual and political claim at the center of public discussion. As individual residents were assembled and coached on how best to present their verbal support of this bill, the group's leaders continued to refine their approach to legislators.

In the days immediately preceding resident testifiers' appearance before the House Committee on Urban Affairs, GBC's outreach coordinator, Barbara Brandt, wrote Kruckemeyer with a few last-minute pointers to shape his speechwriting. Although Brandt misspells her correspondent's name, she is exacting in her instructions:

Dear Mr. Crookmeyer (?)—
Could you base your testimony on the two main points of *housing shortfall* and *increased cost to residents* with highway construction (leading to more highways, parking lots, police, maintenance, etc.). These are both points of special relevance to city dwellers threatened by highways.[44]

Here again, the GBC's hand can be seen actively shaping the public narrative defining the antihighway movement's organizing story. Kruckemeyer is asked to frame his testimony as a response to the "housing shortfall" and "increased cost to residents," two issues highlighted within the committee's legislative analysis. While Kruckemeyer is encouraged to talk "from personal experience," he is reminded by Brandt that she has given him "4 information sheets which I hope will be helpful in writing up this testimony."[45] Brandt's coaching is an expression of the antihighway movement's approach to directing work at the grassroots level as well as the committee's likely assessment that an overly broad and diffuse message would dilute the power of its regional coalition. In short, this geographically and politically expansive grassroots alliance was learning to speak with one coordinated voice.

Heeding his directives, Kruckemeyer grabbed a pencil and several blank sheets of paper and began drafting ideas. When he eventually sat down at his typewriter, his writing task was clear. He produced a two-page, double-spaced testimony that reads as an elegant but firm, data-based rebuke of interstate highways from an impassioned resident: "House bill 2823 will help insure, for both the inner cities and the rest of the Commonwealth, that if interstate highways are constructed, they will be located in direct response to the needs of the areas through which they pass and serve. It will help insure for the City of Boston that if the interstate highways are constructed, the severe effects on the already acute housing shortage and the substantial indirect cost to residents can be held to an absolute minimum."[46] Kruckemeyer's opening paragraph foregrounds GBC's key talking points on the city's housing shortage as well as the cost increase to area residents facing projected rent and property tax increases. He further builds his case by fingering the DPW as an unelected body unresponsive to the transportation planning needs of the state generally and local communities in particular. He argues: "This bill is necessary because the present plans of the Department of Public Works illustrate that it is neither responsive to the balanced transportation needs of the Commonwealth, nor to the intimate requirements of her communities. The DPW and their consultants are not accountable to the electorate nor to the communities through which their highways will pass."[47] By critiquing the DPW in the State House itself, Kruckemeyer succeeds in bringing a searing grassroots debate directly to "enemy" territory.

Though his remarks remain measured and tethered to the bill's aim of reforming the state's overall approach to planning, it is likely that Kruckemeyer's audience of DPW allies did not welcome his critique of the leadership fitness of the DPW "and their consultants." But Kruckemeyer did not linger on this topic; he saved the bulk of his testimony to discuss the damage and disruption a highway and its daily traffic would bring to Boston's residents, especially those living in nearby public housing developments.

> In the South End–Roxbury area, not only have four thousand to five thousand people (at least 1,319 dwelling units) already been displaced, and at least 1,699 workers lost their jobs, but the highway would continue to disrupt the lives of many thousands of residents who live in the immediate vicinity of the highways. The proposed interchange between the Southwest Expressway (I-95 South) and the Inner Belt (I-695) will carry an estimated 160,000 automobiles through the middle of a 2,100-unit complex of low and moderate income housing developments . . . Surely, these two proposed highways are not the result of planning which has given any weight or understanding to the needs of the city of Boston or its neighborhoods.[48]

Traffic counts and the number of low- and moderate-income housing units coupled with resident displacement figures peppering Kruckemeyer's testimony may not read as especially provocative at first glance. However, these details represent an important aspect of the Greater Boston Committee's overall information strategy to use and reuse "figures from official state or city reports."[49]

The committee's organizers were adamant that any data they used must be verifiable by state agencies. Remarking on this tactic and its effect within the committee's ongoing state appeals, Steve Teichner told a reporter, "We forced our opponents to do their homework. With the assistance of UPA [Urban Planning Aid], we were feeding the Governor's office information the DPW couldn't make available—they had the stuff, but they hadn't pulled it together."[50] This data-sourcing strategy required the state to reconsider its existing plan within GBC's political framework. The result was a new debate based on old, yet official, information. Thus the GBC was effective in shifting the state's discussion toward a closer examination of and engagement with the goals of antihighway activists.

Kruckemeyer's quantitative summary of the impact of interstate highways also underscored the displacement and public health threats facing Boston's public housing residents. Public housing developments, including the Whittier Street Housing Project (200 units); Mission Main and Mission Hill Extension Project, "where one ramp passes within 50 feet of the fifth floor windows"; Lenox Street Housing Projects (306 units); and Bromley Heath Project (800 units) immediately abutted the highway's route through the city's center.[51] Kruckemeyer concludes his testimony by assuring his listeners that "House 2823 is not a bill which will stop 'progress.' It is a bill which will insure a better solution to the transportation needs of the Commonwealth by respecting the needs of her cities and towns."[52] His attempt to redefine "progress" for state legislators was earnest but tepid. However, his instinct to address the dominant cultural notion that highways equal progress rightly identifies a major ideological battle for the antihighway movement.

Kruckemeyer's testimony joined a chorus of residents and organizations worried about Boston's public housing stock and the highway's detrimental effect on people living there. Prior to the GBC's legislative organizing efforts with residents, the Black United Front launched multiple outreach campaigns to recruit public housing residents directly as antihighway organizers. Gloria Fox, who would later be elected state representative (Democrat, 7th Suffolk), was one such BUF-mobilized public housing resident. When Fox and her family moved into the Whittier Street housing projects in 1968, "most of the Southwest Corridor was completely leveled." As Fox recalls, the scene outside her Whittier Street window revealed "just one great big vacant lot." But she was most startled by something else: "I noticed my son was wheezing everyday": "I looked around and saw that the earth had changed, there was dust everywhere. The kids were becoming sicker. We were partnered with the Whittier Street Health Center, so most of the kids, including my son and my family, were seen at the health center right across from the projects."[53] The dust along the Corridor shifted and moved with the wind and created a hazard for residents and especially children playing outdoors. For Fox, clearance for the highway was both political and personal. Though the availability of services at a local health center was helpful, the landscape's environmental danger threatened the health of children living on the Corridor and violated the city's pledge of safe, modern housing for the public. The biological impact of flying dust and debris brought a daily reminder of the highway's looming presence. Fox took action. She joined the Black United Front's antihighway subcommittee, Operation STOP, as a resident organizer and persuaded neighbors to join her. She explains her early organizing:

> I-95 would be connecting from Maine all the way down to Florida with us in the middle. What we did was we literally started with an education process with the folks in the housing projects, first in my development saying this is why you're choking. This is why your kids are asthmatic. And we started it as a health issue as well as politically. It was an immobilization issue. They wanted to keep us in between all of these little [traffic] circles that would be created by a highway. So we would be in one little pocket . . . So we saw that plan and if the dust and the dirt and everything didn't kill us, then definitely by the time they built this, it would be so detrimental to us that we would be dead in terms of a community.[54]

Fox's concern for the health of her son and her neighbors catalyzed her decision to become an antihighway organizer. "We became environmentalists long before this became a sexy issue. People always consider that that isn't one of the major issues of black people—environmental issues." As eventual lead organizer for Operation STOP and then a neighborhood liaison for the GBC, Fox held a central leadership position in the political apparatus surrounding the antihighway movement itself.

Although the highway's proposed alignment seemed to suggest a natu-ral protest constituency among Fox's neighbors, many residents were not convinced that publicly expressing their disapproval would effect change in any way. "Some people thought that it could never be done. No one's ever fought a major interstate highway and won. That would have been a first, but we were determined that it was going to be the first."[55] Although Boston would not be the first U.S. city to fight a highway and win, Fox's passionate commitment to defeating I-95 imbued her words with authority. Much of her work as an organizer was to persuade her neighbors with stories, data, and the power of her own convictions. She is not bashful in identifying the reason for her organizing success: "I had the forte, skills, and could relate to all of the people in the housing developments."[56] Fox's fervor, competence and determination were key to furthering the Black United Front's work among Boston's public housing residents.

While the Front's neighborhood outreach efforts took multiple forms, flyer circulation by such organizers as Fox was a primary communications and movement-building tool. The Front's flyers typically used language both alarming and empowering to great rhetorical effect. For example, one antihighway flyer warned:

"The *residents* of Roxbury, North Dorchester, South End, Jamaica Plain SLEEP as two serpents *to strangle* (isolate and destroy your neighborhood), *to poison* (pollute the air and create noise), *to kill* (a danger to you and your children as cars speed by 30, 40, 50 feet above your head and in some cases within 100 feet of your home.) THESE TWO SERPENTS ARE TWO ROADS: (1) THE INNERBELT, (2) THE SOUTHWEST EXPRESSWAY."

THESE ROADS are of *NO BENEFIT* to the *RESIDENTS*. THEY, only, *BENEFIT* the following: 1. *RICH SUBURBANITES* who will have easier access to downtown Boston. 2. The LARGE *CONSTRUCTION COMPA-NIES* engaged in highway building. *YOU CAN STOP THESE ROADS!!!* YOU ONLY!

By *SUPPORTING* "OPERATION STOP" 1. *COME TO THE TENT* at Columbus and Ruggles for information (will be erected July 28th). 2. *CALL UNITED FRONT* 427-5372 to offer your special service.

HELPING PUT the LAND to GOOD USE FOR the *PEOPLE WHO LIVE THERE* by *PARTICIPATING IN & SPONSORING* Outdoor mov-ies, Mass rallies, Folk Festivals, Outdoor Religious Services, Bazaars, Building: Homes, Recreational Parks, Small Businesses.[57]

In this flyer the Southwest Corridor Expressway and the Inner Belt are personified as two serpents slithering across the city as residents passively sleep. The serpents' threat is cast as immediate and potentially lethal; residents are informed that they are in danger of being strangled, poisoned, or killed. Though this flyer was designed for circulation in several neighborhoods across the city, including Roxbury, North Dorchester, the South End, and Jamaica Plain, the analysis provided refers specifically to the highway's impact for public housing residents in the city's heart.

The flyer's reference to the highways as a "danger to you and your children as cars speed by 30, 40, 50 feet above your head and in some cases within 100 feet of your home" is alarming but is based on Urban Planning Aid's research on the interstate highway's impact on residents of Boston's public housing. In this way Urban Planning Aid–sourced data—used here as well as within the Greater Boston Committee's legislative testimonies— provided essential content for the antihighway movement's ongoing public awareness activities. And while the Front's flyers aimed to educate, they also sought to inspire collective action. Readers are told, "You can stop these roads!!! You only." Through these kinds of exhortations, residents are encouraged to join the antihighway movement and, critically, "to put the land to good use for the people who live there."

Following the state's demolition order, multiple waves of change engulfed Fox and her neighbors. Older brick and wooden frame houses were cleared in 1966, as were many business that brought jobs, services, and provisions to the area. Reflecting on the Black United Front's activism among public housing residents, Fox observes, "We had a captive audience of people that were so mad that you would do something to them. And we were the only thing standing. We lost about 500 units of housing." Fox further recounts the businesses losses, including local shops and national food chain Kemps: "Businesses were pushed out as well. We had about 800 businesses that were also along that corridor. They were small businesses, they were lighting companies—they were all kinds of business along that corridor. We had a gas station where the police station was. We had Kemp's so we had some chains . . . along that strip, so we had a lot of jobs that were made to disappear. So one of the things that we naturally began to do now that we're organizing and the mission is to stop the road."[58]

Fox began by sharing information and ideas with her neighbors in Whittier and ultimately built a larger network among public housing residents. The vacant landscape of what had been a dense business and residential corridor signified a frightening act of disappearance for many public housing residents living in the highway's path. But the idea of engaging in a battle to stop the highway also inspired doubt and uncertainty. This was true for urban and suburban communities along the highway's right-of-way. Yet, Fox is unequivocal when explaining what was at stake for her neighborhood: "We had the most to lose. There was the environment that was going to be destroyed from one end to the other. We were the *environment* . . . it was people. So our motto became 'People before Highways.'"[59]

＝＝＝＝

Despite its signature veneer of political bravado, this period of the antihighway movement's history is best characterized as an epidemic of uncertainty. The final highway verdict was uncertain, the landscape remained a dusty wasteland, and antihighway activists were racked with doubt as to whether their ultimate goal of stopping the highway was feasible. Any retrospective analysis suggesting that social movements gain momentum based solely on political victories is misleading. Although the movement eventually achieved several of its goals, many of its early large-scale efforts failed, including the attempt to file a legislative package in 1970. Not one of the GBC's seven bills was passed. Most died in committee. Yet this failure, as others that followed, prompted antihighway organizers to continue looking for winning strategies. This ongoing search prompted by repeated failures built Boston's antihighway movement.

As the movement spread from Cambridge to Boston, the tactics and strategies for mass mobilization shifted to address the specific concerns of local residents. For both cities, the physical form and location of the interstate highway itself created geographically specific grievances. Cambridge residents' battle against the Inner Belt's radial loop through Brookline and Elm Streets prefigured Roxbury residents' opposition to the highway's noodle-like interchange. In both instances the highway's arrival represented yet another state-sponsored displacement scenario for area residents. What specifically galvanized local residents to act and become engaged in a fight that would stretch across two full decades is the backstory that this chapter lays bare. The work to identify, communicate, and mobilize according to what was at stake locally built a platform among Boston neighborhoods that did not initially see themselves in common cause with one another.

But these residents did realize that it was necessary to take matters into their own hands in the face of an unresponsive state and local government.

And, significantly, local control, once a controversial political idea brandished by white southern segregationists, emerged as black nationalist creed and multiracial, region-spanning resident response to absent and abusive government authority. Local control offered an ideological base camp for residents' growing belief in their ability to create better political and environmental conditions for themselves than would the state and federal government. Through grassroots construction projects, doorknocking campaigns, legislative organizing, and countless neighborhood meetings, the Black United Front and the Greater Boston Committee on the Transportation Crisis mobilized neighbors to assume an active role in governing themselves. It is ultimately residents' reliance on themselves, matched with a strong desire to change the cultural values determining political decision making in their names, that sets the region on course to make political history by stopping a highway.

Chapter 4

Planning for Tomorrow, Not Yesterday

"We Were Wrong"

The celebratory lore surrounding Boston's antihighway movement and the Southwest Corridor Park is a point of pride for political activists and longtime residents of Greater Boston. State House marches, multiple press conferences, lists of fiery demands, backroom sparring sessions with mayors and governors, the birth of new grassroots political organizations, and numerous published reports—all of this is recounted in technicolor detail depending on whom you ask. But there are two parts of this story that typically inspire extra word count and wistful reflection: Governor Francis Sargent's decision to call for a formal three-year restudy of the state's transportation plan and the eventual reversal of his prohighway position. For the movement's lead actors, these two actions above all pushed antihighway activists forward in their long-sought victory. Yet, their accounts do not elevate Sargent to the status of political superhero as much as they reveal the inner workings of governmental problem solving and how local activists were able to exert influence within typically concealed political processes.

When Richard Nixon became U.S. president in 1968, Massachusetts would lose its governor. Nixon tapped Massachusetts governor John Volpe to serve as U.S. secretary of transportation and propelled his lieutenant governor, Francis Sargent—known as a mild-mannered nature lover and moderate Republican—to the office of governor. Two days after his inauguration in 1969, antihighway protesters swarmed the State House demanding to know Sargent's official position on the highway plan. As Chuck Turner recalls: "Volpe went to Washington when Nixon asked him to be Secretary of Transportation. So everybody said, you've got the highway builder of the country now heading transportation—there's no way he's going to let you stop a highway. The irony was that Sargent was a conservationist, and his sense of conservation piqued his interest [in our cause]."[1] Turner echoes the initial assessment of local activists that Sargent's gubernatorial rise was a potential benefit to the antihighway movement. Most protesters knew Sargent's prohighway past as head of the Department of Public Works (DPW), but he had also served for ten years as commissioner of the Department of Natural Resources. So his sudden political ascension and environmental leanings were imagined as new bases for negotiation.

Yet neither the antihighway protesters storming the steps of the State House nor Sargent himself knew that within a mere thirteen months of assuming the office of governor, he would utter this dramatic statement: "Four years ago, I was Commissioner of the Department of Public Works— our road building agency. Then, nearly everyone was sure highways were the only answer to transportation problems for years to come. We were wrong." And just like that, the surprise governor of Massachusetts surprised everyone. In a single ten-minute television broadcast, Sargent critiqued the state's transportation policy, announced that a new planning process was immediately necessary and declared that he would travel to Washington to get federal help to do so. Framed as a series of questions and responses outlining a broad set of issues surrounding the state's highway controversies, Sargent's historic announcement was a game changer: "Are we really meeting our transportation needs by spending most of our money building roads? The answer is no. Are the roads we are building too costly—not merely in dollars, but in what they cost us in demolished homes, disrupted communities, dislocated lives, pollution in the air, damage to our environment? The answer is yes—they are too costly. The most important question is this: What should we do?"[2] Wearing a dark suit and sitting at his State House desk framed by the Massachusetts flag, the governor peered directly into the camera. His voice was steady; his words were simple and plain. Yet for Sargent's viewing audience there was no mistaking the drama and complexity of his message. Highway building would be halted while a new study, described as "first in the nation," would convene a group of citizens to examine the state's transportation needs. The final result would be, according to Sargent, a transportation plan based on "not where an expressway should be built, but whether an expressway should be built."[3]

To build or not to build a highway was an important question, but the bigger question asked by antihighway activists and the governor himself probed the process for making such a decision. In this way, Sargent's television address was pivotal for recasting the highway debate as both a transportation and a planning crisis. Although a state-level politician's decision to change course on live television is noteworthy, the real story is how on-the-ground activism grew to influence and shape public policy and how this was accomplished by redefining the relationship between citizens and the plans made in their name. The 1948 *Master Highway Plan for the Boston Metropolitan Area*, its attendant facts and figures, and the state's own highway experts and engineers were now being questioned not just by antihighway activists but also by the state's chief executive.

Furthermore, Sargent critiqued the state's transportation planning process while bringing renewed attention to a strip of land in Boston known as the Southwest Corridor: "The state now owns three-quarters of the land in that Corridor. We are committed to the use of that Corridor. Plans now call for highway construction there—massive highway construction: an eight-lane highway, plus four extra breakdown lanes. The old plan does call for rapid transit in this Corridor. But it does not consider its proper integration, or other transportation alternatives now available to us. And it emphatically does not consider the impact on the environment—on housing, on land use, on people. I have decided it must."[4] By the governor's order, the Southwest Corridor was deemed a landscape in need of special attention and protection. No additional clearance would be permitted there until the current highway plan was reexamined.

Against the backdrop of state and national debates on how best to move people through cities, Sargent's speech brings attention to people living within cities. Sargent's discussion of transportation plans for the Southwest Corridor again redirects public attention away from "to build or not to build" debates and toward a more nuanced issue, the impact of highway construction on local neighborhoods. He informed his viewing audience that the plan for the Corridor was flawed for failing to account for its immediate effects and now "it must." Sargent called for not only a new kind of planning process to address the state's transportation needs but also a new set of criteria for determining transportation planning's effectiveness.

By advocating for a multimodal transportation system integrating road building with mass transit and pausing to consider the environmental and social impact of such a plan, Sargent articulates a radical reversal of mid-twentieth-century professional planning norms that would have lasting national repercussions.

Locally, Sargent was now marked as a detractor, if not full-blown opponent, of the state's powerful prohighway lobby inclusive of the Department of Public Works. Nationally, Sargent would have to appeal to Congress and his former boss, John Volpe, whose permission Sargent's plan required. As federal secretary of transportation, Volpe wielded considerable authority over how federal highway planning dollars were spent and whether these funds could be redirected toward mass transit. This had never been done, and Volpe, with his public prohighway stance and prior stint as an Eisenhower appointee to the Federal Highway Administration, appeared the least likely federal bureaucrat to support such a scheme.[5] The Sargent administration rolled the dice anyway. Although the governor's televised announcement may have been perceived by viewers as a stunning and spontaneous turn of events, the truth was that Sargent and his senior advisers had been studying the issues and how best to address them for months.

America's conventional practice of transportation planning was now on trial, and Sargent made sure everyone could watch. Furthermore, his broadcast delivered a high-wattage rebuke of transportation planning orthodoxies of the day. And Sargent's call for a gubernatorial task force to advise him on the state's transportation plan would fatefully set the basis for incorporating antihighway protesters' goals and approaches into the formal political process. This broadcast was momentous, and pro- and antihighway factions knew it. Sargent's policy reversal and effort to remake the state's transportation planning process are also instructive for what they reveal about America's 1960s so-called urban crisis, namely, that politicians and professional planners themselves held some responsibility for the problems plaguing cities and not urban residents, who were frequently typecast as the problem.

Urban Crisis as Planning Crisis

A politician-commissioned study to examine urban problems in America was not without precedent. Just two years before Sargent made his televised address to Massachusetts's residents and announced a plan to study Boston's metropolitan region, President Lyndon Johnson had appointed three separate commissions to address the "crisis" within America's cities.[6] Each of these commissions would come to be known simply by its chairman's last name—Kaiser, Douglas, and Kerner—and all would release their findings in 1968–69. The President's Committee on Urban Housing, chaired by industrial magnate Edward Kaiser, examined how private industry might help advance the federal government's quest to produce affordable housing for low- and moderate-income Americans.[7] The National Commission on Urban Problems chaired by former Illinois senator Paul Douglas reviewed standard federal tax policies and housing codes so as to increase the supply of housing for low-income residents.[8] And the National Advisory Commission on Civil Disorders chaired by Illinois governor Otto Kerner investigated the root causes of violent uprisings across twenty-three U.S. cities. Although each commission offered data-rich analysis of urban America's racial and economic ills, the Kerner Commission released a thunderclap of commentary that made local, national, and academic headlines.

The Kerner Commission's scathing 1968 report on American cities announced a new racial narrative: "Our nation is moving toward two societies, one black, one white—separate and unequal." The Commission concluded that "white racism" was the number one cause of the riots and further intensified public debate of the Johnson administration's antipoverty agenda.[9] While many critics and civil rights leaders considered the report groundbreaking in its naming of white racism as an active impediment to the functioning of U.S. society, the report's ironic flaw is that by naming "white racism" as a culprit, there were no specific actors to target. In short, the entire society needed to be reformed. Though this general diagnosis was compelling, there were specific actors and institutions that could have been further interrogated, namely, urban planners and policymakers.

Yet, the Kerner Report offers more than a fatalistic treatise on racial separatism in America. It provides the beginning of an important synthesis of the institutional and political failures driving urban unrest. In fact, by linking urban unrest, social distrust, and decreasing economic opportunity to urban infrastructure, the Kerner Commission forcefully challenges the period's essentializing discourse on race and urban space and prompts federal examination of the social and economic conditions plaguing U.S. cities. The time was ripe for federal agencies to take a closer look at their expanding twentieth-century role in producing and regulating urban neighborhoods.

The Kerner Report is also noteworthy for bringing national attention to the ways in which a growing race consciousness and pride among black citizens were precipitating new kinds of political conflict within urban neighborhoods. The commission's authors write: "By and large, the rioters were young Negroes, natives of the ghetto (not of the south) hostile to the white society surrounding and repressing them and equally hostile to the middle class Negroes who accommodated themselves to that white dominance. The rioters were mistrustful of white politics, they hated the police, they were proud of their race, and acutely conscious of the discrimination they suffered."[10] This description of black protesters is neither apologetic nor dismissive. Rather, it attempts to suggest a set of interior motivations leading to street protest. The hostility of protesters is linked to their assessments of "white dominance" and "discrimination." In this way the Kerner Report brings attention to the web of racial and political issues surrounding urban populations and attempts to move national discussion away from still popular biological and pseudoscientific notions of black behavior. While doing so may not have been the expressed intent of the commission, its incisive and unconventional social analysis is a noteworthy contribution.

The report's description of black city dwellers as self-aware political actors advanced a new conceptual framework for understanding urban problems. Here the economic and social conditions surrounding cities are presented as crucial factors informing the actions of some black residents. The Kerner Report does not go far enough in detailing the policies, events, and actors responsible for the conditions within America's 1960s-era urban centers; however, it does begin to examine the effects of metropolitan growth and the often devastating consequences for older cities and their populations.

For the Kerner commissioners, the low employment levels and inadequate infrastructure endemic to older cities only exacerbated the racial and political inequalities found there: "Most new employment opportunities do not occur in central cities, near all-Negro neighborhoods. They are being created in suburbs and outlying areas—and this trend is likely to continue indefinitely."[11] In response to the issue of urban unemployment, the commission advocated federal support for "improved transportation linking ghettos and suburbs," among other recommendations.[12] Not just content to offer a laundry list of urban ills, the commission set forth a series of national recommendations designed to "change the system of failure and frustration." The commission further articulated its concern about cities by suggesting that the government promote policies that would enable more black citizens to move to the suburbs, where jobs are located, and to cease building high-density, high-rise "slums."[13] A main goal of such policies, the commission asserted, would be to improve communication between black citizens and local government via an expansion of "opportunities for ghetto residents to participate in the formulation of public policy."[14] As these examples indicate, the commission recognized policy as key means of social intervention. And although urban planning, as a tool for addressing the needs of citizens and increasing citizen involvement in the governance of place, is not mentioned explicitly by the commissioners, their final recommendations speak to its political importance.

Within its consideration of urban problems and how they might best be addressed, the Kerner Commission highlights a historical clash between the availability of jobs and the expectation of northern-bound black migrants seeking them. The commissioners write: "Throughout the 20th century, and particularly in the last three decades, the Negro population of the United States has been moving steadily from rural areas to urban and from South to North and West . . . Negro migration from the South began after the Civil War . . . The movement of Negroes out of the rural South accelerated during World War I, when floods and boll weevils hurt farming in the South, and the industrial demands of the war created thousands of new jobs for unskilled workers in the North. After the war, the shift to mechanized farming spurred the continuing movement of Negroes from rural Southern areas."[15] Again, the commission's conception of contemporary cities centers itself in structural analysis yet does not address the ways that urban renewal or government-sponsored planning projects (highways, public housing, etc.) facilitated new migration and investment patterns. By failing to do so, the Kerner Report missed a national opportunity to reveal the role of political and economic actors engaged in profiteering development practices that left longtime city residents fending for themselves. While placing the nation's urban problems within a context of white supremacy is useful for explaining structural failings and discriminatory practices, white racism is an insufficient target for correcting the list of maladies engulfing 1960s cities.

Prior to the release of the Kerner Report, Daniel Patrick Moynihan published his national study of black families with the intent of creating new federal social policy. As assistant secretary of labor under President Kennedy and then President Johnson and eventual domestic policy assistant to President Nixon, Moynihan was tasked with creating a comprehensive framework for setting federal antipoverty policy. Already established as an academic expert on America's ethnic communities, Moynihan turned his attention to the status of America's black populations. Moynihan's 1965 report entitled "The Negro Family: The Case for National Action" directed a national spotlight on what he defined as the "pathology" of the black family. In sharp contrast to the Kerner commissioners, Moynihan concludes that the nation's black populations were in crisis not because of racial segregation, a lack of jobs, or a lack of decision-making power but rather because of the dysfunctional workings of the black family itself. He writes: "The deterioration of the Negro family . . . is the fundamental source of the weakness of the Negro community at the present time."[16]

Though civil rights leaders and liberal politicians immediately attacked Moynihan's report as specious and inflammatory, many of his ideas held currency far beyond Washington.[17] Furthermore, his analysis demonstrates the highly impressionistic generalizations of urban life that circulated at the national policy level:

> Country life and city life are profoundly different. The gradual shift of American society from a rural to an urban basis over the past century and a half has caused abundant strains, many of which are still much in evidence. When this shift occurs suddenly, drastically, in one or two generations, the effect is immensely disruptive of traditional social patterns. It was this abrupt transition that produced the wild Irish slums of the 19th Century Northeast. Drunkenness, crime, corruption, discrimination, family disorganization, juvenile delinquency were the routine of that era. In our own time, the same sudden transition has produced the Negro slum—different from, but hardly better than its predecessors, and fundamentally the result of the same process. Negroes are now more urbanized than whites.[18]

For Moynihan, twentieth-century urbanization had produced a racialized social disorder with historical precedent. Like the Kerner commissioners, Moynihan attempts to shine light on U.S. demographic shifts hastened by

new twentieth-century urbanization patterns. However, his characteriza-
tions of Irish and Negro "slums" are steeped in the kind of flawed race-
space typologies popularized by Robert Park and the Chicago School.

More than providing clear analysis for what ails American cities,
Moynihan's descriptions reveal much of the cultural bias present in midcentury U.S. urban research.[19] Politically entrenched ideas about race, "slums,"
and the "pathological" poor generated ineffective and often self-defeating
urban policy. However, the greater public need for a nuanced understanding of the urban environment on which to base policy remained unful-
filled. Two years later the Kerner Commission would provide more cogent
environmental analysis but, like Moynihan, would fall short in authoring
a comprehensive assessment of the underlying issues and actors driving
America's so-called urban crisis. Together and separately, each of these
nationally scaled, politician-driven reports are significant for their ability
to capture mid-1960s-era debates on the relationship between race, class,
and urban development.

As the Moynihan and Kerner Reports were being written, hundreds
of urban renewal turf battles raged across neighborhoods throughout the
country. Residents of urban renewal project areas verbally demanded new
and more responsive local and federal policy on a daily basis. Yet neither
of these reports offer a spatial critique of urban renewal or its role in further disordering cities or undermining citizens' trust in government. The
absence of a substantive discussion of urban renewal, or planning generally, within these reports suggests a glaring, though telling, omission.
Beyond textbook examples of a structural versus behavioral framework for
describing the intersections of race and poverty in America, both reports
deliver important commentary on the nation's struggle to understand the
core of its urban problems. These reports were seminal in influencing late
twentieth-century discussions of America's urban problems; however, both
failed to consider fully the roles played by urban planning policies or professional planners in shaping the present and future of cities. Planners in
the United States took up this critique themselves and joined a growing
cross-Atlantic chorus questioning the usefulness of urban renewal as well
as planners' professional role in producing cities that had become almost
uninhabitable for urban residents.[20]

A review of the American Institute of Planners' bimonthly journal suggests that by the late 1960s the field of planning declared itself in crisis.

The *Journal of the American Institute of Planners'* March 1969 issue was
dedicated to "the cities, the black and the poor." The issue opens as follows:
"The aim of this issue is to provide a forum for discussion of some of the
major planning policy questions posed by urban America's problems of
race and poverty. The need for institutional change is assumed by most of
the authors; it is the type and direction of change that are at issue."[21] This
stated need for race-inflected "institutional change" shared by the journal's
contributors is also reflected in its range of article titles: "Comprehensive
Planning and Racism," "Integration and the Planner," "Model Cities, Model
Airplanes, Model Trains," and "Black Control of Central Cities." These articles ask searching questions about race and cities and delve deeply into
the practice of planning and its perceived shortcomings.[22] Lengthy discussions of race, racism, and the political implications of urban planning are
anchored by multiple references to the Kerner Commission's report. These
cross-disciplinary references demonstrate the currency of this document
beyond Washington and internal federal government debates. Academic
thought leaders in the planning field, including Peter Marcuse, Marshall
Kaplan, and Greater Boston luminaries Alan Altshuler and Gordon
Fellman (Urban Planning Aid), represent a who's who on the field's frontline of practice.

Several authors cite the Kerner Commission's findings, including its list
of cities "in which Negroes will soon attain majorities,"[23] and its observation
that "in nearly every disorder city surveyed, grievances related to housing were important factors in the structure of Negro discontent."[24] These
citations are notable because they demonstrate the academic planning
community's attempt to align its professional priorities with the material
needs of cities and their changing populations. However, ongoing political
debates surrounding the development of cities represent a decidedly bigger
challenge for the profession. One article warns: "Unless future comprehensive plans for major urban areas in the U.S. are developed around a solid
understanding of the implications of racism, they will not only be ineffectual but they may also be agents of disaster."[25] This excerpt encapsulates
the range of issues confronting planners: the need for new plans for urban
areas, the need to scrutinize urban plans for social bias, and the need to
understand the emerging political demands of changing populations.

Planners Peter Marcuse and Marshall Kaplan offer a compelling synthesis of new directions for the field of planning and new types of urban

plans that are urgently required. Marcuse and Kaplan identify the politics of planning as an essential, though traditionally unexamined, problematic. For these authors, it is precisely because planning is not examined in political terms that planners further the crisis within U.S. cities. Marcuse observes: "Most planners have typically viewed their role as a nonpolitical one. When providing decent housing for minority groups or planning for the ghetto, their role cannot be nonpolitical, for the simple reason that decent housing in this situation is housing that its occupants have decided upon, and that it in turn requires political strength to make the decision. Those who live in the worst housing in our country also tend to have the least political strength. Planners must help to change that situation, and it is a legitimate, if not essential, part of their professional job to work for this end." Marcuse admits that his version of the appropriate role of planners within cities "differs substantially from the conventional self-image of the profession."[26] Instead of an expert professional who prescribes and determines answers for a community, Marcuse suggests that planners need to assume a subordinate and supporting role to the decision making of local citizens. His article challenges planners to understand themselves as political agents capable of enhancing the collective power and health of urban communities and not just their physical condition.

Marshall Kaplan similarly describes how new urban-focused federal policies have served only to intensify the political nature of planning: "A major change in urban planning, brought about by the War on Poverty and Model Cities Programs, has been the politicizing of the planning and resource allocation process." He cites these programs as offering "welcome opportunities to redefine urban planning."[27] Kaplan's commentary echoes much of the well-known argument of planner, lawyer, and academic Paul Davidoff, who had published his seminal article "Advocacy and Pluralism and Planning" just four years prior but continued to provide provocative new commentary within the field. Kaplan offers readers a replay of Davidoff's analysis by further critiquing the "general plan" as the planner's main, though inadequate, tool. The general plan is lamented for its embodiment of a utilitarian view of the city based on land use and infrastructure needs and little else. Kaplan, channeling Davidoff, contends that traditional planning does not consider the socioeconomic or political needs of communities and thus reinforces most of the current inequities found in cities.

In "Advocacy and Pluralism and Planning," Davidoff describes urban renewal's failures as necessitating a new political approach to the built environment: "The critics of urban renewal have forced a response from the renewal agencies and that ongoing debate has stimulated needed self-evaluation by public agencies."[28] Furthermore, he rails against the notion that planners should produce only one plan representing the interests of a single group (usually the municipal planning authority): "The recommendation that city planners present and plead the plans of many interest groups is founded upon the need to establish an effective urban democracy, one in which citizens may be able to play an active role in the process of deciding public policy."[29] By 1969, the future of the field of urban planning sat suspended within a lively debate. Yet Davidoff's call for a role change for planners, from that of experts to advocates, would find resonance in politics on the ground in cities across the nation and especially in Greater Boston.

Searching for Solutions: Boston Launches a Transportation Restudy

To this rigorous debate on the future of American cities, Massachusetts governor Francis Sargent brought a state-level demand for new modes for planning and defining the social value of cities. This was a tall order by any calculation. As a U.S. government official, Sargent stood in the middle of two colliding movements: first, technocratic modernism as expressed by an international professional consensus (now weakening) on the primacy of centralized, elite authority in city building and urban revitalization; and second, an expanded U.S. civil rights movement demanding grassroots participation and local decision-making power for communities directly affected by urban plans. The clash between these two movements exposed a larger national identity crisis as U.S. government at all scales struggled to define and assert its role in urban development.

When Sargent called for a restudy of Greater Boston's interstate road building in 1969, federal highway administrators and their prohighway policies were fully under assault. By this time, the U.S. Department of Transportation had been a Cabinet-level department for only three years. Highway controversies across the country had produced a growing number of federal lawsuits, regional antihighway movements, and political barricades for highway boosters. Ground-level opposition was further strengthened by President Nixon's signing of the National Environmental Policy Act (NEPA) in December 1969. While NEPA is often referenced in terms of the array of environmental protections it codifies for the nation, its legislative requirements significantly increased the planning rigor of America's public works projects, including highways. The act established a set of procedural requirements for all federal agencies to assess and document the environmental impact of government-sponsored projects.

NEPA gave additional muscle to multiple federal highway laws previously evaded by zealous prohighway legislators. For the first time in the nation's history there was a comprehensive statute defining and accounting for human impact on the natural environment. The act's mandates required comprehensive planning processes, two-part public hearings, and detailed presentations of multiple alternate plans for submitted development proposals.[30] For antihighway activists across the country, NEPA provided a powerful lever for battling prohighway legislators; in Massachusetts, the timing of its enactment would prove particularly helpful to antihighway interests.

NEPA was just the latest in a chain of legislative acts aimed at increasing local citizen involvement and influence within federally funded public works projects. The topic of public hearings—when to have them, how to publicize them, and whether to incorporate their results into current plans—remained particularly contentious. Along with the 1956 Federal-Aid Highway Act's road-building invitation to cities, a stipulation was included that required each state highway department to hold a public hearing to announce all proposed roads. Citizens across the country complained frequently that hearings were not held, not well publicized, or publicized with inaccurate meeting information.[31] Many of these charges were found to be true and prompted changes in federal law. A wave of additional highway legislation incorporated new legal requirements for public hearings and planning in urbanized areas (Federal-Aid Highway Act of 1962); offered flexibility in route determination (Federal-Aid Highway Act of 1966 and later 1968 Howard-Cramer Interstate Route Additions); increased the number of public hearings (from one to two hearings, Federal-Aid Highway Act of 1968); and mandated the study of planning alternatives (Federal-Aid Highway Act of 1968).[32] The net result of these amendments was a highway planning and building process marginally more responsive to public demands for greater citizen participation and alternative, non-car-based transportation plans. However, the adoption of this constellation of revisions to federal highway law was not insignificant. Each shift signaled successful organizing by antihighway activists across the country. And, because of their forceful mobilization efforts, any interstate highway planning processes launched after 1969 would have to clear a much higher legal bar to secure federal funding. Funding that was seemingly easy to tap during the 1950s and through much of the 1960s now had more strings attached as the federal government maneuvered to shield itself from charges of disregard for the social and environmental impacts of road building.

Following his television appearance on February 11, 1970, Governor Sargent would go on to create the Boston Transportation Planning Review (BTPR) to answer the call for new thinking and analysis on Boston's highway controversies. With a mandate to launch an open, public process to study the commonwealth's transportation plan, Sargent's transportation review group provided a vehicle for catalyzing competing regional demands into potentially new public policy. His decision to examine the state's transportation policy through public deliberation would change the antihighway movement's political trajectory almost overnight. While resident-led press conferences, signature drives, and mass demonstrations pushed Boston's antihighway movement forward, these actions had not translated into formal expression within the political process. The transportation restudy established an official structure for pro- and antihighway factions to communicate directly to the governor with the aim of shaping policy. This was an unprecedented development within the region's then six-year highway fight. Antihighway activists understood the BTPR's structure and process as radical departures from planning conventions of the day and mobilized to ensure their full participation.

Prior to announcing the BTPR, Sargent had assembled a special task force to review the state's transportation policy in light of the controversies. This panel, the Governor's Task Force on Transportation, met privately in the fall of 1969 to discuss the state's highway plan and its opposition and to propose possible next steps for the governor. Sargent appointed Alan Altshuler, a well-regarded MIT political scientist with no previous government experience, as chair.[33] Within a few months, the panel had formalized its recommendations and advised Sargent to halt highway construction and to commission a public restudy of the state's transportation plan for

Greater Boston. Not only did these recommendations inform the content of Sargent's 1970 televised speech, but they also chipped away at his pro-highway stance by convincing him that bold new thinking was needed to address the state's many transportation problems. This was a considerable accomplishment. With nearly $1 billion in federal highway funding on the line and a vocal construction lobby demanding road-building projects to redress the industry's 14 percent unemployment rate, Sargent was forced to weigh his options with care and speed.[34]

When Sargent announced the BTPR's formation, Altshuler knew exactly who should serve as its deputy director—a former federal antipoverty program administrator named Jack Wofford.[35] Wofford was then a lecturer at Harvard Law School and had been directing a study of legal issues in urban transportation; he had also served as the executive director of the special task force that advised Sargent during the previous year.[36] Many political insiders viewed Wofford as a careful and skilled negotiator. While this was true, it was also true that Wofford distinguished himself by an abiding professional commitment to participatory democratic politics. Trained as a lawyer, Wofford had clerked for a federal district judge and then spent two years in Washington as assistant to the director of operations of the newly formed federal Community Action Program (CAP). Under the banner of Johnson's War on Poverty and housed within the newly created Office of Economic Opportunity, CAP was an important new vehicle for creating innovative antipoverty programs at the local level and carried a legal mandate that its projects be developed with "maximum feasible participation of the poor." This charge seeded new models of community-based organizations in low-income areas, and Wofford had developed the initial draft of federal grant guidelines to fund their creation. Wofford's professional experience in Washington as a shaper of federal antipoverty policy would prove critical to highway battles in Massachusetts.

At the first meeting of the Governor's Task Force on Transportation, which preceded the BTPR's work, Wofford recalls panel members wondering aloud whether they should invite the state's highway planners to meet with them at their next meeting:

> I think they said, "Well let's start by having the agencies come in and describe the plans" . . . I actually jumped in and said, "You know with all this opposition the governor faced right after his inauguration, maybe

we should invite the opponents in." I mean I'm coming out of the poverty program where we were stirring things up, right? The Community
Action Program was designed to stir up the old-line social service agencies, and it required that there be a threefold organization to organize
antipoverty efforts at the local level: the municipalities, the traditional
social service agencies, and new neighborhood groups. This was the
poverty program's way to make sure that the mandate for "maximum
feasible participation" would be taken seriously.[37]

Wofford's approach to planning invited constituent contention as a
means of identifying what was at stake for multiple interest groups. He
learned this technique in Washington and brought its lessons to Boston.
The Community Action Program was envisioned as offering more direct
impact for federal resources targeting low-income communities.[38] As
Wofford observes, this approach to program reform and its attendant
redefinition of local "authority" marked a major shift in the federal government's approach to poverty alleviation. Wofford successfully transmitted
his commitment to "maximum feasible participation" to Greater Boston's
transportation planning process. His previous work with federal antipoverty programs served, in his words, as "precursors to what we did."[39]

Alan Altshuler brought similar insights to his role as chair of the
Governor's Task Force and BTPR's executive director. In 1965, he had written a critique of the city planning process from a political perspective,
describing the prevalence of interagency and "political obstacles to general
planning at all levels of American government."[40] Wofford views his own
background working with federal antipoverty programs and the implemen-
tation of "maximum feasible participation" as a compliment to Altshuler's
academic focus on interagency challenges within urban planning. Both
Wofford and Altshuler were concerned with moving beyond seemingly
intractable urban problems and institutions to produce new strategies for
supporting the development of vibrant and healthy cities. Reflecting on his
professional partnership with Altshuler, Wofford notes: "I brought a commitment to listening and taking seriously the concerns of people beyond
the highway department, and Alan brought a very structured approach to
creating an advisory process, with emphasis on advisory."[41] For Wofford
and Altshuler, elected officials, such as Governor Sargent—not BTPR's
members—were the true decision makers carrying full accountability to
the public. The BTPR's values, process, and scope were crafted to opera-

tionalize this distinction, which it rigorously maintained throughout its two years of biweekly meetings.

When I ask Wofford about his role in helping to transfer politically progressive process ideals, he deflects: "These were, you could say, thoughts that were in the air at the time . . . The call for citizen participation wasn't brand new. The new approach that Alan and I brought was applying it to transportation, which had usually been the province of the highway department and their planners."[42] Yet, it is exactly the introduction of notions of citizen participation and devolved governance that were still unique within regional politics—and Wofford's and Altshuler's leadership was key. More than just "something in the air," the specific actions of such actors as Wofford and Altshuler helped advance new models for social change. Popular discontent with top-down models of local development and planning meant that bureaucracy-driven government rollouts like the federal urban renewal program were no longer to be trusted or tolerated. Instead of political appointees or elected officials, local residents would determine and lead their own development plans. This was maximum feasible participation at its fullest expression. This was brand new.

Reflecting on his early days navigating the state's highway controversies, Wofford admits that he did not know enough about the highway plan to have a political position one way or the other. His appointment as executive director of Sargent's private task force served as a primer on the region's transportation issues. Wofford's policy experience in Washington taught him to confront contentious public issues head on by allowing those directly affected to help set the terms of debate. After the task force decided to solicit testimony from highway supporters and opponents, Wofford found himself absorbed by the complexity of issues presented and advocates' use of various persuasion tactics. He recalls the antihighway organizers' first appearance before the Governor's Task Force:

> So the opponents came into that first meeting and they said, "Look at the impact, look at these (land) takings, look at the neighborhood disruption, look at the impact on the environment." And they had the tally of the takings of all these factors broken down by this highway and that highway. They were really prepared even with handmade signs. They said, "Given these impacts, you should study alternative locations for these highways, including the Inner Belt. Why don't we put an Inner Belt as more of a boulevard out in the Brattle Street area? The state shouldn't

do it in the lower income areas of the inner city but it could do it out
there in the Brattle Street area." They even had a rudimentary sketch of a
boulevard. That's a very effective antihighway technique. You get people
to see a specific alternative. And then you say you better compare them,
and all of a sudden you've got two groups really angry and then they
get together and you have a very focused conflict. I was observing this
strategy, and I'm thinking they're pretty savvy.[43]

By proposing an alternate highway route through Brattle Street, a well-
known and wealthy section of Cambridge, antihighway leaders effectively
baited Wofford and members of the task force. The tactic of using the specificity of map drawing to activate an audience was used here not to goad local
residents to action (as Urban Planning Aid had achieved to great effect)
but rather to challenge the perceived assumptions of a panel of governor
appointees. The proposal of a four-lane highway coursing through Brattle
Street did not threaten the personal residences of Wofford or the panel's
members, but it did challenge their tacit understanding of which neighborhoods were off-limits for road building. Thus this strategy exposed an
unarticulated set of spatial and socioeconomic biases being used to justify
the highway's proposed route.

During their presentation to the Governor's Task Force, highway opponents questioned the data, logic, and placement of highways proposed by
the state's planners. This impressed Wofford. The task force had now been
prompted to address the issue of local impact and whether the proposed
plan would provide a balanced transportation solution that minimized
social and environmental impacts. The task force next invited the state's
highway planners to present their views. When a task force member asked
a high-ranking engineer in the Department of Public Works how the state's
plan linking three radial expressways to an Inner Belt would ease local traffic congestion, the engineer replied, "Maybe another Inner Belt, 'an inner
Inner Belt,'" would best resolve the issue. This thinking—more highways
as the answer to the problems of highways—was typically unquestioned
within state highway departments. Wofford recalls a panelist whispering to
him: "My God! It is worse than anybody could have expected!"[44]

As journalist Alan Lupo reported, the Governor's Task Force lambasted
local highway planning as a "pathological planning and decision process."
Task force members directed much of their critique to the state's highway

planning agency, the Department of Public Works. They write, "We find on the one hand extreme citizen distrust of the DPW, on the other extreme DPW rigidity, defensiveness, and insensitivity to broad political and planning values."[45] Following its meetings in the fall of 1969, the Governor's Task Force unanimously concluded that more information was needed by the state before it should continue further road construction. The task force recommended that Sargent impose a moratorium on further highway planning and initiate a broad study of highway and transit in the Greater Boston region. Sargent executed this recommendation and called for a comprehensive transportation policy review. A new and decisive course of action was now emerging.

With Altshuler and Wofford at its helm, the Boston Transportation Planning Review emerged in 1970 as a critical intervention to the state's broken planning process. The BTPR's decision-making process, structure, and diverse membership merged groundbreaking principles of participatory planning with new approaches for addressing America's late twentieth-century urban transportation needs. An informal group of pro- and anti-highway advocates helped develop BTPR's scope and laid the basis for a formal Steering Committee to manage oversight responsibilities. During this early stage of BTPR's participatory planning process, stakeholders advanced a requirement that 10 percent of the restudy budget be allocated to technical assistance and ground-level communication and coordination. This innovative planning approach meant that there "was a staff available to those who would not normally have access to the technical information and thinking of a process of this kind."[46] It also meant that fledgling ideas could be developed into feasible alternatives by professional staff working with advocates. Referred to as "Study Element 2—Community Liaison and Technical Assistance," this critical BTPR feature was designed to "provide substantive technical assistance to those participants who lack sufficient resources to play an effective part in the study and to initiate and maintain communication and interaction mechanisms between the study team and participants for the continuance of the participatory planning process."[47]

In the summer of 1971, with its scope established and its staff and consultant team in place, the BTPR kicked off its technical work to provide "public officials, private groups and individual citizens with a reasoned analysis of the advantages and disadvantages of major highway and transit proposals."[48] Steering Committee members were drawn from Massachusetts state agencies, including the regional public transportation authority (MBTA), the Department of Public Works, the Turnpike Authority, and the regional planning council. In addition to having political representation from Boston, the committee also included representatives from the many municipalities (north, south, and west of Boston) affected by the state's highway routes—Arlington, Cambridge, Lexington, Medford, Newton, Somerville, and Brookline to the west; Dedham, Milton, and Canton to the southwest; and Beverly, Lynn, Peabody, Revere, Salem, and Saugus to the north. The Federal Highway Administration also sent a representative.

Nearly a dozen private groups (both for and against highway building) were also counted as members of the Steering Committee. These groups ranged from prohighway advocates, such as the Massachusetts Association of Transportation Constructors and the Greater Boston Chamber of Commerce, to antihighway advocates, including the Greater Boston Committee on the Transportation Crisis (GBC), the League of Women Voters, the Sierra Club, and Operation STOP of the Boston Black United Front (BUF). Altogether, the BTPR Steering Committee comprised nearly thirty separate groups and agencies. The committee set the agenda for how the full group would address four main issues: the feasibility of highway and transit building; where highways and transit might be placed, if built; possible alternatives that incorporated mass transit; and the detailed economic, environmental, and social impacts of the alternatives. Toward the end of the restudy, the BTPR reported its findings as draft environmental impact statements.

Though Governor Sargent gets credit for commissioning a new kind of transportation planning study, Altshuler's direction setting and Wofford's impartial leadership of the BTPR enabled it to fulfill a higher purpose—remaking the process and goal of transportation planning for the commonwealth and providing national leadership for municipalities attempting to do the same. As a formal structure, BTPR gave the concerns and desires of residents a legitimized political platform. Instead of an overstuffed panel of engineers and highway planners, its Steering Committee's tripartite structure—similar to the federal antipoverty program—mobilized state agencies, municipalities, and private groups to imagine transit beyond highways alone. And, critically, instead of endless debate fodder, BTPR developed competing ideas into alternative plans, all tested for feasibility. A stable of seventy-five paid consultants and technicians ensured that multiple plans were researched and rendered to professional standards. This detail is significant.

While consultants produced professional-grade plans for a wide range stakeholders, BTPR maintained an overall commitment to a decidedly low-tech approach that "downplayed the use of sophisticated quantitative techniques."[49] During the postwar period, complex mathematical modeling prevailed as the industry standard for transportation planning.[50] The decision of BTPR's leadership to buck this orthodoxy while providing professional tools and expertise to grassroots advocates facilitated a highly participatory process accessible to professional planning specialists and nonspecialists alike.[51] For neighborhood activist groups with little to no technical expertise, this was a particular boon. They were often spared excessive professional jargon and models, and their own ideas were developed to the same level of detail as earlier state-generated plans. Through this dynamic yet structured process of knowledge transfer and grassroots capacity building, a citizen opposition movement that began in living rooms and on city streets gained political traction. Further, BTPR's method of studying the region's transportation needs in corridor-based segments remedied the tyranny of abstraction that dominated most state-led metropolitan planning processes of the period. Similar to the Greater Boston Committee on the Transportation Crisis's tactic of showing local groups how proposed highways connected them as a regional interest group, the BTPR elevated public understanding of municipal boundary–crossing issues and how to address them at the local and metropolitan level. Within this emerging geopolitical structure, as noted by urban transportation planner and scholar Ralph Gakenheimer, Sargent acted as a kind of regional mayor, providing direction and leadership for an expansive assortment of Greater Boston municipalities.[52]

Throughout the BTPR's deliberations, the GBC prevailed as the undisputed leader of antihighway interests and maintained the dominant voice of highway opposition. In his incisive study of the BTPR and its outcomes, *Transportation Planning as a Response to Controversy*, Gakenheimer highlights this point: "The GBC emerged into the BTPR process with a reputation as the organization that, more than any other, impelled the creation of the Review and influenced the rules by which the BTPR would be conducted. It had a background in the prior technical studies of the projects involved, and important friends in the governor's and mayor's offices. Most of all, while these were no longer the activist late sixties, the GBC had a background of activism that was a menacing reminder for participants with other orientations.[53] The GBC's ongoing relationships with Urban Planning Aid and local organizations across the region had equipped it with an authoritative command of the issues as well as a bevy of relevant technical details. And, as Gakenheimer notes, the GBC's activist reputation alerted others that street-level organizing was a key part of its policymaking toolkit. Chuck Turner served as GBC's primary leader on the BTPR and kept "a diplomatic but firm hand on the consistency of argument with basic ideology and was also a frequent participant in the process."[54] Though the GBC stood firm in its antihighway position, the BTPR's analysis and persuasion of Governor Sargent would gradually shift the GBC toward a pro-transit position. But for many months only one question loomed: How can an interstate highway be stopped?

How the Highway Was Stopped: "Maximum Feasible Participation" Meets "No Feasible and Prudent Alternatives"

The historic convergence of President Nixon's 1969 National Environmental Policy Act and Governor Sargent's call for a transportation review created a unique moment of reckoning for antihighway protesters' greatest hopes. This coincidental timing would also mean that Massachusetts would submit the first environmental impact study in the United States. Wofford describes the concurrence this way: "[NEPA] required nationwide for any major federal action exactly the kind of study that we were proposing in Boston. So we became a fishbowl nationwide . . . We [produced] the first environmental impact statement in the country, and people came from all over to watch what we were doing."[55] The state's 1948 transportation plan included an extension of Interstate 95 slated to pass through an area southwest of Boston known as the Fowl Meadow, a wooded parkland to the north known as the Lynn Woods, and a marshy greenway near Boston's Museum of Fine Arts. Planning conventions of the 1940s did not recognize these natural areas as off-limits for highway expansion.

Though the legislation that created the federal Department of Transportation (DOT) in 1966 carried a stipulation that no transportation project could pass through a public park or historic site unless there were no feasible and prudent alternatives, state highway planners had been routinely allowed to determine what was or was not feasible or prudent. Referred to as "Section 4(f)," this policy carried DOT's explicit objective "to preserve the natural beauty of the countryside and public park and recreation lands, wildlife and waterfowl refuges and historic sites."[56] This attempt to protect federally significant landscapes meant that highway plans submitted after 1966 were subjected to a new level of scrutiny.[57] Yet, Section 4(f)'s stipulation of "no feasible and prudent alternative" created a lack of clarity as to who and what determined feasibility and prudence. Though this clause was meant to force additional planning and analysis among state transportation planners to justify why a proposed travel route necessitated seizure of public parkland or historic buildings, it often produced superficial assessments framed by dubious analysis.[58] As a result, state highway planners often concluded, not surprisingly, that there were no feasible alternatives to their proposed routes. Many of these procedural and interpretive issues within federal highway planning spawned controversy and mistrust within urban neighborhoods across the country.

For prohighway advocates in Massachusetts, section 4(f) signaled particular trouble. Wofford describes the Fowl Meadow and the northern Lynn Woods as constituting "two huge anchors of a problem with these highways legally." When it became clear that the Fowl Meadow represented an illegal right-of-way for a federal transportation project based on Section 4(f), BTPR staff began developing alternative alignments, including one through the suburban town of Dedham. Wofford recounts the search this way:

> We had to consider impact on the Fowl Meadow, a major public park . . . So we started to look at highway alternatives in this area. We said, "Well, we need to look at a highway that doesn't go through the park." And it so happens that this requires us to develop an alternative through homes in Dedham. So we said, "We need to put these alternatives out to the public, they need to see them." So Dedham suddenly reads in the local press that we were looking at new alignments for the Southwest Expressway, which residents had assumed would go over there in the Fowl Meadow. They're now thinking: "It's going to go through our kitchens? What are these people thinking about?" So we did neighborhood workshops, and then we did big public meetings. We said we need to take these alternatives out to Dedham High School. So there I was with 1,300 or so people in the Dedham High School auditorium—screaming and yelling: "And if you think you're going through our kitchens, you're crazy."[59]

Wofford's memory of Dedham residents reacting to news of a highway going "through our kitchens" illustrates the vortex of competing interests entangling suburbanites, urban dwellers, and the natural environment. Wofford's effort to lead exactly the kind of public planning process NEPA and the federal Transportation Act required had, ironically, made him a target of resident derision. Suburbanites unwilling to assume the physical burden of a road being built primarily for their benefit cast Wofford and the state as unwelcome intruders.

The BTPR had determined that any alternatives to the state's original transportation plan, including alignment changes, would need to be presented to citizens via public meetings and workshops. These public discussions, no matter how contentious, were imagined as feedback loops for the review committee's ongoing planning process. In the end, the residents of Dedham and their nearby neighbors in Canton joined together to reject the suggested highway alignment. With the resistance of these suburban communities and the pressure of environmental groups wary of state promises to mitigate the impact of highway salt runoff into the Fowl Meadow, viable route options for the Southwest Expressway were disappearing. Without a legal place to go and with strong public opposition to proposed alternatives, the fate of the southwesterly extension of I-95 was all but doomed.[60] The review committee recommended that the governor cancel this road, which he soon would.[61]

After formal regional public hearings following the publication of the BTPR Corridor reports and meeting privately with each of the main stakeholder groups, Sargent consulted his advisers to determine his decision. The debate was principally between Donald Dwight, his lieutenant governor, who favored the highways, and Al Kramer, his chief policy adviser, who opposed them. Sargent sided with Kramer. In November 1972, Sargent killed the Southwest Expressway and proposed the relocation of a major transit line from its existence on an elevated structure on Washington Street into a tunnel in the Amtrak corridor where the expressway would have been. He also supported the development of what was to become a prize-winning new public park, the Southwest Corridor Park, above the rail and transit tunnel.

While Sargent's earlier 1971 decision to cancel the Inner Belt effectively ended the Cambridge side of the antihighway fight, the Boston fight surged ahead. The release of the BTPR's final transportation report in

1972 delivered a decisive one-two punch of analysis that definitively ended Boston's highway battles.

Sargent Decides—Breaking "Loose from a System That Doesn't Work"

When Governor Sargent reappeared on television on November 30, 1972, he was ready to discuss what he had learned from the restudy process. In yet another dramatic evening broadcast, Sargent shared decisions directly affecting citizens of Massachusetts.

> I present to you tonight decisions touching the lives of all of us. I will ask that you share the risks. I'll show you the opportunities. The problems of transportation have held us prisoner for 40 years and recently that captivity has become intolerable. You, your family, your neighbors have become caught in a system that's fouled our air, ravaged our cities, choked our economy and frustrated every single one of us. To move ourselves, our goods and our services, we've built more and more and bigger and better super highways and expressways. They seemed the easiest, most obvious answer to our multiplying needs. What we misunderstood was what those highways would create: massive traffic congestion . . . The side effect, billions of dollars spent and more and more cities torn apart. More and more families uprooted and displaced. Worst of all *failure* to solve the problem that started it all: how best to get from one place to another. Massachusetts, indeed America confronts the same old problem now complicated by a growing paralysis on our superhighways. The old system has imprisoned us. We've become the slaves and not the master of the method we chose to meet our needs. How do we break loose from a system that doesn't work?[62]

By detailing traffic congestion, population dislocation, and environmental pollution as evidence of an inadequate system holding the state "prisoner," Sargent frames his address as an opportunity for immediate and rectifying action. The craft and grace of Sargent's language here knits together a broad set of contentious and jargon-filled political debates not easily summarized or interpreted for a nontechnical audience. Not only does he effectively translate complex ideas for a mass audience, but he is also persuasive in communicating that a collective "we" must work on "our" problems together. His choice of pronoun also marks a political shift toward a more localized and shared approach to the state's transportation decision making.

And Sargent's rhetorical technique of reminding the electorate of what he said he would do and that he did it and what should follow reflects a conception of political leadership wedded to public accountability. "In February 1970 I spoke to you on television to declare that it was becoming clear superhighways and some of our old transit plans were not doing the job." When making the case for what to do next, he first reframes for viewers what is at stake. He asks: "Shall we build more expressways through cities? Shall we forge new chains to shackle us to the mistakes of the past? No, we will not repeat history, we shall learn from it. We will not build expressways." Following this policy overview, Sargent details his solution: "Instead of a Southwest Expressway, forever ruining the cherished Fowl Meadow area and further ravaging an already devastated section of the city, we shall build a transit and commuter rail system that will move people faster than rubber tire vehicles can move them." Here Sargent articulates a dramatic shift in values defining the region's transportation planning agenda. He rejects plans that would destroy significant natural resources as well as human communities threatened by highway expansion. Further explaining the social threat of road building through Greater Boston's core, he warns: "It would have also involved the further dislocation of about 370 families and 800 jobs. Finally, it would have involved the overruling the clear preference of most of the elected officials and private citizens in the Southwest Corridor who have made their views known."[63] The BTPR's multistakeholder process and analysis delivered not only a new transportation plan for the region but a new, progressive set of values for guiding regional growth and development. Sargent was its proud and vocal champion.

Before the transportation review was created, no one knew whether or not the southwest extension of I-95 or the Inner Belt could be stopped. No one knew that the commonwealth would create a new public transportation line or a 52-acre park. After the BTPR's transportation planning process was completed, these were nearly forgone conclusions. But before any final decision, BTPR participants and the entire commonwealth waited for an official answer. Transportation planner and scholar Ralph Gakenheimer writes: "While the announcement surely did not come as very surprising to knowledgeable observers, in the sense that they might not have thought it possible, certainly no one was counting on it until it was made. While anti highway representatives of interest groups and governments expected a somewhat favorable decision, they were by no means confident of getting this one."[64] Sargent's announcement permanently changed the course of history for Boston's regional transportation planning, advanced a citizen-centered development agenda, and developed a new broad policy that Boston's interior core should be served primarily by public transportation, not additional highways. Although highway opponents agreed that smashing roads through Boston's dense urban centers and suburban bedroom communities was not the optimal solution to the region's transportation problems, there was less agreement on what should take the place of highways and what a new public transportation system might look like.[65]

To further complicate this discussion, the means for funding anything but highways remained undetermined. The federal government's ample 90 percent reimbursement rate for states applied only to highway spending. Neither the state nor the federal government had appropriated significant resources for mass transit. Governor Sargent's public promise to appeal to Congress for mass transit funding meant that he was not willing to let the federal government off the hook for nonhighway transportation expenditures. Wofford recounts Sargent's position: "I mean these are big banner headlines—'I'm going to Washington to persuade Congress to change federal law,' he said on TV. 'So that we can use this highway money for (mass transit).'"[66] With careful planning and lobbying, Sargent and his team achieved exactly that.

Altshuler led the fight to support what initially was called "the Boston provision." This provision soon gained the support of several metropolitan areas around the country. But, in his televised address, Sargent stressed to everyone that he could not do it alone. He would need the financial help of the federal government as well as the political support of the commonwealth: "What I propose tonight cannot be done without the help of Washington and I must go to the Congress and the bureaus and the agencies of the federal government to ask for that help. But most of all naturally what I propose cannot be done without your help. You must join with me in this massive endeavor, you've done so before in other major undertakings and we've won the gambles that we've undertaken. We can do so again." Shortly after his November broadcast, Sargent rallied fellow state governors and traveled to Washington to make his appeal for funding from the Highway Trust Fund: "A vigorous national effort [must be made] to free up the Federal Highway Trust Fund so that states all over the country can have greater flexibility to use such revenues for the mix of highway and transit investments that they think best."[67] Through lobbying and numerous congressional appeals, Massachusetts's political leaders forced an additional provision within federal highway law. Referred to as the "Interstate Transfer Provision" and later named the Interstate Withdrawal-Substitution Program, this provision made it possible for Massachusetts and other states to secure federal aid for public transportation projects proposed in lieu of highways. The provision is Section 137(b) of the Federal-Aid Highway Act of 1973: "Upon the joint request of the State Governor and local governments concerned, the Secretary could withdraw his/her approval of unbuilt Interstate routes or portions thereof within an urbanized area, if he/she determined that the withdrawn segment was not essential to completion of a unified and connected system. Transit projects in or serving the same urbanized area could be substituted for the withdrawn segment with funding from the General Fund in an amount equal to the Federal share of the withdrawn Interstate facility."[68] This legislation meant that public transportation projects, with the request of their governors, could replace highway projects with mass transit and receive a comparable level of federal funding, landmark legislation for Massachusetts and the rest of the country. Although federally approved public transportation projects would be funded from the Treasury's General Fund and not the Highway Trust Fund per se, the fact remained that significant resources for mass transit were now nationally available.

Though the state's transportation restudy led to the reform of outdated planning processes and the creation of a national model for involving citizens in transportation planning, many people in Massachusetts do not remember it. Jack Wofford knows this well. "I talk to people about the BTPR—they go, 'What?' And we had this steering committee. 'You had a what?' It's like yeah and it really worked! It wasn't separate from the politics 'cause it was tied into the politics which really worked."[69] While many Massachusetts residents may be unaware of the transportation review's seminal work to reform the state's planning process, the federal Department of Transportation has hailed the BTPR for its important contributions to the history of urban transportation in America. In "Urban Transportation Planning in the U.S.—A Historical Overview," the department's official history, Edward Weiner writes: "The BTPR occurred at the height of the citizen participation movement in a highly charged atmosphere outside the mainstream of decision-making in Boston. Although it is unlikely that such a study will be repeated elsewhere in the same manner, the BTPR has left a permanent impact on urban transportation. The legacy of the BTPR has been to demonstrate a more open form of planning and decision-making that has greater concern for social and environmental impacts and the opinions of those affected by transportation improvements."[70] In Massachusetts these new federal funds were used to extend the geographic coverage of existing public transit services and to create a new rapid transit line through the heart of Greater Boston. Massachusetts was the first state approved for use of federal substitution funds, but it was not the last. Nearly two dozen urbanized areas representing every region of the country took advantage of this change in federal law. Many metropolitan regions, such as Boston, San Francisco, New York, and Washington, D.C., that had been embroiled in citizen-led highway controversies in the 1960s and 1970s now had direct access to federal funding for mass transit alternatives.[71] A partial listing of highway-replacing transit projects shows that highway segments were canceled and substituted by mass transit in the following cities: Tucson, Arizona (I-710); San Francisco, California (I-280); Waterloo, Iowa (I-380); Duluth, Minnesota (I-35); Chicago, Illinois (I-494); Washington, D.C. (six routes replaced); New York City (I-495 and I-478); Pittsburgh, Pennsylvania (I-579); Memphis, Tennessee (I-40); and Atlanta, Georgia (I-420). By 1989, the Department of Transportation had allocated $6.7 billion for substitute transit funds for petitioning states such as these listed.[72] The cancellation of these interstate highway segments resulted in the removal of 343 miles of federal roads.

≡ ≡ ≡

This chapter has charted how citizen protest and resistance effectively pressured state and federal highway leaders to reconsider their espousal of undemocratic transportation policies. An unremedied crisis in the field of planning fueled a dysfunctional set of new debates and, worse, new master plans targeting the future development of U.S. cities. Politicians, planners, and social scientists agreed that something was wrong, but no one seemed able to identify exactly what. Citizen opposition in Boston to interstate highway expansion led the Massachusetts governor to reverse his stated position on road building, convene an innovative transportation restudy, and expand mass transit opportunities for the nation. On the ground, citizen-led activism in Boston and beyond convulsed in the mid-1960s to demand new policy and processes for developing cities. Top-down planning dished out by federal and state officials had proven inadequate and even damaging to the formation of vibrant urban neighborhoods. Furthermore, residents demanded change within their neighborhoods and within federal law. In the end, a shifting set of values articulated by grassroots protesters and 1960s-era liberation movements helped devolve decision-making power to local communities and funneled federal resources toward mass transit projects.

In Massachusetts, the Boston Transportation Planning Review and the leadership of Governor Francis Sargent were instrumental in creating a formal mechanism for pro- and antihighway factions to voice their concerns, discuss alternatives, and produce a set of recommendations that would stop I-95's passage through Greater Boston's dense urban core. As many of the antihighway movement's lead actors themselves have observed, Governor Sargent and the transportation restudy helped citizens begin to repair their trust in political authority while emboldening their own leadership and vision for the commonwealth. In this way, the victories of Massachusetts citizens in overhauling the state's transportation planning process and ushering in a wave of public transit construction projects memorialize both the defeat of unlimited interstate highway growth and a collective unwillingness to forget the state and federal abuses of the past.

Chapter 5

New Territory

City Making, Searching for Control

On the rainy evening of February 10, 1970, just hours before his historic announcement suspending state highway construction the next day, Governor Francis Sargent walked along the Southwest Corridor. Sargent wanted to view what everyone had been discussing. Though he had been learning about this landscape for weeks through briefings and private meetings, he now wanted to see the local effects of clearance and economic disinvestment firsthand. Shielded by a beige trench coat and opting not to make official comments, Sargent walked quietly among a throng of aides and newspaper reporters.[1] His personal tour of the Southwest Corridor would help lay the basis for state policy and insert an important addendum to his road-building agenda: "But before we go further, let us know certainly where we are going, how we are going. One important footnote. While we consider a new plan for the use of the Southwest Corridor, Boston faces a major housing shortage. Today, there are 475 livable housing units standing in the Corridor. I have ordered a halt to their demolition."[2] Here Sargent advocated not for a revised plan to determine how commuters can get from here to there but for a "new plan" to consider how Corridor land could be used to address specific issues for nearby residents. His call for a cessation of highway construction within Greater Boston (inside Route 128) ordered transportation planners to stop demolition along the Southwest Corridor and to recognize additional development needs, such as housing. In this way, Sargent prompted residents to think about their future in terms broader than transportation.

Over the course of nearly a decade, powerful resident organizing coupled with the detailed analysis of the Boston Transportation Planning Review (BTPR) had yielded a unified public position stressing the importance of implementing a resident-defined plan for redeveloping the Southwest Corridor's cleared land. Activists from Urban Planning Aid, the Greater Boston Committee on the Transportation Crisis, and the Black United Front had helped shape public opinion on the Corridor, and the governor took note. Reflecting more than three years of public information gathering, the restudy's 1973 final report concluded:

> The Southwest Corridor has the greatest overall need for investment in improved transit service. Transit investments are urgently needed in this Corridor, both to provide improved mobility for the residents of the Southwest area and to spur the renewal of the land which has been cleared for the Southwest Expressway. The early provision of transit service in this cleared land area has been identified as a key component of the program for revitalizing this area . . . The decision not to build an expressway in the Southwest Corridor necessarily brings with it the need to implement a program for the sound and sensitive redevelopment of the cleared land in the Corridor and for the equitable treatment of those who have been affected by the demolition in the Corridor.[3]

The scene was now set. A series of investments in mass transit would form the centerpiece of a revitalization plan to improve "mobility for the residents of the Southwest area and to spur renewal of the land."

With analysis from the BTPR and consensus between Governor Sargent and antihighway activists, the development of the Southwest Corridor emerged as a primary goal following the highway's cancellation. The state's new transportation plan emphasized public transportation over highways and aimed to address the economic needs of urban residents over the travel desires of suburban commuters. Such a dramatic planning turnaround was a political victory for Boston's antihighway activists for sure; however, how to maintain resident engagement in a battle that was not quite over defined the antihighway movement's next organizing challenge. The landscape's unique mix of problems and possibilities would inspire an innovative set of grassroots solutions over the next decade.

Following his decision to cancel the Southwest Corridor Expressway, Sargent called for a new future for a landscape that had known many failed plans. From railroads to factories to public housing developments, the Southwest Corridor had hosted a historic array of place making and remaking efforts. Each of these visions represented not only new uses for the Corridor's land but also the familiar start-and-stop pattern of capitalist economic investment. Changing land use goals among an oscillating set of public and private owners had produced grave consequences for residents living on the Corridor during its many land use transformations. The failed plans of zealous industrialists, public housing reformers, and highway boosters ultimately helped birth a grassroots political agenda based on self-governance and local control. But more than a reactionary, insular politics, this resident-led synthesis of progressive ideas would lead to new cutting-edge models of participatory democratic practice. In the end, an urban planning movement seeking to repair a mangled landscape and the damaged political trust of its residents would reset the Corridor's late twentieth-century development path.

During Boston's antihighway fight, the landscape of the Southwest Corridor sat at the center of statewide debate. What would happen to this land if the highways were successfully halted? was the seminal question fueling a fresh round of public debate and ground-level strategizing. Yet, the Southwest Corridor's longer historical timeline reveals that road-building bureaucrats and antihighway protesters were only the most recent set of actors aiming to inscribe their hopes and dreams within this landscape. A three-century-long contest to claim new uses for the Corridor has littered its terrain with physical markers of past projects promising a new future for anyone in need of one. Innovative ideas for city making have been spawned here from its earliest days as a semi-rural hinterland outside of Boston.

Southwest Corridor Beginnings

The Southwest Corridor's location at the center of the Stony Brook Valley and proximity to the Dedham-Hartford Turnpike imbued its landscape with early industrial and travel importance. Completed in 1807, the Dedham-Hartford Turnpike was built to strengthen Boston's trade connections with Rhode Island and Connecticut. However, the road's uneven surface coupled with toll pricing disputes among connecting states led to its eventual abandonment. New roads and then railroads were laid to bolster the global and domestic circulation of Massachusetts-produced leathers, cotton textiles, beer, and shoes. Each of these transportation innovations would prove critical for establishing the Southwest Corridor as a vital transit route for the region's economic productivity.[4]

The maturing demands of New England's industrialized economy propelled a diversity of transportation technologies along the Corridor. These changes also shifted the landscape's residential character. In the eighteenth century, English colonialists viewed land on both sides of the Stony Brook Valley as suitable locations for their private estates. By the nineteenth century, the advent of horse-drawn commuter carriages coupled with Boston's commercial growth transformed the Corridor from a distant, pastoral retreat to a bustling suburban satellite for well-to-do merchant families. Yet the Corridor was able to maintain its reputation as an idyllic escape from the city—that is, until the railroad arrived. The advent of the Boston and Providence Railroad in 1834 brought an urbanizing crush of new factories and workers to the Corridor's center, eastern, and western boundaries.[5] Whereas the Dedham-Hartford Turnpike had proved a financial and travel disappointment, railroad development spurred an economic boom and delivered unrivaled comfort, speed, and service reliability to cash-flush passengers.

From nineteenth-century attempts to build an interstate road to early passenger rail service, to globally-scaled industrial manufacturing plants, to mid-twentieth-century construction of public housing, to postindustrial land rehabilitation strategies, the Southwest Corridor has been home to a wide array of avant-garde urban development projects. However, not all the Corridor's projects were success stories. Many failed to deliver what they originally promised. Fires, abandonment, and dramatic population shifts reveal a complex history of a landscape under continuous economic pressure. In 1972, many Corridor residents worried that the next wave of development following the interstate highway's cancellation would also be a failure.

Translating highway opposition into the creation of a new blueprint for the city's development was neither an easy nor an obvious next step for antihighway activists. However, the idea that nearly two hundred acres of land in the heart of the city could be repurposed to meet the needs of nearby low-income residents provided the incentive to spur a new phase of organizing. Before the reality of a new mass transit line and a city park appointed with basketball and tennis courts, bike lanes, outdoor amphitheaters, and community gardens came to life, the Southwest Corridor sat idly as the focus of a resident-led planning battle. Governor Sargent's decision to cancel the Southwest Corridor Expressway redefined the Corridor as the front line for a new grassroots fight for land rehabilitation. Highway clearance along the Corridor beginning in 1966 had pushed the landscape into a development never-never land where no one was exactly sure what would happen next. Wrecking balls had replaced blocks of businesses and homes with a long stretch of empty, treeless land. Unlike the city's previous clearance project on the Corridor that had led to the development of modern public housing, the state's failed highway agenda resulted only in a dormant territory warranting public concern.

Factories, Housing, and Fear of the Future

In 2010 I visited two public housing developments on the Corridor in hopes of interviewing residents involved in the 1960s fight to stop the Southwest Corridor Expressway. Instead of hearing new perspectives on the Boston antihighway fight, I was told repeated stories of the wintry night in 1976 when the Thomas G. Plant Company's shoe factory burned down in Jamaica Plain. Residents of the Bromley Heath Housing Development described this terrifying event to me in vivid detail. Thomas G. Plant brought his eponymous factory to the Southwest Corridor in 1896 and began an ambitious global quest to dominate the women's shoe industry. Over the next three decades, the Plant factory would indeed rise to become a major U.S. producer of fashionable women's shoes and one of the largest industrial employers in the city of Boston.[6] While its success gave proof that the Southwest Corridor was a profitable location for big business in the early twentieth century, by the 1950s the factory had lost significant market share and closed its doors. Its hulking building sat dark and menacing until February 1, 1976, when it burned to the ground.

Bromley Heath resident Barbara Hall recalls, "I remember the fire, it was really bad. I lived at 10 Bickford Street and my grandmother lived in the seniors' building and they all had to go to the neighborhood house [Bromley Hall]. It seemed like the world was coming to an end." Resident Lorenzee Cole also remembers the night: "All the seniors had to be roused up in the night and moved to temporary quarters for safety. The fire was so hot it melted fixtures in the seniors' building and caused millions' worth of damage."[7]

When the Plant Company shoe factory first arrived on the Corridor in 1896, low-cost wooden buildings constituted the primary affordable housing option for the area's mix of German, Irish, and Italian working-class families. These dwellings were typically owned by private individuals, who rented apartments and rooms to the public. Affordable housing options did not keep pace with continued migration of Western European laborers to the Corridor. Though the early arrival of the Boston and Providence Railroad and the later arrival of the New York, New Haven and Hartford Railroad symbolized economic growth and prosperity for enterprising industrialists like Thomas Plant, the railroad's presence created abysmal living conditions for area residents.

Workers whose economic limitations required them to live within walking distance of their employers were left to choose among grim housing conditions just as the railroad spurred numerous suburban housing developments for middle-class and upwardly mobile white families.[8] Black workers experienced extreme housing discrimination and, in areas like the South End, were frequently relegated to buildings that flanked the railroad track at the edge of neighborhood streets. In this way a pattern of class and racial segmentation typified by the industrial economy was further amplified by technological changes in the landscape. This pattern was not unique to Boston. The outward migration of middle-class families and workers from older industrialized cities reflected a national trend that would later be referenced by highway proponents to justify the need for federal road-building projects. Yet, the need for new housing in the central city remained even as transportation improvements and white middle-class residents moved elsewhere.

When it was announced in 1940 that Boston's housing authority had secured a $2.7 million grant to construct a new public housing development in Jamaica Plain, local reactions were mixed. Shops and homes would be cleared across 110 land parcels to make room for two projects: Heath Street (1942) and Bromley Park (1954), two separate developments that would later come to be known simply as "Bromley Heath." A journalist capturing conversations in local stores and across fences revealed that while small business owners along Heath Street were not happy with news of the new housing and their displacement, many low-income residents, similarly facing displacement, supported the construction of new afford-able housing options.

Michael Quinn, a white resident living with his wife and seven children in a five-room wooden tenement, gave the development his full support. "It's a wonderful thing to get rid of these dirty old houses and build new ones for people to have a decent chance to live clean in." Despite the fact that Quinn's own house would likely be razed for the new development and that he might not be able to live there himself, he maintained his posi-tion. Referencing his own house, he mused: "You get nothing. Soft wood floors that hold the dirt, and windows that let in the cold. It's the thing to do to clear them out."[9] In this early instance of clearance on the Southwest Corridor, a large, white, mostly working-class community of Italian, German, and Irish families were displaced. Many of these families left the area and did not return.

In the years immediately following its completion, Bromley Park was highly sought after by working-class white families and later white veter-ans returning from World War II.[10] Heath Street's low- and mid-rise brick developments boasted sunny views, modern amenities, and comfortable living for families eager to leave aging tenement dwellings. But by the mid-1950s, the development's reputation slowly began to change, along with its demographic mix. A community that had been almost exclusively Irish, German, and Italian was now gaining African American and Latino resi-dents. By the 1960s, anyone who could get a mortgage and head to the sub-urbs did.[11] White residents occupied 80 percent of Boston's public housing units; however, declining federal expenditures for public housing, coupled with a loss of local political muscle (tied to Boston's white ethnic polit-ical machine and its exiting constituencies), meant that public housing developments, like Bromley Park and Heath Street, lost both their inves-tors and champions. Without the financial resources and political backing that birthed it, Bromley Heath and its surrounding area became forbidding examples of urban neglect and disrepair. Gone were the bustling factory days when work was plentiful. Steady-paying jobs and modern housing were now located elsewhere. And a new group of migrants arrived to claim Bromley Heath as its own.

Housing the City: The Birth of Tenant Control at Bromley Heath

Mildred Hailey and her soon-to-be neighbor Anna Mae Cole were among Bromley Heath's first cohort of black families who arrived in the 1960s.[12] Hailey and Cole would come to share a lasting friendship and mutual disdain for the failing physical condition of their housing. They wondered together what might be done to improve the development's future. As Boston's urban renewal program further reorganized the city's overall residential geography, Bromley's demographic composition shifted from predominately white ethnic to more racially mixed. Anna Mae Cole had been renting an aging apartment along the Boston and Providence Railroad tracks in the South End and had imagined that the move to Bromley would mean a housing upgrade for her family. She was wrong. Local filmmaker Richard Broadman featured Cole, along with a small group of black, white, and Latino residents, in his 1978 documentary film *Mission Hill and the Miracle of Boston*. Broadman's film offers a compelling first-person account of urban change and revitalization in Boston during the 1960s and 1970s. A Mission Hill resident himself, Broadman produced and self-financed the film as a searing, resident-led critique of the city's urban renewal and pro-business development policies. In one scene, Cole recounts Bromley Heath's racial divisiveness: "The older side, which was the Heath Street side, was all white. I don't think it was any black families there, maybe one or two. So it was a certain reluctance to go there (Heath Street) because it was kind of like a territorial feeling. I don't know if anybody said that to me but when you looked around, you just didn't see too many people you could identify with so you just didn't venture into that area."[13] Cole's commentary describes the environment she encountered as a new tenant and her protective decision to avoid crossing racially segregated territories within Bromley Heath, namely, the "old side." When Bromley Heath's first units were built on Heath Street in 1942, the apartments were leased exclusively to white tenants. Local and federal pressure to make public housing accessible to all low-income residents of Boston led to the gradual integration of Bromley Park when it was constructed more than a decade later.[14]

Cole's relocation from the South End, where blight and urban renewal had significantly decreased affordable housing options, to Bromley Heath placed her well inside the crosshairs of Boston's turf-based affordable housing struggle. Federally financed public housing was not outside the racialized bounds of this issue. Cole's displacement, though technically voluntary, was indicative of the limited supply of housing for working families as well as the ways that racist housing assignment practices further complicated the few options that did exist.[15] Poor whites and blacks competed for whatever affordable housing they could find, but their fights were waged separately. Cole cites the failure of Bromley Heath's tenants to forge an interracial alliance as evidence of shortsighted racial politics.

> In the meantime, we were all living under the same kind of conditions. Poor blacks and poor whites—but white people never realized what was going on with them. They just felt, "You know I'm white, it's been a white society." So the difference between poor blacks—and it's no difference. There's no difference. If I'm hungry and my kids are not wearing shoes, it's no different than anybody else. If my husband can't get a job, it's no different than a white person. But they've never wanted to identify with us in that sense because we were black. And that's why I always said, I wouldn't care if it was rural or anybody else, I just assume to join a coalition of people fighting for the rights of all of us who are poor. And I wouldn't have to love rural or any white person but just let us get our equal share of the pie, which we're entitled to and that's what it's all about.[16]

Here Cole advocates a collective politics that transcends race to consider place, strained material conditions, and human rights. For her, these categories offer the potential to build a politically viable cross-racial coalition. Cole's conception of racial equality calls out a shared economic struggle of black and white citizens confronting poverty. Her rhetoric reflects her political belief that there is "no difference" in the experience of being in need. For Cole, the only difference lay in available options, and for poor people of any race, these options were limited at best.

As Bromley Heath's racial composition shifted, physical violence among residents made an already tense situation decidedly worse. Richie Jarrell and his mother left Bromley Heath as a direct response to racial violence. As white residents, Jarrell and his mother perceived the development's black and Latino residents as immediate threats to the neighborhood order. Jarrell confided to filmmaker Richard Broadman: "I used to fight colored kids. I used to fight white kids but it was over Mickey Mouse shit. It was only being kids. Then at one point it became a heavy-duty thing. [If] you stepped out over here and you stepped into a different turf, you could be hurt seriously. If the project is three-quarters white and a quarter black . . . through a change up of power, and the change up of people turning over and gaining control of a certain area, which is territory . . . you get into a violent thing because nobody gives anything up without violence."[17] For Jarrell, the transgressive act of stepping into what was considered "white" space justified physical violence. Though Bromley Heath was federally defined public space subject to the constitution's equal protection clauses, a resident-enforced social and spatial order coded by race dictated its daily life. Fearful white residents used bodily intimidation to keep nonwhite residents within the development's segregated boundary lines. However, these efforts ultimately backfired. White residents' use of force could not fully suppress the presence or movements of nonwhite residents, so they eventually stopped trying and decided to leave Bromley Heath all together.[18]

Ann Mae Cole summarizes Bromley's 1960s-era white exodus this way: "So a lot of whites said, 'Well I've had it. I'm getting out of here. I can't stand it anymore.' So they moved on to other projects or either other available apartments, which was also more accessible to whites than blacks. So if you wanted to move into a fairly decent neighborhood, they still had a choice where we didn't. So we had to stick it out, stay here. And eventually Heath Street side became all black and that's the way it is today."[19] The out-migration of Bromley's white residents issued a call to action for those who remained. Cole and Mildred Hailey began their neighborhood organizing at this moment.

As it became clear that neither Bromley Heath's long-term residents nor the city's housing authority officials were fully committed to addressing the development's many needs, Cole and Hailey inserted themselves into the leadership void. But the range of issues they confronted was daunting. At a congressional Housing Committee hearing years later, Hailey described the development's early conditions: "When the tenants first became involved, there were 4,000 broken windows, tons and tons of garbage and debris, leaky roofs, inoperative boiler plants, and volumes and volumes of work orders. Work orders that could have filled the local library. Crime was so bad the outside referred to Bromley Heath as the 'Concrete Jungle'—so bad—tenants couldn't get basic deliveries, such as milk."[20] Despite this sprawling list of material needs, Bromley Heath's problems were not just physical for Hailey and Cole. Hailey once summarized this position for a newspaper reporter: "We looked not just at housing conditions, but the need for some community control."[21] Hailey and Cole's desire to arrest the development's further social and physical deterioration led them to rally their neighbors to discuss Bromley Heath's most pressing issues. And what began casually as a small series of resident-led cleanup days and safety patrols would seed Bromley Heath's national rise as a leading example of successful public housing reform.

The Civil Rights Act of 1964 earmarked funds to pilot the idea of tenant-managed public housing developments. Though these funds were set to be administered by the newly created Office of Economic Opportunity (OEO), few national or local housing leaders envisioned who would qualify for this unprecedented project. Ellis Ash, the director of the Boston Housing Authority, bucked the trend. Ash imagined this new funding opportunity as a boon for residents living in Boston's largest public housing development, Columbia Point. However, when the residents of Columbia Point declined Ash's invitation, Bromley Heath's residents asked to be named the city's OEO designee. In 1968, Bromley Heath's residents applied for and won a federal demonstration grant of $168,000 to test the feasibility of tenant management in public housing.[22] This action represented the first application of resident management as a management model for U.S. public housing and would launch a forty-four-year experiment in tenant-led activism and public housing administration in the city of Boston.

Formally incorporated as an independent nonprofit in 1971, Bromley Heath's Tenant Management Corporation (TMC) later named Mildred Hailey as its executive director and Anna Mae Cole as chair of its board of directors. Under Hailey and Cole's leadership and with the financial support of the federal government, TMC emerged as an important political actor shaping Bromley's post-1960s development. When the Massachusetts highway plan was canceled in 1972, TMC flexed its newfound political authority to ensure that the Southwest Corridor's redesign reflected the needs and wishes of Bromley Heath's residents. Alongside Hailey and Cole, a third resident leader, David Worrell, would later become the organization's deputy director.

Though only a teenager when Hailey and Cole began their resident organizing, Worrell well remembers the development's deteriorating condition in the 1960s. "Bromley Heath, at one point, people considered it one of the worst places in the city. At one point nobody would deliver anything here. This was a while ago, but you know how you used to have like your diaper services—they wouldn't come in here, furniture deliveries wouldn't come in here, the milkman wouldn't come in here. I mean people would just not come in here; it was that bad—they were always getting robbed. So the environment was that bad and that was prior to '68 and our real community involvement piece, that had happened [later]."[23] Worrell's discussion of the lack of services available to Bromley Heath's residents illustrates the degree of privation plaguing the area. Beyond just a comment on crime levels, his analysis highlights the interplay between uneven resource distribution and the geographic divisions within cities. Bromley's reputation as a dangerous and forbidding location created an invisible stop line separating its residents from the larger community of Boston. For diaper, milk, and furniture companies considering delivery to Bromley Heath, the risk of loss was perceived as greater than the potential commercial gain, so services were suspended. For these businesses, Bromley Heath did not exist and thus was not serviced. Such treatment by Boston's business community further illustrates the financial drift of the Southwest Corridor. Once a competitive and crowded terrain of wholesale manufacturers vying to establish themselves on a global scale, Bromley Heath and its surrounding area now repelled even retail trade. The decline of light and medium industry along Bromley Heath's border between Jamaica Plain and Roxbury meant not only the exodus of bottling companies, breweries, tannery shops, and shoe manufacturers for which the area had been known but also a devastating loss of locally based food and clothing shops necessary to sustain working families. Against this backdrop, the 1970s redesign of the Southwest Corridor offered a unique opportunity for Bromley Heath's residents to revive their social and economic relationships to the city of Boston.

The Next Movement—City Making, Electoral Politics, and the Southwest Corridor Coalition

The 1976 Plant Company shoe factory fire marks a defining local memory fully dramatizing the disappearance of the neighborhood's industrial past. For many Corridor residents and organizations, the fire signaled the ultimate end of one kind of economic development trajectory and the urgent need to create a new one. As the antihighway fight progressed

from protests and demonstrations to planning negotiations, residents of
Roxbury, Jamaica Plain, and the South End created a new umbrella organization called the Southwest Corridor Land Development Coalition, known
popularly as the Southwest Corridor Coalition (SWCC). Chuck Turner
and the Boston Black United Front's antihighway committee, Operation
STOP, launched the SWCC in 1972 because, as he stated, "We needed an
entity that unified us with other groups along the Corridor."[24]

Turner's role as chairman of the Black United Front and cochair of
the Greater Boston Committee on the Transportation Crisis meant that
he was continuously responding to the antihighway movement's shifting political needs. The decision to form an umbrella group composed
of as many Corridor abutting neighborhood organizations as possible
expressed antihighway activists' desire to forge a broad, planning-based
pressure group. Turner's organizing of the Corridor Coalition reflected his
knowledge that the state-sponsored transportation restudy was redefining
the Southwest Corridor as a new kind of multineighborhood territory and
that no single neighborhood alone would be able to influence its overall
development outcomes.

The Southwest Corridor Land Development Coalition began as a loose
planning alliance but solidified its structure and agenda with the attain-
ment of a $25,000 grant from the federal Model Cities Program. The grant
allowed groups along the Corridor to hire their own planner and develop
an independent, resident-informed plan for what the Corridor might
become. For Turner, winning the Model Cities grant marked a pivotal
moment for the Corridor's neighborhood groups to articulate a blueprint
for future development that included greater access to higher education
and the construction of a community college in Roxbury: "What [the
Model Cities grant] meant was that we then pulled together a team that
had a vision about what it [the Southwest Corridor] would look like. We
had the Corridor Park, RCC [Roxbury Community College] . . . It was
a logical plan. Essentially we had the plan and success in the [antihigh-
way] struggle."[25] The Corridor Coalition's plan advocated new recreational
spaces, educational facilities, and business development as essential to
transforming the Corridor into a productive landscape of opportunity for
area residents. Through meetings, published reports, and newsletters, the
Corridor Coalition tasked itself with bringing public awareness to the pre-
carious status of the Southwest Corridor's land.

In the summer of 1976, the Corridor Coalition's newsletter splashed the question, "Can we afford not to build?" above a series of photographs showing the Thomas Plant factory engulfed in flames. The accompanying text reads:

> Fire is another form of demolition which has a long history within the Corridor . . . Due to the time lapse in rebuilding the SWC [Southwest Corridor] many of the remaining businesses have suffered and adjacent communities are experiencing loss of additional businesses through liquidations, abandonment, and a rash of unexplained fires throughout the SWC of older factories, some of which are occupied and others vacant. These structures are potentially re-usable as housing or other developments. Displaced firms have included a full range of manufacturing, retail, wholesale and service establishments and most recently the 500,000 sq. ft. shoe factory at 307 Centre Street, one of the city's largest industrial buildings.[26]

For the Corridor Coalition, the factory's fire typified the ongoing threat of clearance and blight along the Corridor. Although Governor Sargent had officially halted government-sponsored land acquisition and demolition four years prior, Corridor residents continued to watch the landscape outside their windows be destroyed. And just as grassroots planning efforts to reclaim the Corridor raised residents' hopes, unexplained fires and vandalism strained resident optimism about what was truly possible following the highway's defeat.

Moreover, the state's legal responsibility to protect this landscape and its residents meant that unexplained and dangerous events like the Plant factory fire furthered soured public opinion on the efficacy of state authority. "Where can residents turn for political assurance?" seemed to be the collective lament. As the state's slow process of land reallocation and planning dragged ahead, the Corridor Coalition encouraged residents to rely on themselves for answers while continuing to hold state and local government leaders accountable. Though there were times when the Corridor Coalition staggered under the weight of its ambitious political agenda, the group remained focused in its belief that a "unique opportunity exists for the Commonwealth of Massachusetts and the city of Boston to turn the Southwest Corridor area into a healthy residential and commercial urban area."[27] It would take several years and many additional actors to push this

vision to fruition; however, the Corridor Coalition served as a crucial vehicle for aligning residents from multiple neighborhoods within a Corridor-
focused interest group while rebuilding local trust for a state-led plan slow
in execution.

While the Corridor Coalition worked to build relationships among
Corridor residents, new political candidates sought to do the same. South
End resident and activist Mel King ran for state representative for the 4th
Suffolk District in 1973. King's outrage over the Corridor's many parcels
of cleared land as well as his active involvement in Boston's anti–urban
renewal battles helped set the basis for his statewide political campaign
(figure 7). King walked the Corridor, surveyed its needs, and talked to area
residents at length: "One of the things that happened in the campaign was
meeting around what was to happen all through [the Corridor]. The question came up at one of the meetings from the Latino residents: 'Well, if we
support you, will we be able to grow fruits and vegetables on this land?'"[28]
King's reply: "Of course." The land was dormant and area residents were
interested in farming it. This agreement with residents sharpened King's
campaign strategy and his eventual legislative agenda. King's promise to
the Corridor's Latino voters inspired other Corridor constituents to lobby
him with their ideas. A growing network of urban gardeners, residents, and
community activists had found a political champion.

Born in Boston in 1928 to parents from Guyana and Barbados, Mel King
has lived his entire life in a neighborhood central to the city's most turbulent urban renewal and highway battles. During his student days at Claflin
University in South Carolina, his parents frequently mailed him clippings
from Boston's newspapers. One day in 1948 he unfolded one such clip-
ping to read that urban renewal officials had labeled his home a "slum." In
fact, all the houses in his New York Streets neighborhood of the South End
were declared slums and set for demolition. "I was alarmed . . . I thought
I lived in a great neighborhood. I had a lot of friends and great relationships."[29] For King, his family, and his neighbors, urban renewal was not an
abstract argument over the most effective way to revitalize an aging city or
a theoretical discussion of the merits of centralizing planning but rather a
personal affront and a seminal lesson in local politics gone wrong. By the
time King graduated from college, his family had already relocated from
his boyhood home. He returned to Boston to find many other changes that
he did not like.

WE NEED A CORRIDOR DEVELOPMENT CORPORATION — to make creative use of the land idled and wasted by the plans for I-95 and the Inner Belt.

WE NEED GOOD HOUSING — especially low cost, owner occupied, tenant controlled, self-help, and family units, financed by state guaranteed loans for rehabilitation and construction.

DEAR FRIENDS AND VOTERS,

People who don't consider the city home talk of it in negative terms, exploit it, and then desert it. We know better: we call it home.

As I have gone throughout our district in the last month, I have been impressed by the number of groups making great efforts to build a really humane and viable community in Wards 10 and 4. I've found people protecting the interests of low rent housing and business space, building teen centers and recreation programs, growing gardens to create a beautiful and refreshing environment, and making sure that the planning for hospital expansion is in the interest of the community. I've seen people working to get housing to meet code standards, planning for health care delivery, fighting drug abuse problems, organizing food coops and consumers protection groups. And I've met people running high school equivalency and day care programs, maintaining their property and even re-routing traffic for the safety of their children — all people who care. People see the problems, but they also see the opportunities.

We must insist that we get the support we need to take advantage of the opportunities and to solve the problems facing our neighborhoods. I'm confident that the way to save our cities is through our neighborhoods.

Where do we start?

WE NEED HIGHER INCOME — from better paying jobs and adequate welfare handled by Federal authorities.

WE NEED NEIGHBORHOOD SECURITY — safety from crime, protection from institutional expansion such as the Harvard power plant and I-95, and enough funds to stabilize our neighborhoods with new development.

WE NEED NEIGHBORHOOD DEVELOPMENT CORPORATIONS — to provide the vehicle for new jobs, training, construction, business, and housing organized and run by residents.

WE CAN SAVE OUR NEIGHBORHOODS, and we can begin now by getting the representation we need in the State Legislature. Through legislative action we can get the tools we need to take the initiative and make our neighborhoods healthy and productive. I ask your support in this effort.

VOTE FOR ACTION ON SEPT. 19

VOTE FOR RESULTS

VOTE FOR MEL KING STATE REPRESENTATIVE 4th SUFFOLK DISTRICT DEMOCRAT

FIGURE 7. "Vote for Mel King" flyer from King's successful 1973 run for Massachusetts state representative, 4th Suffolk District. Source: Mel King Personal Archives.

With strong Corridor resident backing, King swept into public office pledging to honor the Southwest Corridor's community-driven development vision as a political priority. But this would be an uphill battle. Illegal dumping and a toxic mix of industrial contaminants had rendered much of the Corridor's soil hazardous. Undaunted, King used his first speech before the Massachusetts Legislature to focus on the Corridors' gardeners and the state's need to "turn the land back to the people": "The first bit of money that I was able to raise was money to clean the land so that the folks could put their gardens and things in it. So I got $15,000 or so in the budget and it happened so they cleaned it. At the same time I filed legislation for taking state land for community gardens. The other gardens are up there because any land that the state owned, we could take over for community gardens. It was a whole movement."[30] King sponsored House bill H2426 to further this appeal. His work on urban gardens increased public and legislative awareness of the ongoing need to designate diverse uses for Corridor land. King served in the Massachusetts Legislature for three terms (1973–82) before later running for mayor of Boston. As an important ally to Corridor residents and the Southwest Corridor Land Development Coalition itself, King's political rise signaled a kind of institutionalization of radical redistributive politics born on the ground and anchored by notions of local control.

Controlling the Land: "Planting Hope, Growing Neighbors" on the Farm

As the Southwest Corridor's official development plan began to take shape, vacant land parcels were numbered by the state and integrated into a comprehensive land reuse strategy. The good news was that many of these parcels would be used for the creation of mass transit and open space and not a limited-access highway. The bad news was that several of the Corridor's large parcels, not included in the state's plan and thus called "surplus land," would remain sites of neglect. For example, clearance on both sides of Lamartine Street had left behind a vacant block of land between Hoffman and Roys Streets. When the highway plan was aborted, the eastern side of the street was earmarked to support mass transit and a strip of landscaped parkland, but the western side was left idle. Over time, the western side of Lamartine became a dusty pit of overgrown weeds and illegal trash dumping. It was here that residents Femke and Peter Rosenbaum organized their neighbors to clean up the ground, lay fresh topsoil, and claim the area for community-based urban agriculture. And with that, the Southwest Corridor Community Farm was born as an urban farming experiment led by a group of multiracial, multiethnic residents living in Jamaica Plain and Roxbury.

When Femke and Peter Rosenbaum moved to Jamaica Plain, the Corridor's vacant terrain caught their attention. They immediately imagined this open strip of land as something beautiful, productive, and able to bring neighbors together: "We got here in '73. So the road had been stopped, but they were still talking about the arterial road . . . It would have been a four-lane highway. So people still wanted a highway even though there was going to be public transit here. When we heard about that, we got involved. We knocked on doors and talked to people about it with petitions and that was [with] the Southwest Corridor Coalition—that was the organization that was active at the time."[31] At least initially, the Southwest Corridor Coalition offered Femke and Peter just the organizing vehicle they needed to become involved in the Corridor's revitalization. Femke's reference to residents' discussion of the four-lane arterial road through Jamaica Plain offers a historical glimpse of the then bubbling neighborhood debate on surface road improvements. For some residents, the construction of an arterial road would provide a necessary neighborhood buffer against commuter traffic destined to pass through Jamaica Plain in the Southwest Expressway's absence, but for others, such as Femke, any mention of new roads simply meant that more resident activism was needed.

While supportive of resident-based planning strategies, Femke and Peter were skeptical about the grassroots efforts of the Corridor Coalition as well as the formal planning process led by the state. Femke believed that unless residents personally planned and maintained the Corridor's land themselves, even the best-designed plans would deliver only a short-term solution. Pointing to a photograph of land once used as play space, Femke reflects on failed approaches to repurposing the Corridor's vacant areas: "This used to be a playground, and the kids took it apart in three months' time. It was destroyed. When people started talking about a park, I thought, 'It's not gonna last.' That's when I started advocating for people to do something with the park—that the people had to create the park themselves and that would be the way for them to actually look after it."[32] Femke's activism was grounded in her belief that the participation of residents was key to the Corridor's ongoing maintenance and survival. She and Peter shared a commitment to the idea that "people had to create the park themselves." This principle formed the central organizing tenet of the Southwest Corridor Community Farm. Residents would determine, develop, and manage the land for themselves.

The farm comprised more than forty ten-foot-square individual plots cultivated by residents as well as common areas of berry bushes and fruit trees.[33] Early images of the farm show residents tending plots of sunflowers, rosemary, and basil; spreading manure; watering young green sprouts. In one photograph, a group of residents gather around the farm's horticulture expert to learn planting techniques best suited for urban crops (figure 8). The landscape encircling the group describes another lesson, the physical

FIGURE 8. Southwest Corridor Community Farm, 1981. Carmenza Fonstad, horticulture expert and outreach coordinator for the farm, is shown here instructing a group of residents. Photo courtesy of Read Brugger.

and social effects of unsustained urban investment. The farm hosted classes for residents, a seed-selling program, and garden plots in the middle of two shadows of arrested development. On the photograph's left side, the background presence of a large brick warehouse and several utility poles wired for phones and electricity remind viewers of an abandoned industrial landscape stuffed with businesses and houses that no longer exist. The houses were demolished long ago, but the survival of their towering utility poles casts everything in miniature while memorializing a residential population that once thrived here. In the photograph's foreground, parcels of open land offer panoramic sight lines of Boston in each cardinal direction and mark the start and stop of a federal highway. By pushing beyond the land's past uses to cultivate vacant ground as well as social connections among residents, the Southwest Corridor Community Farm established itself as a vibrant model for grassroots-fueled urban redevelopment.

In another archival photo, Femke's husband, Peter, pushes a wheelbarrow and smiles into the camera. Behind him the landscape is abuzz with activity and chatty neighbors. Peter laughs at this image of himself. When I ask how they decided what to plant at the farm, he smiles broadly and describes how residents' individual interests and cultural backgrounds played a defining role in determining the farm's planting mix: "At the time we started the Southwest Corridor Community Farm, there were a lot of people from Bromley Heath who had come up from the south in that [post–World War II] migration and who were rural black folks who had grown gardens—who had grown food their whole younger adult lives, and they knew what to do (laughter). Whether it was collard greens or what, they really knew, and I'm afraid most of that generation is gone now, but they were very active. A lot of the things that I learned, I learned from them. In the sense that collard greens weren't part of my tradition, but they grow well here—it's that kind of thing."[34] Far from a sentimental back-to-the-land project, the Southwest Corridor Community Farm advanced a radical political understanding of the utility of local decision making and knowledge dissemination. With the motto, "We plant hope, we grow neighbors," the farm charted a local development agenda that relied unapologetically on the knowledge and work of residents themselves. From collard green plantings to soil rotation methods to produce-based revenue strategies, neighbors working the farm authored a future-focused practice of urban revitalization based on the daily exchange of rich cultural knowledge.

Bromley Heath's community of black southern migrants brought new cultivation strategies to Boston's northern soil while educating their white neighbors, like Peter, on expanded varieties of leafy greens. Leroy Stoddard, one of the farm's early directors, further discusses the circulation of cultural knowledge among neighborhood residents and farm staff: "I think of two Italian families that lived there. They came in the '50s after World War II (to) work in the shoe and brewery industries that were going strong before the clearing for the highway ... I was taught how to prune by this man who knew that planting fava beans took nitrogen from the air and helped build the soil for the crops that followed. Of course they made tomato sauce. They were virtually self-sufficient farmers in their little tiny plots in the city having brought Italian urban agriculture practices so we had nothing to teach them. Here, in fact, we were students of what they knew how to do."[35] Migrants carrying a formidable base of agricultural knowledge enabled the Southwest Community Corridor Farm to thrive. In 1979 Femke decided that the farm needed an annual celebration that would kick off the growing season, bring residents together, remind everyone of the antihighway fight's history, and highlight the city's multiracial populations.

The Wake Up the Earth Festival was launched in the spring of 1979 and has run every year since. On the Festival's ninth anniversary in 1987, its organizers published a commemorative newsletter to showcase the farm, the festival, and its sponsors. The newsletter featured a front-page reflection on activist planning for the Southwest Corridor:

> *We Planned.* For eight years, ever since the first Wake Up the Earth Festival in May of 1979, we had been planning the perfect celebration of the Corridor communities' survival and renewal. Completion of the mass transit and park systems would symbolize that renewal, but the rebirth we wanted to proclaim was social, even spiritual not transitory.
>
> *We Dreamed.* In spite of the four-mile-long tear through the fabric of our communities, we were able to stitch together Black, Brown and White threads every May, and to pledge annually to work together so we wouldn't be unraveled.[36]

Although this commentary was written to address a perceived slight by the state's transportation authority for not contracting the festival's organizers to plan the Southwest Corridor Park's opening ceremony, it illustrates how local activists viewed their planning aims for the Corridor's reuse. For these activists, the Corridor's grassroots revitalization potentially delivered a transcendent experience for residents. The demolition that tore "through the fabric of our communities," as they describe, necessitated not just economic development but social and spiritual healing. For Femke and her allies, the Southwest Corridor Community Farm and Wake Up the Earth Festival provided living models for achieving healthy reconnection among groups that had been physically displaced and psychologically battered by the Corridor's own history. A desire to "stitch together" the landscape and its neighbors propelled this work then and now.

Commenting further on the local impact of land clearance on the Corridor, former farm director Leroy Stoddard observes: "What the state did back in '66 was not just to remove people's livelihoods and homes but to create a nuisance of vacancy that never yielded a tax dollar and never did anything but grow weeds. When you disinvest in a city that way, plenty of high-level planners never dreamed that they were creating such a problem."[37] Though planners and policymakers may have been unaware of the long-term effects of their land development strategies, Corridor residents were intimately familiar with the overreach of public and private power and its historic role in shaping their neighborhoods. From globally scaled industrial factories to public housing construction to highway expansion, each of these development projects in various ways inspired local residents to reimagine the landscapes around them and assert their own authority as political stakeholders and self-taught urban planners. While groups such as Bromley Heath's Tenant Management Corporation, the Southwest Corridor Land Development Coalition, and the Southwest Corridor Community Farm originated bold, new urban plans to shape the Corridor's future according to their own visions, the state's planners continued to evaluate possible uses for the landscape's string of vacant parcels.

Controlling Economic Development: CIRCLE, Inc.

Five years prior to his run for state representative, Mel King and fellow activist Hubert "Hubie" Eugene Jones organized a retreat for leaders of several neighborhood-based community organizations, including the NAACP, the Urban League, and local settlement houses. The result was the formation of a new coalition group called CIRCLE with a young MIT political science professor named Willard Johnson chosen as its executive director.[38] As a coalition-based umbrella organization with a race-informed political agenda for Boston's residents of color, CIRCLE shared a structure and membership similar to that of the Black United Front. However, CIRCLE predates the Black United Front and focused its activities almost exclusively on local enterprise and neighborhood development goals. CIRCLE is significant to the Southwest Corridor's development history because of its success in operationalizing key black nationalist values and approaches prominent during the 1960s and 1970s. From late civil rights–based principles of economic justice and opportunity to Pan-Africanist ideas of postcolonial diasporic unity to Black Power models of community control and collective economics, CIRCLE laid the foundation for a new kind of land development organization steeped in multiple black political agendas.

CIRCLE's formation, like the subsequent formation of the Black United Front, signals a growing grassroots hunger for greater local control and coordination in addressing Boston's urban development challenges.[39] Johnson notes: "This is before King's assassination, but already it was troubled times. Watts riots, Detroit burning, and so forth, so it's clear the country is in turmoil and we've got to pull together and think about this."[40] Urban uprisings, failed policies, and a large variety of nonprofit, antipoverty organizations prompted CIRCLE's membership to develop a pragmatic economic development and planning agenda. Taking a leave from MIT, Johnson led CIRCLE for the next couple of years and committed himself to "developing a common strategy for dealing with the problems that were besetting the city." For him, the continent of Africa, not an MIT classroom, held the key to what would become CIRCLE's visionary approach to economic development.

Johnson's prior graduate study at Harvard had carried him to Cameroon, where he observed postwar efforts to unite the nation's English-speaking and French-speaking territories into one political entity. Independence and decolonizing movements across the African continent drew Johnson's intellectual curiosity toward the question of, "How?" How could geographies and populations sidelined by economic development be remade by redirecting state-led economic investment? For Cameroon, this was a bold new question.

Cameroon's leaders did not seek political independence from colonial rule but rather a process of integrated reform. In 1961 Cameroon's political leadership set the legal terms of agreement for unification of east and west Cameroon and prompted public debates on how best to spark new economic growth.[41] Johnson observed these debates in person and tracked ground-level efforts by the Cameroon Development Corporation to boost business activity in previously underinvested areas. He refers to his study of the Cameroon Development Corporation as "the relevant dimension that was guiding me" at this time.[42]

> The Cameroon Development Corporation was created to supply Britain with colony-derived resources during the War. What it meant was that you had the power of the state, both its money power and its legal power, behind the creation of an organization that operated as a business development agency. So it had the full faith and credit of the state behind it, but its mission was to succeed in developing the businesses, so I thought that would be a model for us. We couldn't tap the state's money, but we could organize the community as a kind of collective owner and beneficiary and then operate the organization itself as a job creation mechanism.[43]

As Cameroon moved toward cultural and economic integration, Johnson deepened his understanding of how this "model" might be applied in the context of U.S. urban renewal and civil rights organizing. For him, Cameroon's postcolonial redevelopment efforts offered a compelling model for Boston's own Roxbury neighborhood.

Johnson recalls interjecting his voice into the discussion during CIRCLE's founding weekend retreat. Reflecting on his time in Cameroon, he urged Mel King and Hubie Jones and all the meeting's attendees to think formally and long-term: "My suggestion to the group was that we institutionalize—that we create a corporation, an organization down the line. That we go about the process of both creating and acquiring capital assets that could be used for job creation and so I have in mind [Cameroon] and I had also seen the same thing in Uganda. So we decided to do that. We turned the name 'circle' into an acronym which we called Centralized Investment to Revitalize Community Living Effectively, the CIRCLE."[44] The organization was established as federation of twenty-eight community-based organizations that marshaled the skills of its members to run a consulting business while developing itself as a proto–community development corporation. Within a year of winning a series of increasingly lucrative marketing,

media, and communications contracts, CIRCLE had amassed a staff of
sixty people.[45] Buoyed with the success of its consulting practice, CIRCLE
pursued and won a $100,000 foundation grant to create a training institute
called the Roxbury Institute of Business Management (RIBM), a training
vehicle for managers of CIRCLE-launched businesses.

In supporting the launch and development of local business enterprises
working in demolition and construction, CIRCLE "would take us straight
into the [Southwest] Corridor issues." The corporation eventually won a
contract from the Boston Transportation Planning Review to conduct a
mobility study on the Corridor and develop an engagement strategy for
soliciting resident input.[46] "We had some discussion of [the antihighway
fight] but it was raised initially within the framework of 'we need to control our land' so it was bigger than the highway. The highway was gonna
cut straight through the community. There was no doubt that that was
a problem."[47] The group assumed a more authoritative local voice as the
state's public planning process for the Southwest Corridor became formalized.[48] Having exhausted his MIT leave, Johnson returned to academia and
turned CIRCLE's work over to Chuck Turner. Under Johnson's leadership,
CIRCLE grew from a weekend brainstorm in 1967 to a fully staffed development and planning organization by 1968. Turner's regional approach to
organizing, political knowledge, and web of social networks positioned
CIRCLE well to take on one of its first big land issues "to get Roxbury
Community College located on the Corridor."[49] During the late 1960s, a
groundswell of grassroots activism surged to prominence with the objective of founding a state-sponsored community college in Roxbury. With
Turner's guidance, the Southwest Corridor Coalition had been lobbying
the state to designate the college's proposed campus on Corridor land.
Now CIRCLE was also poised to join the fight.

Controlling Access to Education: Roxbury Community College

As Governor Sargent was assembling his advisers to deliberate on Greater
Boston's transportation controversies, an additional crisis was brewing on
where and how to administer the Massachusetts Legislature's 1968 appro-
priation of $361,280 for Roxbury Community College.[50] Over the next few
years a battle to determine the location, legal status, functional autonomy,
and curriculum of Roxbury Community College would entangle local and

state officials, including Sargent himself, within a turf war to determine Roxbury residents' pathway to higher education. Though the legislature's act appeared to be an obvious win for local advocates, ongoing tensions between the governor-appointed advisory body named the Roxbury Community College Board and the state's college governing board, the Massachusetts Board of Regional Colleges, revealed an overall mood that was less than celebratory.

The Roxbury Community College Board and its chairman, Kenneth Hubbard, stood opposed to the legislature's act because this law did not recognize the new college as an independent institution within the state's community college network. Instead, the proposed Roxbury Community College would sit within the governance structure of another state college. Hubbard and his board read this as an operational slight suggesting a subordinate state status for Roxbury Community College and its projected majority black student body. In response, Hubbard and the board voted to reject the oversight authority of the Massachusetts Board of Regional Community Colleges, and a heated battle ensued. Widespread community endorsement of Hubbard's stance prompted local residents and their allies to send Hubbard spirited support letters like this:

> Black people must be provided with services, among which are education institutions which offer skills needed by all segments of the Community. However, an even greater need is the ability to determine the nature of these services and the ability to control the goals and means of these services. As it now stands, the proposed "Roxbury Community College" remains in the hands of people outside the Community. Some suggest that this position be accepted by the Community in return for assurance that in 1970 an autonomous community college will be established. Basically, this requires us to forfeit immediate control in the hopes of future control . . . We must demand control of all services entering into the Community from the start.[51]

The writer's stance advocating control of the nature, content, and goals of the college's services reflects a clear political demand informing the Southwest Corridor's on-the-ground planning objectives.

Within the struggle for Roxbury Community College's earliest beginnings, the principle of local control is consistently articulated as a means to ensure that services and resources intended to benefit underinvested populations actually would. Local control was viewed by its proponents as a more just means for guaranteeing equitable distribution of public resources and decision making. And, for black communities in particular, local control seemed to offer a liberatory corrective to inadequate, unresponsive, and, likely, racist political and economic systems. A group called the Boston Association of Afro-American Educators released a position paper in support of the Roxbury Community College Board's official stance and made clear that anything short of black community control would be "unacceptable and non-negotiable": "We must be continually wary of external forces which cloak themselves in the guise of paternalism and well meaning. We must make certain that our actions are consistent with our philosophy at all times that the liberation of our people demands that we control and influence those institutions which design our destiny."[52]

The fiery correspondence between the Roxbury Community College Board, its allies, and the Massachusetts Board of Regional Community Colleges carries all the drama of a page-turning mystery novel despite knowing that the Roxbury Community College Board would ultimately secure its demands and land a permanent home for Roxbury Community College (RCC) on the Southwest Corridor. Yet, plot twists, canceled meetings, rhetorical excesses, strained lunch dates, biting wit, and hearsay fuse a blistering trail of letters, meeting minutes, and newspaper articles and suggest a negotiation route all but straight for RCC's founders.

Robert Putnam, member of the Massachusetts Board of Regional Community Colleges, the state governing body that RCC's advocates opposed, wrote to Hubbard after getting an insider's meeting tip: "I heard from my daughter the other day that there was some serious question at your last meeting as to whether it would not be better to wait a little while, and have a separate Community College just for Roxbury."[53] Employing his persuasion skills, Putnam goes on to provide legal and fiscal details as to why a separate, autonomous college is not advisable in his opinion. He concludes: "I think it would be a great mistake to insist on a separate college. It will mean the postponement of any accredited institution for at least five years and of any institution for two, and might well mean a totally different Advisory Board. We are just as anxious as you are to bring the advantages of Community College education to the area, and I hope your group will permit us to do so. We are ready to recommend to our Board, and I am sure the Board is ready to act favorable on any reasonable method of doing this."[54] Putnam's conciliatory tone only slightly conceals his position. And his choice of the words "reasonable method" makes clear that he expected a course change from Hubbard and the Roxbury Community College Advisory Board. But it would not come.

By the early summer of 1969, the Massachusetts Board of Regional Community Colleges issued its decision not to support Hubbard's proposal for an autonomously controlled community college or its potential placement in Roxbury. The state's community college system was already grappling with fiscal and enrollment challenges; however, based on supporting correspondence, it appears that the idea of a locally controlled public college in Roxbury was what gave state officials most pause. Following his attendance at a public hearing on the proposal, Daniel H. O'Leary, president of the State College at Lowell and member of the Board of Regional Community Colleges, wrote to inform Hubbard of his conclusion:

> It was evident yesterday that widespread citizen support is not yet aroused on this issue. Less than fifty concerned residents attended the public hearing, and only six of them voted in favor of a Roxbury Community College under control of the Board of Regional Community Colleges. Those present chose to endorse a Roxbury Community College under local black control . . . I speak only for myself, and only as a single fallible individual who knows much less about the needs and aspirations of the present residents of Roxbury than you do. I do know something about what a college is and what it needs to develop academic excellence. I recognize and respect your zeal and your devotion.[55]

In the end, O'Leary and others endorsed a Dorchester location for the college but did not change its decision. In response to this recommendation, Hubbard writes to Theodore Chase, chairman of the State Board of Regional Community Colleges: "Having a Roxbury Community College in Dorchester is like locating the Massachusetts Institute of Technology in Providence, Rhode Island . . . It is an insult to this Community to be deprived of an autonomous institution with which it could identify in the field of Higher Education. The people of every community which receives your services have been elated to have such a component within their midst and that pride should not be denied Roxbury." He concludes: "With these considerations in mind the Roxbury Community College Board has voted to '"Decline the present allocated funds unless provisions for meaningful voice of community participation and concern can rightfully be administered.'"[56] The Roxbury Community College Board formally rejected the state's funding grant as well as any administrative and operational options short of its demand for autonomy. This brief snapshot of Roxbury Community College's founding history illustrates how a maturing political ideology of community control was guiding both land and institutional development along the Southwest Corridor and creating new bases for public negotiation and mobilization on the street and within the halls of government. Governor Sargent would soon intervene and, once again, show the state's ability to listen.

= = =

Community control as an edgy expression of homegrown do-it-yourself city planning and place remaking would populate the Southwest Corridor with bold examples of engaged residents designing a future to address their current needs and hopes. During the intervening years between the end of the highway fight and the launch of formal planning and development for the Southwest Corridor, Boston activists produced a daring collection of creative land-based, citizen-led interventions intended to reverse a long history of disinvestment and material decline. Chronic systems failure had pushed many Corridor residents far away from access to decent jobs, education, housing, political leaders, planning tools, and opportunities to control and enhance the direction of their lives.

Instead of waiting for an unknown savior, Corridor residents and their allies produced their own solutions to vexing problems that state, federal, and local government officials seemed unable, or unwilling, to address. By fighting to stop the highway, activists had succeeded in their claim to imagine a new kind of city making that included them not just as passive beneficiaries but also as engaged planners, theorists, and leaders identifying actions and strategies to advance their collective social, economic and political interests. They wanted control. Yet their control impulse often revealed a deeper dream for a type of redistributive justice that residents themselves could lead. In the years to come, Southwest Corridor residents and their allies would again have their ideals tested to determine how much they were truly willing to do to secure a future nearly three decades in the making and how much of it they would be willing to share.

Chapter 6

Making Victory Stick

New Park, New Dreams, New Plans

For Boston's antihighway activists, Sargent's cancellation of the Inner Belt and I-95 represented a decisive win despite raising new concerns about how to secure a long-term highwayless future. While there was general public agreement on the need to develop mass transit along the Southwest Corridor, there was less agreement on the idea of creating a public park. In 1973 Sargent appointed architect Tony Pangaro as the Southwest Corridor Development Coordinator. Recalling the early days of his job, Pangaro shrugs his shoulders: "There were a lot of people who said, 'Oh, don't build a park. Nobody will take care of it. It will be full of crime. It will fall apart.'"[1]

The Southwest Corridor—A Park?

David Lee, principal architect at the Boston architectural firm Stull and Lee, originated the idea of the Corridor's linear park and would later become responsible for creating overall design standards for the Corridor, its eight-station transit line, and coordinating planning and engineering among the project's many contractors. Though Lee was eager to implement his breakthrough idea, he found few initial supporters. Like Pangaro, Lee remembers encountering resistance:

I remember going to the MDC [Massachusetts District Commission, state park authority] at the time and saying, "I got this idea for how we could have 90 acres of new parkland running the length of the Corridor," and they said to me, "Are you crazy? We can't even manage what we have and now you're talking about bringing more." But ultimately they bought into the idea. What led me to thinking about it was looking at the Olmsted Emerald Necklace and looking at the proximity of the Corridor for various communities . . . I drew this diagram that showed how the Corridor could be like a strand, if you will, of the necklace and connect important places in the community.[2]

Lee's drawings present an updated version of Frederick Law Olmsted's historic idea of a "strand" linking urban recreational space to nearby areas of cultural and historic significance (figure 9). Using a simple but elegant design, Lee proposed a landscape with direct spatial references to the greenway known as Olmsted's Emerald Necklace spanning the Back Bay Fens, the promenade of Commonwealth Avenue, and the Boston Public Garden.

Lee credits his own prior antihighway activism with giving him the inspiration to create a park to connect the Corridor's collection of surplus land:

It was during the environmental impact studies that I came up with the idea for a linear park. What led me to thinking about it was looking at the Olmsted Emerald Necklace and looking at the proximity of the Corridor for various communities' cultural centers . . . I drew this diagram that showed how the Corridor could be like a strand of the necklace and connect important places in the community, so I drew this diagram and wound up writing for the environmental impact statement. We had excess land because they had cleared all this land for all these highways and now you didn't need that much so the rest of it was left over. So a portion of it went for the park system, and a portion of it was parceled out for development.[3]

Lee convinced the state of the viability of his plan and then began the arduous process of trying to convince neighborhood residents that an urban park running through the middle of Boston was a worthwhile idea.[4]

Looking at the Southwest Corridor Park today, it is hard to believe that anyone would question its safety or necessity. Bike riders zoom by in both directions, late summer tomatoes grow in garden plots, moms push

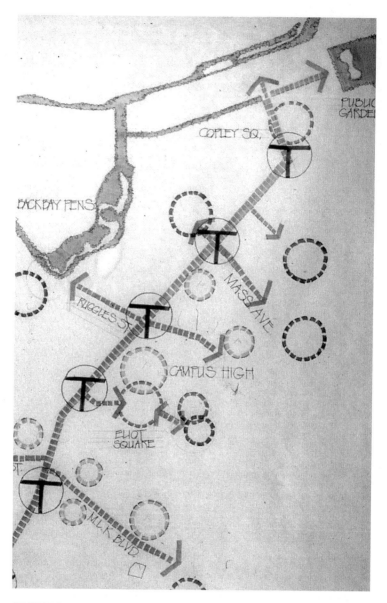

FIGURE 9. David Lee's original freehand drawing proposing the creation of a linear park on the Southwest Corridor. Source: Stull and Lee Corporate Archives.

toddlers in strollers, and screaming kids play pickup basketball like there's no other place any of them would rather be. Yet, as Pangaro attests, the 1970s offered a different context for the social meaning of city parks. Ken Kruckemeyer, who worked alongside Pangaro as one of two assistant project coordinators, recounts the challenge of persuading skeptical Corridor residents that a park could be beneficial to them

> In the 1970s people didn't have much respect or understanding of the positive nature of public space. They tended to be afraid of public space. And to some degree the continuous bombardment about how beautiful the suburbs are and about how that's the place to go left the people who were captives of the city—because the suburbs didn't welcome them because of their race or because the suburbs didn't work for them because they didn't have a car or because they couldn't afford the suburbs because there just wasn't enough money to buy a house out in the suburbs—they were sorta left here and feeling abandoned by much of the rest of society that was paying so much attention to making the world beautiful in the suburbs, and so folks left in the city were at the same time being rather alienated by their own parks and things they had heretofore thought of as the respite for city life.[5]

Kruckemeyer's assessment of changing social perceptions of public space ties transformations in urban settlement patterns to new dilemmas in open space planning. These shifts, coupled with the quickening pace of urban economic disinvestment and an intensifying racial polarization between metropolitan spaces, meant that unclaimed areas such as parks could be envisioned as threatening mainly because of who, not what, might be in them. When residents cautioned Pangaro against building a park along the Southwest Corridor because it would be "full of crime," they echoed this idea of forbidding types of action and persons defining a socially unregulated, and thus unsafe, place. The notion of "public" space as shared, communal, and socially heterogeneous was, for some residents, anxiety producing and potentially dangerous. By the 1970s, many of America's urban parks were widely perceived as frightening zones of encounter to be avoided. This sentiment could not have been further removed from Olmsted's original intentions for U.S. parklands.

More than one hundred years before the Southwest Corridor Park's creation, renowned landscape architect Frederick Law Olmsted planned

Boston's municipal park network as the first comprehensive urban park system in the United States.[6] Olmsted's "Emerald Necklace" was created as the pastoral antithesis to the chaos, congestion, and class segregation of the nineteenth-century industrial city. Connecting several neighborhoods across Boston through a series of walkways, manicured greenways, and rolling hills, Olmsted's parkland set a national standard for the aesthetic form and social purpose of urban parks. For Olmsted, the natural beauty, harmony, and peace of his parks were intended to instruct human social relations in the city. Thus, in addition to his picturesque designs of American landscapes, Olmsted's lasting professional contribution lies in his success in making the socialization of urban residents a public priority worthy of political attention, financial resources, and physical space.

Olmsted imagined urban parks as essential spaces for bringing citizens together for a type of democratic rehabilitation from the social rigidity of hierarchy-bound, industrially ordered cities. In contrast to the industrial city's commercial and residential buildings, parks would provide equal access for people of all classes to mingle and socialize. Yet, far from a proponent of a socially unregulated society, Olmsted saw parks as a civilizing tool for working classes and what he deemed as uncultured groups. And, interestingly, he paid particular attention to the public behavior of men.

Olmsted believed that using nature to cultivate women's behavior would have a positive spillover effect on the people they cared for and especially park-visiting men. Architectural historian Dolores Hayden has commented on the centrality of women within Olmsted's conception of public open space. Referencing his 1870 Boston address titled "Public Parks and the Enlargement of Towns," Hayden writes: "Olmsted defined a backward society as a nonurban society where the 'men counted their women with their horses.'"[7] For Olmsted, more equitable gender relations were a key measure of his conception of a forward-moving civilized society. Instead of being reduced to the status of possessions to be counted and commanded, women were endowed by Olmsted with the capacity to inspire and facilitate the social advancement of humanity. He declares: "We all recognize that the tastes and dispositions of women are more and more potent in shaping the course of civilized progress, and we may see that women are even more susceptible to . . . [the] townward drift than men."[8] Here women are simultaneously understood as linchpins of human "civilized progress" as well as highly "susceptible" to an *uncivilized* "drift" toward saloons and other unmentionable urban establishments. Although Olmsted's logic reflects Victorian era idealizations of middle-class white women and their prescribed social role as nurturing moral stewards, it is significant for its effort to consider the physical presence and social contributions of women outside the home and within the public domain of parks.[9] Planners of the Southwest Corridor Park did not articulate such prescribed ideas about women's roles in shaping public behavior in parks; however, the experiences and memories of women in their own lives would prove critical to the conceptual development of the park in several important ways.

In addition to the Corridor's early planning activism by Anna Mae Cole, Mildred Hailey, and Femke Rosenbaum, the experiences of female relatives of the Corridor's lead staff would leave an indelible imprint on the Corridor's reuse plan. In the end, it is the activism and experiences of women that worked to subvert 1970s-era fears about the creation of open space in the heart of Boston. Kruckemeyer traces his appreciation for urban open space to his mother's childhood memory of the park in her Cincinnati neighborhood: "I remember my mother talking about the park across the street from her house when she was growing up. This was in 1910. They would go over to the park and sit there any time day or night just because it was a great place to go. They were middle-class Cincinnatians growing up in the city. But the park, which was a pretty rambling park, it was not a park where you could see every corner of it and know whether there was anybody there or not. It was this thing that went up and down in the little hollows and everything else, but her recollection of the park in 1910 as a little girl was that it was the most fun, safest place to go."[10] This image of a rambling urban park enjoyed by people day and night and regarded as fun and safe persuaded Kruckemeyer that there were important lessons about the future that only the past could teach. Smiling widely at the recollection of his mother, Kruckemeyer reveals not only his personal musings but also the ways in which his mother's environmental experiences would compel him as an architect and transportation planner. Referencing the decisions of the Corridor's coordinating team, he confides, "I think we were comparing how people had cared for things in the past and believing that that could be accomplished again."[11]

Similarly, Kruckemeyer and Pangaro's eventual boss, state transportation secretary Fred Salvucci, cites the experiences of his grandmother as formative for his understanding of public planning and space making.[12] During public lectures and discussions, Salvucci has frequently referenced an earlier wave of highway building in Massachusetts that led to the demolition of his grandmother's house. While this story is often told to explain Salvucci's activism as a radical planner, it also illustrates his deliberate act of applying lessons from his grandmother's life to his own. "In 1959 when they [state planners] took my grandmother's house, there was no process." Salvucci's grandmother lived near railroad tracks in Boston's Brighton neighborhood. All of the houses on her side of the street were razed to make room for the Massachusetts Turnpike. In Salvucci's assessment, the state "behaved atrociously" because it failed to provide a fair public planning or relocation process for residents. Salvucci identifies his grandmother's story as core to his conviction that something was wrong with the state's approach to transportation planning.[13] This conviction sparked both his early pledge to fight the highway and his subsequent commitment to create an open and participatory process for planning the development of the Southwest Corridor.

The male dominance of planning as a professional field of practice meant that Salvucci, Pangaro, Lee, and Kruckemeyer all enjoyed a privileged position of access to training, resources, and expertise. However, during the 1960s and 1970s, so-called expert knowledge was being attacked and redefined by grassroots activists. For many, the cancellation of the Massachusetts highway plan coupled with the governor's admission that "we were wrong" proved that the old rules and ways of knowing were officially dead. And, in their place, the collective memories and experiences of nonprofessional actors—chiefly neighborhood residents—forged new knowledge systems. Women were critical to this epistemological shift. From leading public housing reform to envisioning urban agriculture, to disciplining the professional practice of their sons and grandsons, women's contributions to the planning and development of the Southwest Corridor succeeded in creating a landscape and parkland that would make Olmsted himself envious. Furthermore, the expansive visions of resident actors pushed beyond transportation and park planning to stake a claim in building not just a new territory but also a renewed notion of community. These visions, joined with the creative development options authored by resident coalitions, would directly inform the Corridor's final plan.

Planning the Southwest Corridor

As the state-appointed official leading the Southwest Corridor's development, Pangaro led a mandate "to bring together the many public agencies
and numerous citizens' groups to plan the development of the Corridor."[14]
By 1973, Boston's I-95 segment had been canceled, and Governor Sargent
had successfully lobbied Congress to secure federal funding for mass
transit through the "Boston provision" of the 1973 Federal-Aid Highway
Act. The Corridor's new future was taking shape. Pangaro and his team
began meeting with citizens and neighborhood groups and assembled the
Southwest Working Committee to draft a set of community goals and land
development opportunities for the Corridor.

The 1976 release of the Southwest Corridor Report summarized more than
a year's worth of Southwest Corridor Working Committee discussions and
set the course for a wider public planning process. The report outlined a comprehensive vision for the Corridor's future: "The Southwest Corridor must be
a place where people can live, work and do business. Since it is the first time
an area cleared for an Expressway has been redesignated for alternative uses,
it presents the unique opportunity for sound planning so that new development will not only serve regional transportation and recreation purposes but
also local neighborhood needs. From an area of controversy in the past, it can
become the model for urban living in the future."[15] The Southwest Corridor
Working Committee viewed their planning process as exceptional—"the first
time an area cleared for an Expressway has been redesignated for alternative
uses."[16] While it is difficult to disprove this claim fully, what's significant is the
way in which this self-tagged distinction emboldened the Corridor's planners and activists with a zeal-like sense of purpose. The Corridor Working
Committee's focus on the unique planning opportunity created by land
cleared for the highway highlights how the land's political history guided the
present approach to its development. This was not large-scale construction
as usual. Activists, architects, urban planners, and the governor himself had
made clear that this was a landscape to be treasured for its past victories and
protected for its future redevelopment promise "of equitable treatment of
those who have been affected by the demolition in the corridor."[17]

Stretching eight miles from the edge of Boston's downtown and across
several neighborhoods, the Southwest Corridor defined a massive new

territory to be created inside a centuries-old city.[18] The super-sized physical scale and economic impact of the Corridor's construction packed its
public reports with strings of superlatives: "Economic development of the
Southwest Corridor is potentially the single most exciting and productive situation to face the City of Boston in this century. It is estimated that
construction expenditures will total $540 million, and will provide 18,500
jobs, with $245 million in wages during the 6–10 year construction state.
The result will be a new transportation network, large-scale commercial
and housing development . . . new open space and recreation areas, as well
as capital improvement for necessary city services."[19] Mass transit improvements, job creation, housing rehabilitation, outdoor recreation opportunities, and sidewalk and infrastructure upgrades would all be made possible by
federal highway dollars, with additional support from the state and the City
of Boston. The Corridor's new plan called for demolition of the elevated railway (the old Orange Line) and a rerouted train line (the new Orange Line)
to run though a depressed track within the historic Penn Central right-of-
way. The Corridor's new rapid transit line would be anchored by eight new
train stations providing upgraded intercity commuter rail as well as Amtrak
service connecting Corridor-abutting neighborhoods directly to the Greater
Boston region beyond Route 128 and the wider Northeast Corridor.

In addition to these significant transportation enhancements, the
Southwest Corridor would be home to a 52-acre park offering "tennis and
basketball courts, and a bike path running the full length of the Corridor.
Children's play areas, victory gardens, amphitheaters, and extensive land-
scaping."[20] Each of these outdoor and recreational features was the result
of lengthy discussion and negotiations between Pangaro's team and area
residents. Thus these features represent not only specific planning details
but also material manifestations of public will for and investment in the
Southwest Corridor's viability and use. In short, they represent wins in
local citizens' ongoing struggle to direct the Corridor's future. No feature
would represent this more than the designation of a permanent campus for
Roxbury Community College.

Governor Sargent, the Massachusetts Legislature, and relevant state
authorities had yielded to the demands of local advocates and leaders of
the Roxbury Community College Advisory Board. The result was a sin-
gular victory in the historic fight for access to higher education for residents of Roxbury and Greater Boston: "The new $36 million Roxbury

Community College has been approved by the Commonwealth's Board of Regional Community Colleges. It will have the facilities for 3,000 students and will bring to the area new educational and economic opportunities."[21] The location of Roxbury Community College on the Southwest Corridor as an independent state college with its own governing board and president demonstrated to its supporters the efficacy of a community controlled agenda within public resource battles. David Lee recalls this moment well. Lee's involvement in the Corridor preceded its planning and design phase. He was active in the Southwest Corridor Coalition working with its executive director, Elbert Bishop, to provide technical support for the group's land planning agenda and its lead recommendation: the construction of Roxbury Community College. The coalition's hope was that the development of a state-funded public college would protect the Corridor from future highway encroachment: "It was very important to get the College designated because what that established was that once and for all, this was going to be a transit Corridor and you weren't going to have somebody come along ten years later, after everybody got tired and went away or whatever, and come back in and ram a road through."[22] With an ambitious citizen-supported planning process, the Southwest Corridor's 1970s-era development would prove nearly as action packed as the 1960s antihighway movement before it.

The organizing idea that the Southwest Corridor's development could create a new "model for urban living in the future" resulted in an innovative range of planning responses to the social and economic needs of its residents. David Lee notes the conceptual framework guiding his approach to the Corridor: "A seminal moment was when we got people to understand that this wasn't a transportation problem—this was a community development problem with a transportation component. And once you looked at it through that lens, you were able to do other kinds of things . . . All of the land uses—Roxbury Community College, Ruggles station, and later the police headquarters—were part of a land use strategy too. Because once the Corridor was established . . . we wanted to do what is now called 'transit-oriented development' or 'joint development.'"[23] This was urban planning with a point of view, not neutral, not removed from the lived experiences of everyday citizens or designed for the benefit of someone elsewhere. An integrated approach to addressing residents' needs informed the Corridor's architecture and development.

The Corridor's planners understood their task this way: "The Southwest Corridor is not seen as a city unto itself, but rather as a means of reinforcing existing communities."[24] In every sense, this new territory would serve as an integrated zone for boosting social connectivity, mobility, and economic investment for the Corridor's neighborhoods. And, critically, the public planning process for achieving these results also carried a social mandate. Echoing many of the insights of Paul Davidoff and the 1960s advocacy planners he helped inspire, the Corridor's planners viewed planning itself as a negotiated relationship: "It should be noted that progress in planning has been sustained by a partnership between city, state and citizens. This relationship must continue so that public agencies can take effective action based on reliable and realistic information."[25] This emphasis on sharing reliable information as an essential feature of better planning processes is itself a not-so-subtle recognition of planning's past practices to the contrary. By prioritizing the relationships among city and state agencies and local residents, the Corridor's planners envisioned a revised approach to large-scale urban revitalization that sought to reverse the historic trend of social and political alienation as a primary outcome. The success of the Boston Transportation Planning Review coupled with numerous on-the-ground interventions generated irrefutable contemporary evidence for the necessity of building new public planning processes based on transparency, communication, and mutual respect.

Trust

When I met Tony Pangaro at his downtown office in April 2010, I most wanted to know how he was able to build trust among neighborhood residents rightfully leery of government employees and their plans. After all, it was such employees and their plans that provoked the antihighway movement in the first place. When Pangaro was appointed by Sargent as project coordinator and lead architect of the Southwest Corridor, he seemed intuitively to understand what was at stake for residents and the state in the years following the highway's 1972 cancellation. For Pangaro, it all boiled down to listening. Careful listening and note-taking delivered a slow and steady process of civic remediation during the Corridor's planning period from 1976 to 1978. Pangaro's vision made this possible and was instrumental in creating a legitimate (and legitimately functional) public planning process. When I ask him what prior experiences or political theories helped him understand how to achieve this, he talks about respect: "If there were one word that would be the significant hallmark of what we were doing is we were trying to be very respectful of people's opinions. No comment was too insignificant; no comment was out of order in our view, as long as it was delivered to us with some kind of respect. Respect is a two-way street. So that's what we tried to do. The process had to have a lot of integrity and we were very conscious of keeping that too."[26] An ethic of respect enabled residents to hash out their differences, or sometimes maintain them, and work toward a physical solution that reflected their mutual desires. In short, the point was to lead a planning process that enabled people to listen to one another.

More than simply coordinating meetings or producing minutes, newsletters, and maps, the institutionalization of the act of public listening reveals one of Pangaro's key contributions to the two-year urban planning process that created the Southwest Corridor. Pangaro himself would likely agree with this assessment. He cites the process of carefully listening to Corridor residents and translating their wishes and concerns into public architecture as the most crucial project element for him and his staff to safeguard at all times. He explains:

> That's why we paid such attention to the minutes, why we paid so much attention to publishing what was said and trying very hard to record what was said. I reviewed and edited every set of minutes, nothing went out that I didn't see . . . it took a lot of time but after a while, you know, people get good at writing it down and recording. And we didn't cut much, but there's always—making sure somebody who said something that was significant was noted. And I think that sorta paid off because when things pass from one director to another from one agency head to another—because this thing took forever to do, right?—there was a record that people could point to and feel comfortable saying, "Well this was a commitment or that was a commitment." And, you know, a recorded history of it showed that.[27]

Minutes from the Corridor's community meetings were published within roughly ten days of each meeting. This was followed with a bimonthly Southwest Corridor newsletter and a regular circulation schedule for all drawings. Through these vehicles a vital public communication system between residents and government appointees gradually built a new civic relationship founded on trust and transparency.

Neighborhood resident Janet Hunkel reported directly to Pangaro during her seven-year tenure as Corridor community planning liaison for the South End and the nearby St. Botolph Street area. One of several community planning liaisons for the Corridor, Hunkel was tasked with ensuring that the Corridor's engineers and architects created plans reflective of the concerns and needs of local residents. Hunkel recalls the grueling process of note production for hundreds, if not thousands, of community meetings on the Corridor: "I'd write up the minutes. I could not send minutes out without Tony's [Pangaro's] approval. I don't know how Tony ever did this. I mean nobody ever slept during the entire time he was the project manager. And Tony would actually come through and . . . he would edit everything and he'd get it back to you and that was the work. And then you could send it out into the community."[28] Hundreds of evening meetings across each of the Corridor's three sections—South End, Roxbury, Jamaica Plain—were synthesized into typed meeting minutes that Pangaro personally reviewed, approved, and circulated back to neighborhoods. These minutes read like crisp mini-novellas where action is captured in brief sentences among endless characters.

In one early Jamaica Plain meeting, residents discussed the possibility of building a regulation-size baseball field on their section of the new park. During this meeting, consultant Marvin Sanders of Roy Mann Associates, lead coordinator of the Corridor's landscape architects, presented a series of drawings related to a resident-commissioned baseball feasibility study. Citing several nearby baseball fields, the high cost of retaining walls, and a poor orientation to the sun at home plate, Sanders recommends that a baseball field not be built. Once he ends his remarks, residents weigh in:

JUAN HARNETT: We need a swimming pool and skating rink in this area; the closest one to this area is at Roxbury Crossing.

DIEGO ALVARADO: The sun aspect is not a problem in either of the two baseball alternatives.

UNIDENTIFIED: Stray balls will create a safety hazard.

NATE SMITH: I would like to see a swimming and hockey facility in this area.

MARVIN SANDERS: A facility of that size would reduce the width of the Parkland, which we are trying to keep open.

AZIZ BANGEN: There could be baseball; the constraints (wall, sun, trees) don't seem to be a problem.

JUAN HARNETT: I am not condemning baseball, but we need water in the summer, and not just a spray pool.

FEMKE ROSENBAUM: We need an outdoor swimming pool.

MADELINE BRADLEY: Our water pressure is reduced because of open hydrants. We need a compromise.[29]

This meeting snapshot illustrates the iterative nature of the Corridor's public planning process as well as the documentary role of meeting minutes. Some residents agree with the landscape architect and move on to new suggestions. Others disagree with his recommendations and begin to discount his rationale. All input is recorded and attributed even if the speaker's name is not always known. The discussion of an outdoor swimming pool spins the conversation in yet another direction. A few more people offer their remarks and soon Ken Kruckemeyer, Pangaro's second in command, raises additional engineering issues to consider related to building an outdoor swimming pool. The baseball issue is not resolved by the meeting's close; however, the public transcript provides a compelling snapshot of the myriad space dramas and players vying to determine the Corridor's final form.

Pangaro cites Corridor minute keeping as key to moving the process forward in a consistent way as issues and actors changed almost daily. His professional dedication to the capture and public circulation of community commentary reveals a self-conscious effort to chart the Corridor's planning process, aid its momentum, and provide an open record for future stakeholders. Pangaro notes, "Being an architect was helpful because architects always want to build something and there's always an outcome that's more important than process—ultimately more important—but the process is what sustains the outcome and protects the outcome. And over the 30-year time frame it's essential because if you don't have a process to build on, people are very willing to say, 'Well, how we got here doesn't make sense to me.'"[30] In a way, Pangaro's leadership guided residents in the creation of a future-focused social insurance policy. Like many antihighway activists and Corridor residents, Pangaro was concerned about making the antihighway victory stick and used multiple means to try to ensure it.

By designing a strong participatory public planning process for the Southwest Corridor, Pangaro and his staff looked ahead not just to the project's completion date but also to the years of maintenance necessary for the ongoing life and function of a public landscape. Pangaro's focus on process meant that the Corridor's development was an act of cocreation between the state, local residents, and professional architects and engineers. Residents, in particular, were understood as the primary beneficiaries and stewards of this project and were treated as such.

The Corridor's planning process was designed to guarantee that residents' needs and desires were recognized as a base logic for engineering the park, nearby developments, and its mass transit system. And, most important, the Corridor's planning process was imagined as a means of cultivating residents' care and ownership for a territory that they would share for many years to come. In these ways, the Corridor's planning and construction fulfill several key goals of the antihighway movement. Antihighway activists lobbied for more progressive state-sponsored transportation planning practices, and just over twenty years later the Corridor's planning process delivered exactly that. And yet, the everyday project challenges of communication, cooperation, funding, and finding consensus among a multiracial, multiclass constituency representing nearly one-third of the city of Boston's population strained the Corridor's planning process from start to finish.

Closing the Ground—Sharing Space

When architect David Lee began attending public meetings along the Corridor, he was struck by the range and complexity of engineering, design, and social needs driving the project. Before the first portion of the Corridor Park was opened to the public in 1987, fourteen years of planning, construction, and frantic fundraising would consume its interdisciplinary team of thirty consulting firms and twenty-five neighborhood committees and task forces in collaboration with federal, state, and city agencies and thousands of residents who collectively attended an estimated one thousand community meetings.[31] One of the first major design issues to resolve was how to address the open cut of land that the Penn Central Railroad had sliced through the South End, Roxbury, and Jamaica Plain.

The Corridor's plan to bring mass transit into the heart of the city meant that an increased level of noise, exhaust, and rail traffic would greet residents whose homes flanked the tracks. Reflecting on her early years living and working next door to the railroad tracks, Janet Hunkel remembers exploring these issues in detail:

I moved to the St. Botolph neighborhood in '73 or '74 with my then partner and our house was 60 feet from the railroad tracks. I was quite horrified the first time I heard the train going through and the house was rumbling. At that time I had just started grad school for city planning. Here I had this transportation project right outside my front door. I was at BU [Boston University]. So I used it for quite a few of my class projects. This is the thing that got me really involved—not the protest because by 73–74 they had already decided not to tear down any more houses and not put the highway through. In one of my papers, I figured out that there was something like 986 trains that were going to pass every single day and everybody from the state is saying that's not true. Well it takes a student to say, "Ok, every six minutes that Orange Line train is going to come and they run from five until one or whatever. Then I got the Amtrak schedules and I got the commuter rail schedules. And I showed it to them and everybody's like, "Yeah, I guess it is gonna be like 986 trains." I found that some other people in the neighborhood and some people from the South End were concerned about it.[32]

Hunkel's graduate school research helped feed a firestorm of neighborhood opposition to the state's proposal to run mass transit through the South End in an open railway cut. As local opposition grew, area residents brainstormed persuasive tactics for convincing the Corridor's decision makers that their designs were wrong and that the South End and St. Botolph Street neighborhoods needed their portion of the railroad track to be covered with surface decking to contain excessive noise, vibration, and exhaust.

Two particular neighborhood meetings would seal the deal. Fred Salvucci describes one meeting at Ann Hershfang's house as "an ambush" and a second meeting as "clearly a set up." Salvucci and Hershfang had forged a friendship during their days as antihighway activists.[33] In recognition of this, Hershfang offered Salvucci a private audience to present her opposition to his official decision to run trains through the South End without covering the railway cut. "Ann Hershfang invites me as secretary to her house. So I go into this ambush and they said, 'We'll you've been a good ally in stopping the highway so we're not gonna organize and stop you.' And I said, 'How am I going to get the money to lower the grade and build this park over it?' This is the best fight I ever lost."[34] Salvucci would later face the public version of Hershfang's private demand. His defense that limited federal funds meant that expensive "extras" like decking to cover the

FIGURE 10. Decking construction along the Southwest Corridor. Photo looking southwest from South End to Jamaica Plain with Massachusetts Avenue intersection toward the top of the image. Source: Janet Hunkel Personal Archives, circa 1979.

train's cut literally fell on deaf ears. Ken Kruckemeyer, Tony Pangaro, and David Lee also remember attending the public meeting convened at the Harriet Tubman House. South End residents scheduled a meeting to discuss plans for the Corridor but had something else in mind entirely.

> PANGARO: In the meeting at the Harriet Tubman House, Evan Kuntz [local resident] says, "Ok, sit down we're gonna play some recordings for you! So we want you to start the meeting and we're gonna play the recordings during the meeting." And it was train squeal noise and locomotive noise for an hour and a half . . .
>
> KRUCKEMEYER: At the decibel level that was predicted if this was an open cut. So they had taken a faucet with a microphone, recorded it at exactly 87 decibels or whatever it was that was predicted by the noise study. They said, "Ok, pretend this is our living room. Heeininig [mimicking sound of train wheels]!!" When we did the noise measurements, they were in one of these units that had windows facing out onto the Corridor and the tracks at that time were immediately adjacent to that brick wall. So when a train was starting up from Back Bay station with the diesel going roarrr!! It went off the scale at 120 decibels which is the same scale that they use at the airport. It was what this was like living here.[35]

David Lee also recalls the Tubman House meeting as loud and disorienting yet highly effective in making the residents' case for a more suitable planning solution for their needs.

> We came into the room to make a presentation. They had a couple of speakers set up and they had some tape recorders and we didn't know what the heck was going on. We go to start our presentation and every once in a while, this sound would come on . . . We would start the presentation and then they'd raise the sound and then someone would say, "What did you guys say? Because I can't hear you!" And someone on the other side of the room would say looking at their meters, "Yes, but its 66 db." So it became very apparent that that wasn't going to work down there, and as a result they got a full blown deck. They were very savvy, very smart.[36]

By recording the sound of a running faucet and raising the volume up and down throughout the meeting, South Enders had removed the technical abstraction of decibel range debates and showed state officials that their chosen noise standard was unsuitable for daily life in the neighborhood (figure 10). Lee, Salvucci, Pangaro, and Kruckemeyer all laugh at the memory of this meeting and admit that it was an important early lesson and reminder of their shared commitment to public listening and all the promise, challenge, and complexity it would bring.

A few years later that same willingness to listen and partner with local residents would save Salvucci and his Southwest Corridor team from a project-halting funding gap. The Corridor was plagued by numerous early project delays due to a lack of agreement and coordination among federal agencies responsible for overseeing its progress and funding. Between 1973 and 1976, the project constantly faced cash shortfalls, often because the feds were not communicating in a timely manner. During one such emergency circa 1976, Salvucci and Pangaro were desperate to contact anyone in Washington who could address their concerns, but they had no direct personal or professional connections that could help.

> At the state level, we had Senator Edward Brooke, the only black U.S. Senator since reconstruction. Brooke was a good friend of William T. Coleman [U.S. secretary of transportation]. One of the activists from Roxbury, Marvin Gilmore, said that Brooke had roomed in his house when he was attending college. So we're meeting saying we've got this federal blockage and wondering how we are going to get it to move. And Marvin says, "I'll just call my friend Ed Brooke and see if he can help." So they set up this meeting. Somewhere I have a photo of all these community activists—Tony and me, allegedly public officials, in Senator Brooke's office in a meeting that Marvin Gilmore delivered because of his relationships. We're there with the federal highway administrator, the federal transit administrator [urban mass transit administration], and the railway administrator. And Coleman says, "You know I've never had these three guys in the same room at the same time before, but my friend Ed Brooke has a problem and we're not getting out of this office until my friend Ed Brooke is happy." And that was it.[37]

Salvucci's recognition of and deference to local black professional networks enabled a federal negotiation to proceed and bring resolution to a Corridor funding crisis (figure 11). His prior concession to South End residents' demand for deck cover had earned him trust and on-the-ground

FIGURE 11. Funding victory! Members of the Southwest Corridor Land Development Coalition convening a meeting with U.S. secretary of transportation William T. Coleman and Senator Edward W. Brooke. Massachusetts transportation secretary Fred Salvucci (2nd from right) would cite this meeting to close a Corridor funding shortfall as seminal to the project's success. Left to right: Barbara Rucker, Elbert Bishop (executive director), Senator Edward W. Brooke, state representative Mary Goode, Marvin Gilmore, Dee Primm, Secretary William T. Coleman, Ron Hafer, Emily Lloyd, Fred Salvucci, Tony Pangaro. Source: *Southwest Corridor Land Development Coalition, Inc. Newsletter*, Summer 1976, SC1, Boston Black United Front, box 14, folder 1, Roxbury Community College, Roxbury, Mass.

allies that would prove invaluable in ways that Salvucci himself could not have imagined. Describing Marvin Gilmore's successful deal brokering, he concludes: "It's better to be lucky than smart. Had we dug in our heels and said we're not gonna put the park on the roof, it's gonna be open, screw you—you had it that way 150 years. We don't have the money blah, blah, blah. We wouldn't have had the coalition with the community. It was the community coalition that delivered the money. Who could have predicted that Gilmore knew Brooke and Brooke had a relationship with Coleman or even that the three agencies were gonna drive us nuts the way they were?"[38]

A lifelong Republican, William T. Coleman was appointed transportation secretary by President Gerald R. Ford in 1975, becoming the second African American to serve in a White House Cabinet.[39] Like that of Massachusetts senator Ed Brooke, Coleman's career as a moderate Republican earned him allies on both ends of the political spectrum and a wide assortment of friends stretching from D.C. to Boston. The process of planning and constructing the Southwest Corridor would demand new alliances, new methods, and an even bolder commitment to participatory planning than Salvucci, Pangaro, Lee, and Kruckemeyer may have first realized, but they were learning quickly.

With the political commitment to deck cover and some funding concerns allayed, Lee delved further into planning the Corridor's overall look and feel. Drawing inspiration from the federal interstate highway system itself as well as the contemporary development of urban metro systems in Toronto and Washington, D.C., Lee created a set of design and construction standards for Boston that balanced aesthetic uniformity against local neighborhood appeal. "One big idea was that the system should be understandable for anybody riding, whether it was a first time or whether it was the one hundredth time you were taking the Orange Line. So I was thinking about the interstate highway system where, you know, if you miss your turn, you go up one more exit. You go up and around and it's sort of intuitive how to get back on and go on in the right direction. But Boston being a very eclectic kind of a city, we made a conscious choice that for each individual stop there should be room to reflect the neighborhood."[40] Lee's decision to bring design uniformity to the platform level of the Corridor's below-ground train stations meant that street-level innovations, including murals, mosaics, and even landscaped flora choices, could "reflect the tastes of persons who live in the immediate area."[41] The predictability of station platforms invited a sense of security for travelers who had been accustomed to riding an elevated train but were now negotiating a new subterranean geography.

While Lee was defining the design and construction standards that would unify the Corridor's development and help inform forty-seven separate construction contracts supported by thirty consulting firms, resident groups along the Corridor continued to push their own land use agendas. The official decision to create decking along the Corridor's train tracks to mitigate the unwanted effects of the new transit system ushered in a complex set of new planning dilemmas for Lee, Pangaro, and Kruckemeyer.

For the purpose of planning and construction, the coordinating team divided the Corridor into three sections to bring focused attention to the diverse set of needs defining each neighborhood it intersected: the South End, Roxbury, and Jamaica Plain (figure 12). Each section had a section planner "who played a key role in developing and maintaining an effective relationship between the project and the community."[42] The section planner and section engineer for each section also received coordination support from a team of community liaisons who served to operationalize the formal agreement signed by state officials and local organizations active in the antihighway movement. The agreement "mandated that 10% of planning and 5% of basic design contracts be used for community participation and technical assistance."[43] This provision ensured that residents received professional-grade technical support to aid the development of their visioning and planning assessments.

During the mid-1970s, Corridor neighborhoods were already experiencing social and physical changes indicative of a wider set of economic forces shaping the Greater Boston region. Corridor planners viewed these changes with the hope that the Southwest Corridor itself could deliver a stabilizing influence for communities facing further displacement in the 1970s and 1980s. Section One included the South End and St. Botolph neighborhoods, which were in the process of gentrifying. In-migrations of professional-class, young white families drawn to the neighborhood's urban character and affordable stock of mid-Victorian rowhouses brought new residents to a predominantly working-class community of black, Latino, Asian, Middle Eastern, and European ethnic groups. Section Two spanned an edge of Roxbury that had experienced "considerable disinvestment over the last quarter century."[44] Roxbury's population of low- and

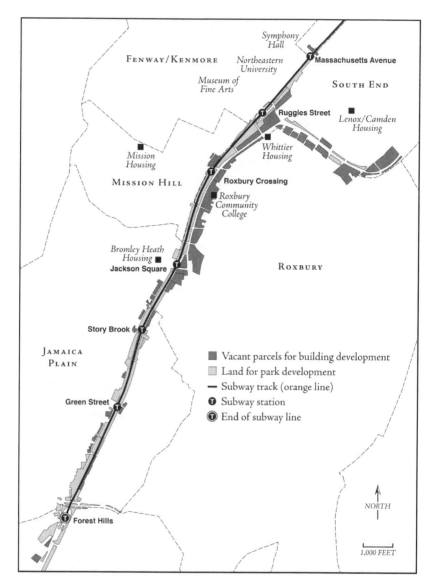

FIGURE 12. Southwest Corridor Map. Memorializing the shape of the canceled highways, the Southwest Corridor integrates mass transit, open space, and developable
land into a holistic contemporary urban plan. Map by Kate Blackmer, © 2017.

middle-income black and Latino residents had mobilized heavily to stop the encroaching highway and expected a plan that considered their current and future economic development needs.

Section Three comprised the Jamaica Plain neighborhood of largely working-class Irish Catholic families. Like the South End, this neighborhood was also showing signs of gentrification.[45] Jamaica Plain's mix of single- and double-family wood frame houses surrounded prominent medical institutions that were scaling in response to regional economic growth in the health services sector. This combination of economic pressures brought by wealthy institutions and incoming young, middle-class families meant that Jamaica Plain's longtime residents were skeptical of projects big on future promises and short on local benefits.

By removing the railroad's stone embankment and inserting decking along segments of each section of the Corridor, the Southwest Corridor planners knit together neighborhoods that had been physically separated for more than a century. Not every resident viewed this as social progress. Fred Salvucci describes the dynamic within Section One this way: "There was a big socioeconomic divide caused by the railroad break. There were through connections at [certain streets] and there were some pedestrian connections but were very dangerous places because you could get mugged if you used them and then the other streets just dead-ended."[46] The existing railroad right-of-way created a dividing line between the South End and St. Botolph neighborhoods. Though these two areas held only slightly different economic profiles, their racial and ethnic compositions could not have been more opposite. St. Botolph residents constituted a largely homogenous block of white families and some professionals working in the city. Though they themselves were city dwellers, many St. Botolph residents looked askance at the idea that deck cover would allow other urban neighbors easy access to parts of their neighborhood previously blocked by the railroad. These residents used the Corridor's public meetings to voice their opposition.

As Salvucci notes, "This distinction of the two sides was a big deal and then after the commitment that there was going to be a park and everything Ken [Kruckemeyer] and Tony [Pangaro] had to negotiate."[47] Pangaro and Kruckemeyer recall their efforts to find a solution:

PANGARO: We offered them a lot of choices. The choice I liked was that we'll put a big swinging gate and someday you'll unlock it and they said, "No, we don't want any part of it." But others were much more liberal . . .

KRUCKEMEYER: Well, actually the places that went through were the places with the overpasses—

PANGARO: That was the rule. That's right—that was the deal.

KRUCKEMEYER: If you have a connection now, you'll get in the future. If you don't have it, you won't have it unless everybody agrees. It'll be what it is today, unless everyone aggress to change it.

Pangaro and Kruckemeyer worked to resolve a design tension fraught with race and class overtones and in many ways threatening to the Southwest Corridor's planning aspirations as a unifying territory. Yet, by listening to and respecting the concerns of residents, they were able to identify an architectural strategy that was responsive to the demands of St. Botolph's residents but did not subvert the overall public planning agenda for the Corridor. In the end, Kruckemeyer and Pangaro worked with a landscape architect to develop designs for a removable fence that could be unbolted at a later date should the neighborhood change its mind. Unfortunately, the design was compromised by another decision to lay granite at the base of the fencing, and when St. Botolph's residents did, in fact, reverse their decision and requested direct access to the Corridor Park, it was no longer possible.[48]

The seeming contradiction of a connective landscape needing to reconcile itself with existing race and class divisions and residents' divergent opinions on what to do about them brought heightened intensity to the work of the Corridor's coordinating team. And, interestingly, although David Lee conceived of the Southwest Corridor Park as a linear connecting territory through the city, he did not imagine that neighbors would actually share space along its length. In fact, he says that this aspect of the Corridor's contemporary life is something that surprises him the most.

> Initially we figured, ok, we'll try to provide some open space for people at the end of their block. In Jamaica Plain, for example, this thing had been up—the embankment—and you had all these triple deckers [houses] . . . but once the clearance started, you're staring at this huge wall that's where people painted "Stop I-95, People before Highways." So we thought we could mitigate some of the starkness of that with

decking in some places but also providing open space resources at the
end of each block. We hadn't anticipated the happy outcome where people use the whole thing. They ride their bikes from one end to another.
If there's not a tennis court at the end of their block, they'll go several
other blocks to play tennis. Or people just go for walks. They don't just
limit themselves to their own little piece of it.[49]

Lee is surprised that residents share the Corridor, and I'm surprised that
this was not part of the original intent. The Corridor is not used solely by a
few nearby residents; it has its own independent ecology that bypasses the
separations between adjacent neighborhoods. It is an open territory for the
many youth, adults, residents, and visitors who crisscross it daily; yet, it is
a private sanctuary to its many abutting neighbors. And, as a connective
landscape spanning multiple racially, ethnically, and linguistically diverse
urban neighborhoods, the Corridor also represents a type of historic line
in the sand signaling the city's commitment to a demographically inclusive,
locally controlled, and coproduced modern future.

　　Two years before the Southwest Corridor Park was officially completed,
Massachusetts governor Michael S. Dukakis, Boston mayor Raymond
Flynn, officials from Northeastern University, and dozens of community
leaders hosted a press conference to celebrate their joint public commitment to create thousands of permanent jobs along the Corridor.[50] This
intergovernmental approach to land development represented a full reversal of the state's official position just twenty years prior. Standing next to
the partially completed $34 million Ruggles Street Station designed by
Stull and Lee, Dukakis was in a jubilant mood. He was eager to announce
an unprecedented agreement between the state and the City of Boston to
launch a parcel-to-parcel development program bundling downtown parcels with neighborhood parcels to create a new strategy for driving the
investment of private capital beyond the city's central business core. The
day was billed as a historic moment of progress in the development of the
Southwest Corridor, and Dukakis wanted everyone to know:

　　Had it not been for the vision and courage of so many of you, we
　　wouldn't be standing at Ruggles Street Station today. We'd be standing
　　at the interchange of the Southwest Expressway and the Inner Belt. The
　　construction of the public facilities in this Corridor is nearly at an end.
　　Commitments we made to each other a decade ago—a magnificent

transit line, a new park through the heart of this city, and a community college for the people who live in this neighborhood—have been
kept . . . The creation of new jobs, hundreds of new housing units, and
a new era of economic hope for Roxbury, Mission Hill, the South End
and Jamaica Plain is about to begin.[51]

The governor's words were both descriptive and prophetic. He charted
what was achieved—the defeat of the Southwest Expressway and its intra-
city connector—and what was hoped for—the economic revitalization of
neighborhoods long in need of it. It was 1985, and the future seemed bright
and close at hand. A new strategy of land development would succeed
where federal projects, including urban renewal and the War on Poverty,
had failed. Governor Dukakis was confident that state and local government could deliver on its promises to residents and that new jobs and
housing units would be the result. In 1985 this belief did not seem at all
far-fetched, especially in the wake of defeating a federal highway project.
However, in the end, the creation of jobs and economic opportunity along
the Southwest Corridor would prove more difficult than anyone could have
imagined on the day of Dukakis's joyous speech.

Governor Dukakis and Mayor Flynn kicked off the press event by grab-
bing shovels and planting a tree in memory of the late local activist Alice
Taylor. The signed development agreements, the governor's remarks and
the near completion of Ruggles Station would have all pleased Alice Taylor
very much. Taylor had worked as a teacher's aide at a nearby school and
served as president of the Mission Hill Tenants Organization. To each of
these pursuits, she brought an unwavering commitment to economic justice, education, and neighborhood organizing.

Taylor had also served in WWII and, like many African Americans in
the postwar period, opted to leave her home in the South for the hope of
new economic opportunities in the North. She settled in Roxbury to raise
her family and became a strong advocate for the Corridor's development.
As Tony Pangaro later recalled, without "the heart and soul" of resident
leaders such as Alice Taylor, the Southwest Corridor's development could
not have been realized.[52] She worked closely with David Lee on the design
and physical orientation of Ruggles Station. Taylor understood that this
new train station would provide her and her neighbors in the Mission
Extension Housing Development with direct access to public transporta-

tion and jobs, and she was compelled to make sure all local residents could take full advantage of both.

Taylor's leadership served as an essential counterweight to Northeastern University's early opposition to the placement of Ruggles Station next to its campus.[53] Not unlike the disagreement between South End and St. Botolph neighbors regarding pedestrian access to the Corridor, Northeastern's offi- cials were worried that "unwanted" travelers would have increased access to its campus. This worry led the university to dismiss the idea that its own student body, composed primarily of commuters, might benefit from a new rapid transit system. Despite the university's initial resistance, Taylor and her allies prevailed, and Ruggles Station was built on the backside of the univer- sity's campus, directly across the street from Mission Extension.[54] Pangaro reflects: "Alice was a wonderful woman who was a strong personality—had people in the projects who trusted her. She was a role model, grandmother. We always felt comfortable that she was not only sincere but consistent. So we began to talk to her a lot at meetings in her apartment. Her interest was really in the project. She was not afraid of the station being nearby."[55]

Today, an amphitheater bearing Alice Taylor's name marks an outdoor gathering space on the Corridor for passersby, performers, curious chil- dren, and anyone interested (figure 13). An accompanying plaque reads: "In memory of Alice Taylor in recognition of her vision for Ruggles Street Station and her dedication to her community." This memorial is a spare but elegant modern structure. Three sunken, granite semicircles provide public seating, and two large Brutalist-style columns—doing double duty as vent lines for train exhaust below—offer a corrugated, concrete back wall for the stage. Also in Taylor's honor, the Mission Extension Housing Development was later renamed the Alice Taylor Housing Development. Alice Taylor and the legacy of her successful organizing are present on the Corridor. While politicians and their staffs were essential for setting policy, securing resources, and executing legal agreements, neighbors organizing neighbors made this dream reality and challenge easy assumptions that lasting social change is achieved by any other means.

Conclusion

America's mid-twentieth-century quest to reimagine its older cities brought urban planners, government officials, and local residents into sharp public

FIGURE 13. An
outdoor amphi-
theater near
Ruggles Station
commemorates
the civic lead-
ership of local
resident, Alice
Taylor. Taylor and
her neighbors
were critical
actors in devel-
oping accessible,
modern transit
and recreational
pace for nearby
public housing
residents and
area college
students. Photo
courtesy of the
author.

debate. Ambitious plans featuring multilane, limited-access roads and new configurations of place and population introduced a bold vision of the modern city. But for whom? This single question unleashed an electrifying surge of radical activism. Like their allies in many other U.S. cities, Boston's antihighway activists rejected the idea that modern roads and displacement of longtime residents meant progress and an expansion of democratic ideals. They argued that, in fact, the opposite was true. For them, the state and federal government's zealous road-building commitment represented not an expansion but a denial of their citizenship, their right to claim ground, and their freedom. Boston's protesters and their allies attacked the base logic of government officials who suggested that highways, cars, and suburbs represented economic opportunity and social mobility for all. In so doing, these protesters exposed the multiple ways in which private cars and the public roads that carried them further limited the housing, transit, and job opportunities available to city residents.

Greater Boston's efforts to remake itself in the 1950s and 1960s through highway expansion, urban renewal, and other modern development projects attempted to build a new city on top of the presumed ruins of the old. Though this approach may have worked within abandoned cities of the ancient world, Boston's bustling midcentury metropolis was full of people who blanched at the thought of government-sponsored redevelopment projects pouring asphalt on top of them. The city was not a site of ruin to be cleared and shaken empty but a home for thousands of multiracial, working-class, poor and middle-class residents holding ground and ready to chastise a government hostile to its own democratic mandate. The actions of Boston's antihighway activists also reveal how the physical conditions of urban neighborhoods further propelled the ideological and tactical ferment of 1960s-era liberation movements. The cross-fertilization of multiple nationally scaled campaigns for justice, including the antiwar movement, the civil rights movement, and the Black Power movement, spawned new ways of thinking about power and acting upon space. Bulldozed blocks, abandoned buildings, arson attacks, illegal dumping, and wrecking balls signaled a city in a vigorous state of remaking. The ground itself became a type of political instigator, and antihighway activists tracked its meaning. They read the cautionary messages of a landscape teeming with warning signs that the city's intended future would not include the majority of its current residents. Multiple race and class-based histories entangled within shifting highway routes and municipal boundary lines had incubated a new kind of urban planning blueprint. The specificity of place-based racial politics and twentieth-century land fights had inscribed distinct cartographies within the identities and regional memories of an entire generation. The result was a battle of the century and a new urban geography sealed with the promise of a progressive democratic future.

In response to government-sponsored visions that they did not accept, Boston's antihighway activists pushed for and ultimately secured an alternative type of twentieth-century modern urbanism. Their insistence on more, not less, grassroots participation as the hallmark of Boston's revitalization meant that elite, technocratic models of professional knowledge were no longer the sole factor driving urban plans. Antihighway activists did not stand in opposition to modern technology or economic growth but rather to unbridled government-led strategies that cannibalized poor communities under the guise of securing a more productive future. Here, again, they asked, A city for whom? And instead of simply hoping for the best, radical planners, concerned neighbors, activist priests, and seasoned organizers said "no" to the state's errant decision-making apparatus and said "yes" to their own homegrown visions.

Recognizing their political agency, these activists deputized themselves as land planners, organizational strategists, and leaders of a movement to secure the survival of an inclusive and democratic modern city and their place in it. Their collective invocation of local control as a counterattack to failed governance and economic disinvestment advanced a new approach to local problem solving informed by black nationalist ideologies and not dependent on the political will of dominant institutions. Beyond a "politics of frustration" or a paradoxical refashioning of conservative appeals to states' rights, local control emerges as a productive democratic intervention during a time when one was sorely needed.[56] Intersecting 1960s-era social movements and overlapping activist networks nurtured an outpouring of resident-led solutions to address urban problems from within urban neighborhoods themselves. As a result, the 1960s and, especially, the 1970s emerge as time of creative experimentation with progressive policy, grassroots activism, and institutional forms. Ironically, just as this vital collection of grassroots strategies and ideas had matured to address many of the issues identified within the 1960s so-called urban crisis, the federal government was moving on to other, nonurban concerns. President Richard Nixon began shifting federal funding away from large-scale urban revitalization projects and toward smaller, scope-specific block grants and business entrepreneurship. Nixon's policies ushered in a new period of federal disinvestment that would leave cities to seek private capital for public projects and otherwise fend for themselves.

This book has attempted to sketch a multistream thought process of thousands of actors and the transmittal of their ideas across a metropolitan region and several decades. By documenting the hopes, emotions, and memories of a small but influential group of Boston's antihighway actors, I have aimed to bring additional insight into how a social movement was formed when its organizers chronically doubted any chance of its success. And although Boston's organizers did not lead the first or only successful American antihighway movement in the twentieth century, their contributions continue to shape federal transportation policy and local planning politics in lasting ways. Boston's antihighway organizers fingered interstate highways as material proof of government policy that had failed to put the needs of city residents before profit-seeking business interests or the convenience of suburban drivers. "People before Highways" as a mobilizing slogan and political demand made clear that grassroots coalitions expected a course correction by their local and federal leaders even as they doubted their own ability to secure it. These coalitions wrapped their demands within a myriad of examples demonstrating their vision for a more humane, democratic, and people-centered future. Maps, public demonstrations, position papers, do-it-yourself land use projects, new institutions, new organizational models, and their own memories and lived experiences delivered searing critiques of how modern city making was failing the constituencies that needed it most. The clear conclusion was that the progressive ideals of local coalitions could and should fill the void.

The Southwest Corridor is a functioning memorial both to the antihighway fight that made its existence possible and to the panoply of ideas, memories, and political strategies marshaled to make its highwayless existence permanent and an ongoing and multigenerational benefit to Boston's residents. Its basketball courts, streets, gardens, bike paths, tot lots, empty parcels, trains, and development projects are historical textbooks for understanding multiple attempts to redefine modern city making as a political, cultural, and social right for all citizens to protect for all time. Yet, despite the seismic victory of defeating a federal highway, ushering in one of the largest public construction projects in Boston's history and changing federal transportation law, many antihighway activists expressed ambivalence when I asked whether they consider the antihighway movement a success. Long quiet pauses and halting half-sentences flooded my audio recorder and further illustrated that this story is far from finished. These activists spoke longingly of the state's decades-long promise of adequate replacement service for the former elevated train on Washington Street and voiced disappointment in the pace and local impact of economic development across the Southwest Corridor. And their greatest shared frustration was that forty years later, many of the Corridor's same residents continue to struggle to hold ground in the city as they confront yet another battle, not against a federal highway but against the hastening threat of neighborhood gentrification as the region undergoes its latest wave of industrial transformation. Time will reveal the true conclusion of this narrative and whether a powerful twentieth-century urban social movement was fully able to deliver on its democratic promises.

Epilogue

J ust as transformations in Boston's regional landscape seeded a new set of grassroots politics resisting urban renewal, highway expansion, and the displacement of poor and working-class people, the creation of the Southwest Corridor Park has inspired new, coordinated responses to the challenge of land management. During the end of my fieldwork, public safety surfaced as a pressing concern for Corridor residents. My reflections here are limited in scope and time; however, contemporary users of the Southwest Corridor shed light on how this territory functions within the neighborhoods it was meant to anchor and protect.

As if running back full circle to 1970s-era fears of the safety and utility of an urban park, a series of serious crimes on the Corridor between 2008 and 2010 provoked resident discussions of personal security and the Corridor's function as public open space. From teenagers hanging out after school, to abutting working-class and well-to-do residents passing through, to police and community activists keeping a watchful eye, the Southwest Corridor holds a diverse set of users in its 52-acre embrace. More than a park and site for rail, bus, and pedestrian travel, the Corridor is a connecting point within a socially and economically splintered metropolitan region. It is a thread stretched taut by the dreams, fears, and needs of thousands of Bostonians who move across its surface every day.

As part of this study of the Corridor, I hired four young residents of Bromley Heath as research assistants. Ranging in age from sixteen to twenty-one years old, these students interviewed family members and photographed various areas along the Corridor that held meaning for them. Their field research made it possible for me to understand life on the Corridor from the direct perspective of its residents. The documentary work of these students was later featured as a formal presentation to three hundred neighborhood residents during Bromley Heath's Annual Family Day Celebration.

Finding Safety on the Corridor

Walter Lewis and Maleik Tarrant are seventeen and sixteen years old, respectively, and attend East Boston High School. They are close friends, their peers would say "boys."[1] They have grown up together in Bromley Heath. They are leading basketball players for their high school's team as well as Boston's youth league. When I asked the young men to photograph a significant place or two in their Jamaica Plain neighborhood, it came as only a mild surprise when both snapped photos of Bromley's "old side"— local shorthand for the Heath Street section of the development built in 1942—basketball court. They supplemented these photos with video footage welcoming viewers onto the court. Maleik's clip starts with a wide framing shot of blue sky pelted by wispy clouds. Panning downward, he focuses his lens on a white basketball backboard. The rim's net juts in the breeze. The camera pans low again, now to Walter, our narrator: "This is the basketball court where I grew up. This is like the second home to me. We had leagues over here. We played baseball, basketball, football—all the sports you can name here. My grandmother used to live over there, so this is where I stayed most of my time."[2] Walter squints his eyes against a blaze of afternoon sun but looks directly into the camera to describe the basketball court, his "second home." He's easy and comfortable here remembering the games played when he was younger and visits to his grandmother's Bromley Heath apartment.

The link between family, friends, and sports travels through Walter's recollections of the basketball court's physical architecture. His memories of playing with friends on Bromley's courts do not include stories of an elevated train or the stone embankment wall that once ran alongside the development because none of this existed when he was a kid. Walter was born in 1993—well after the embankment wall and elevated train were demolished, well after the highway battles reset Bromley's physical and political orientation to the rest of the city, and well after the 1989 dedication of the Southwest Corridor. This grassroots activist–produced landscape is the only one he has ever known. For Walter there is nothing notable about Bromley's basketball courts, except for the sprawling personal memories they possess.

He shows vague interest when I explain to him that the sagging condition of Bromley's older courts in the 1970s was a prime factor in convincing tenant activists to lobby the state for a new basketball court on the Southwest Corridor. These specific details do not matter so much to Walter. What does matter is that this landscape evokes many stories of his young life. For Walter the court is an important historical object of his childhood and adolescence in Bromley. It is familiar, nurturing, and a source of pride, a place where "he stayed most of his time." When Walter's photo of the court is shown on a video screen during Bromley Heath's Family Day event in 2010, the crowd erupts in a loud cheer of recognition. Walter's description of "a legendary court right here" triggers ripples of excited side conversations across the audience. Middle-aged men and women laugh into each other's ears and clasp their hands in revelry of their shared memories of Bromley's recent past.

Like me, some of these viewers know how this basketball court helped define Bromley's 1970s-era open space and recreation needs. The "old side" basketball court near Heath Street was well loved and well used but barely met the constant demand of Bromley's dedicated ball-playing crews. When Bromley's resident leaders sat at the table with the Southwest Corridor's planners to negotiate the use and design for vacant land abutting Bromley, a new basketball court sat at the top of their priority list. The Corridor's planners turned this priority into a blueprint, but there was one problem: the plan allowed for only a half-court. David Worrell, Bromley's deputy director, recalls the discrepancy.

> The basketball court in our opinion was not correct. In other words, you don't do all this work and then give us a little rinky-dinky half-court basketball court, which is what they did. So originally, they gave us a basketball court that was like this [gestures on map], it went across and was too small. What you see out there is the largest outdoor court

in the city—probably. When we got through working with them and letting them know how dissatisfied we were, we came up with the new plan. That basketball court out there is 94 feet long—that's the size of an indoor court. Most of your outdoor courts are only 84 feet. So not only do we have a very good size court, but we have lighting on the court and the community has control of that which is good.[3]

For Worrell and Bromley's residents, a ninety-four-foot basketball court was an important victory not only because of the social benefit of expanded recreation space for park users but also because of the political significance of a formal planning concession intended to meet the needs of public housing residents. With the negotiation of a regulation-length outdoor basketball court, Bromley's residents asserted themselves not just as users of the Southwest Corridor Park but also as its planners and stewards. These residents were instrumental in leading the public message that the Corridor's land was for the benefit and enjoyment of Bromley's residents and all of Boston.

Walter and Maleik talked to me repeatedly about Bromley's citywide basketball tournaments and how important the courts were to them and their friends. I walked the courts myself one afternoon, hoping to somehow conjure the many scenes that Walter and Maleik had described. I did not see much aside from a couple of scruffy courts and a few trash-talking teenagers trying to dunk on each other. The teens laughed, bounced the ball in elaborate patterns (to avoid a muddy puddle under the basket), and seemed generally lost in after-school euphoria. As I listened to their funny taunts and eyed their half-open backpacks lying near the baseline, it became obvious to me why this place was so important for these kids and Walter and Maleik, too. It was a safe, secure, and fun spot for city kids to be carefree, at ease, and away from the annoyance of supervising adults. So there I was courtside at a ninety-four-foot sanctuary for kids teasing their friends, avoiding homework, sweating in the afternoon sun, and generally just being kids. How vital and necessary for all kids to have neighborhood places just like this. Now that I had finally spied some of the magic of Bromley's basketball court, I was ready to discuss my field observations with Walter and Maleik. Nothing could have prepared any of us for the news we received on May 8, 2010. A middle school student was shot and killed on the court in broad daylight.

Jaewon Martin stopped by the basketball court to say hello to a friend before buying a Mother's Day card for his grandmother. An unknown assailant opened fire, and Jaewon was shot at center court. He was fourteen years old. Three days later, I approached Bromley's beloved basketball court with slow, deep breaths and a speeding heart rate. I see two people quietly standing at the court's center. Adorned with tall votive candles, stuffed animals, flowers, and duct-taped notes, the court has been refashioned as a memorial to Jaewon.

When the story first broke, I contacted each of the four young people working with me. All said they were okay. But how okay can you really be after a murder happens in your neighborhood? In such a community as Bromley, which has endured more than its share of homicides, each new violent death is a fresh reminder of every one that preceded it. A young woman standing next to me leans over and adds a note to the message-crammed poster board taped to the ground. She reads a few other notes, takes a photo with her cell phone, then leaves. A young man comes over next. He removes his fitted cap and silently crouches down at the edge of the circle. I'm stunned by this scene and the quiet reverence it exacts from a steady stream of teenage visitors. On most sunny afternoons this basketball court hosts chatty, even boisterous, young dunkers, but today its function is solemn. Today the court is a gathering place for reflection and remembrance. Friends of Jaewon pen notes of "I love you," "I miss you," "RIP." Bromley's director of programs, Jacque Furtado, tells a reporter, "It may look like a shrine to us, but it's more than that . . . It's a place where they can go back and probably talk to Jaewon."[4] A shrine at center court. Just a few days prior, Walter and Maleik were snapping photos here.

A fourteen-year-old middle school student on the honor roll killed while traveling through a neighborhood to buy a Mother's Day card for his grandmother was a crime headline few could ignore.[5] The city's media outlets belched shock and grief. Statements from the governor, the mayor, the police commissioner, and local ministers condemned the violence and spewed outrage at the loss of such a "good" kid. These statements and a flurry of newspaper stories offered a grim yet familiar urban choreography charting youth homicides: police tape is tied across a murder scene, journalists interview people who knew the victim, the mayor arrives at the family's home. Each of these actions was known to Southwest Corridor residents because Jaewon was not the first teenager killed in the park.

On April 21, 2008, Luis Troncoso was killed one subway stop away from Bromley Heath on a basketball court near Stony Brook train station. He was shot in the head in the early afternoon while horrified children and neighbors watched helplessly. Paramedics were summoned, but Troncoso did not survive his injuries; he died at the age of twenty.[6] The year before, thirteen-year-old Luis Gerena had been approached by two young men demanding his cell phone. When he hesitated they stabbed him repeatedly. Gerena took off running toward Jackson Square train station and collapsed just before reaching the station's door. Each of these murders sent a loud clap of anguish and anxiety across the city. And because Luis Troncoso, Luis Gerena, and Jaewon Martin were assaulted on the Southwest Corridor, public land under the jurisdiction of the state, the investigation of their deaths received high levels of police and media attention. For many teenagers and especially young men of color, the Corridor signals a menacing and dangerous place. Youth-on-youth crime has marked this landscape with a kind of death-dealing uncertainty that demands public attention. Following Jaewon's death, increased police presence on the Corridor Park represented a familiar proxy for public attention.

Janet Hunkel is president of the Southwest Corridor Parkland Management Advisory Committee (PMAC), a multistakeholder volunteer body that convenes representatives of the major institutions along the Corridor, state and local park managers, and relevant public and private security personnel. Having served as a community liaison during the Corridor's planning and development, Hunkel knows this landscape inside and out. She keeps close watch on the Corridor Park's public safety and considers that a central part of her job as head of the Parkland Committee. "I became the president about a year and a half ago, and I really did not want to do it because I really didn't have the time. But I said ok, I'll do it. I had one issue and one issue only, and that was security. Because if the park isn't safe, it's not a park; people won't go to it."[7] Under Hunkel's leadership, increased public safety has been the impetus for improving communication and coordination among a wide range of Corridor stakeholders. The unique set of historical circumstances and actors that led to the creation of the Southwest Corridor Park define who is responsible for managing the park today.

The Massachusetts Department of Public Works first began acquiring land along the Corridor in 1965–66. Although some land and housing were eventually returned to private individuals when the interstate highway plan was canceled, the state emerged as the Corridor's primary landlord. As a result, state police patrol the Corridor. And because dozens of city streets intersect the Corridor's fifty-two-acre strip, Boston's district police also patrol several segments within the park.

The issue of who protects the Corridor landscape is further complicated by the nearby presence of public housing, university, and transit police. Hunkel believes a focus on public safety has been vital for increasing the participation of police in the Parkland Management Advisory Committee's meetings. "Bromley Heath at Jackson Square is a real hotspot . . . that's where last May a kid—Jaewon Martin—was killed, and I think that's why the state police took increased interest."[8] According to Hunkel, state police officers increased their participation in the Parkland Committee's meetings in 2010, though she said it was unclear whether Jaewon Martin's death had inspired the uptick in meeting attendance or whether recent media scrutiny of state police details had prompted new public assignments. What drove state police to become more active in committee meetings may not have been clear; what was clear was that their presence raised the relevance of the committee's work for everyone involved, including Hunkel.

Parkland Committee meetings typically begin with police reports. State police, Boston police, and, if they are present, public housing, public transit, and nearby campus police discuss reported crime incidents within the Corridor's footprint and immediate perimeter. A series of reports on recent bike thefts and a robbery at a local convenience store fills the first half of one meeting and prompts a lively discussion among several officers who have been patrolling the Corridor for many years. One state officer remarked, "I think the Corridor has actually become quiet in the twenty-five years since I've come on as metro police. We used to have shootings here every night. The kids would shoot and all of a sudden march beyond us and start shooting. It was crazy in '87, '88, '89." His comment sparks agreement from a Boston police officer sitting across the room: "We used to get a lot of purse snatchings too, and now it's not as bad as it used to be." This exchange does not follow the agenda, it's personal and almost nostalgic. The Corridor's early days are conjured as a time of unprecedented crime and newness. Two other officers offer memories of what the Corridor was like when it first opened in 1989, and each concludes that "crime has come down a lot."[9] This dialogue is strangely wistful—there is a rush of excitement as the officers share a string of gang names, offenses, and street chases. These observations remind everyone that things could be much worse.

An officer asks Hunkel whether she agrees that crime on the Corridor has decreased. She responds, "Last year in the spring we were all commenting on how there hadn't been any crime in the Corridor, and then a fourteen-year-old kid was killed on the basketball court."[10] Hunkel's sobering reply tempers the officers' sense of self-congratulation. But the officer fires back, "But you're always going to get those; we live in a city—there's no way to really stop that."[11] Here another pivotal question presents itself: Can violent crime on the Corridor be stopped, or is this just a taken-for-granted aspect of life in the city?

The murders of Jaewon Martin, Luis Troncoso, and Luis Gerena puncture the celebratory lore surrounding the Corridor's history and demand a moral reckoning. The deaths of these young men also reveal the limits of police protection. By almost all accounts, the Southwest Corridor, with its multiple police jurisdictions and several layers of paid security, is one of the most heavily guarded areas in the city of Boston.[12] Yet despite its roster of security personnel, young people are not always safe here. In the years since the Corridor Park's 1989 dedication, some of the neighbor-to-neighbor trust, connection, and communication that first mobilized highway protesters and made the Corridor itself possible seems to have withered.

When I returned more than a year later for a fall meeting of the Parkland Committee, the group was discussing whether surveillance cameras were the best way to ensure the safety of people on the Corridor. The debate ranged from brainstorming where cameras should be placed to whether they should be Web-based to enable direct access by all officers (including the transit police) to a forthright evaluation of the relationship between police officers and public housing residents. Jerry Smart, a Boston police officer assigned to District E-13 in Jamaica Plain, and David Worrell discussed Corridor safety in its barest terms. When Hunkel asks Smart what might be done to improve the barriers between officers and residents, he sighs resignation: "I wish I had the answer. You know we've tried many things. It's kind of cyclical sometimes. You get a group and they start working, but that's not the only answer; it's multipronged, but getting people to talk [is key] because we'll respond."[13]

Officer Smart pushes the meeting's safety discussion even further: "Yes, very close families have lived [in Alice Taylor] for years. There's a lot of good happening there, but there's still a lot of fear. So when things happen, they're not as outward talking to police as we would like it, but we understand why."[14] For Smart, residents' fear of criminal activity in their neighborhood, coupled with their fear of the police, makes his job a challenge. His observations refocus attention to the needs and challenges of residents living on the Corridor.

David Worrell adds his own reflections:

> Yes, I think there are a lot of good things that happen in a lot of these communities, especially around the Corridor. But I know, speaking for Bromley Heath, to me there seems to be a consistent path that it seems to be going on and it's a backwards path . . . It is a big deal when you have residents that are afraid to come out of their apartments, and we have to work on a way for them to be able to communicate with the police. Because their biggest concern is, "I don't want anyone really to know that I'm talking to anybody." We have shootings in some areas. But for Bromley Heath, really over the last ten years, in my opinion, [crime] has been really kind of mild . . . So I think that somehow, like Mr. Smart was saying, that there are barriers that we have to break down.[15]

Worrell's comments specifically challenge state and local police to consider less obtrusive ways of communicating with neighborhood residents. He cites loud radio broadcasts in parked patrol cars and showy displays of force when there are no reported crimes as alienating to residents who might otherwise be a source of police information and local cooperation. Worrell highlights the fears that Bromley's residents harbor against the police as well as some of their neighbors. These fears are amplified by individual residents' worry that someone in the development will "know that I'm talking" to someone, namely, a law enforcement officer.

This growing set of fears among residents also drives Worrell's concern that if the situation is not addressed, it will get worse. He's worried about increased crime levels as well as the communication impasse between Corridor residents and police that will likely lead to more crime in the future. Young people fear other young people, adults fear young people, residents fear police and one another, and area agency staff analyze the future consequences of so much fear and poor communication. Listening to this conversation, I ask myself, How did this become the state of things on the Southwest Corridor? A landscape hailed as a cherished living memorial to the necessity of courageous resident-led politics is now battling a fear of itself. I'm confident that this is not the final chapter for the Southwest Corridor, but I do not know what it will take to make this territory a safer space for its current and future users. Yet, for the young men and women who have inherited this victorious landscape, greater safety, social support, and knowledge of past political struggles are critical for ensuring the Corridor's long-term vitality, sustainability, and relevance.

Selected Timeline

1944   Federal-Aid Highway Act authorizes 40,000-mile interstate
        highway
1948   *The Master Highway Plan for the Boston Metropolitan Area*
        released
1949   Housing Act (Title I authorizes "urban renewal" clearance)
1954   *Brown v. Board of Education*
1956   Federal-Aid Highway Act
1966   Highway clearance begins in Boston
1966   Cambridge residents rally to protest highways at State House
        (Governor Volpe)
1969   "People before Highways Day" protest at State House
        (Governor Sargent)
1969   Sargent convenes special task force on transportation
1970   Sargent calls highway moratorium
1972   Highway plan canceled
1973   Boston Transportation Planning Review releases final report
1973   Federal-Aid Highway Act authorizes "interstate transfer
        provision"
1979   Construction begins on Southwest Corridor
1987   Orange Line and Southwest Corridor Park dedicated

Interviews

Charles Bell
Ansti Benfield
Eliza Blanchard
Doris Bunte
Peter Calcaterra
Tom Corrigan
Jamie Demas
Michael Dukakis
Lenny Durant
Jane Ernstoff
Gloria Fox
Robert Goodman
Kelly Groomer
Floyd Hardwick
Ann Hershfang
Herb Hershfang
Nichlos Holley
Janet Hunkel
Willard Johnson
Charlotte Kahn
Mel King

Ken Kruckemeyer
David Lee
Tunney Lee
Chuck Levenstein
Robert Lewis
Jamal Nelson
Anthony Pangaro
Ronald Perry
Stephen Power
Donna Richardson
Jerry Riordan
Joe Robinson
Femke and Peter Rosenbaum
Byron Rushing
Fred Salvucci
Sarah Ann Shaw
Leroy Stoddard
Chuck Turner
Jack Wofford
David Worrell
Frank Young

Key Resources

Archives

Charles Bell Personal Archives
Ansti Benfield Personal Archives
Peter Calcaterra Personal Archives
Ann Hershfang Personal Archives
Janet Hunkel Personal Archives
Mel King Personal Archives
Ken Kruckemeyer Personal Archives
Femke and Peter Rosenbaum Personal Archives
Stull and Lee Institutional Archives
Tenant Management Corporation Institutional Archives
Jack Wofford Personal Archives
Boston Housing Authority
Bostonian Society
Boston Public Library Norman B. Leventhal Map Center
Boston Public Library Special Collections
Cambridge Historical Commission
Cambridge Historical Society
City of Boston Office of the City Clerk, Archives and Records Management
Episcopal Divinity School Library Archives
Massachusetts Historical Society
Massachusetts Transportation Library

Northeastern University Libraries, Archives and Special Collections
   Department
Roxbury Community College Library Special Collections
Schomburg Center for Research in Black Culture, New York Public
   Library
University Archives and Special Collections Department, Joseph P.
   Healey Library, University of Massachusetts–Boston

Reports

Boston Transportation Planning Review, Massachusetts Executive Office
   of Transportation and Construction, Department of Public Works,
   Massachusetts Bay Transportation Authority. *Draft Environmental
   Impact Statement.* June 1972.
Charles G. Hilgenhurst & Associates, John T. Galvin, and Anthony Pan-
   garo. *Southwest Corridor Development Plan.* Boston: Massachu-
   setts Bay Transportation Authority, 1979.
Kaiser Engineers, Inc., Fay Spofford & Thorndike, Inc., and Ray Mann
   Associates (prepared for the Massachusetts Bay Transportation
   Authority). *The Southwest Corridor Park: A New Strand in Boston's
   Emerald Necklace.* Boston: Massachusetts Bay Transportation
   Authority, 1986.
Massachusetts Bay Transportation Authority, *Eastern Massachusetts Re-
   gional Planning Project.* Boston: Massachusetts Bay Transportation
   Authority and Eastern Massachusetts Regional Planning Project,
   1968.
Massachusetts Bay Transportation Authority. Stenographic Record of
   "Public Hearing on Construction of the Southwest Corridor
   Project from South Cove to Forest Hills: (A) Transit Capital Grant
   Application (B) Highway Location and Design." July 15–16, 1976.

Publications

Altshuler, Alan A., and David Luberoff. *Mega Projects: The Changing
   Politics of Urban Public Investment.* Washington, D.C.: Brookings
   Institution Press, 2003.
Appadurai, Arjun, ed. *The Social Life of Things: Commodities in Cultural
   Perspective.* New York: Cambridge University Press, 1986.

Beauregard, Robert. *Voices of Decline: The Postwar Fate of U.S. Cities.* New York: Routledge, 2003.

Castells, Manuel. *The City and the Grassroots.* Berkeley: University of California Press, 1983.

Connery, Robert H., ed. *Urban Riots: Violence and Social Change.* New York: Vintage Books, 1969.

Davidoff, Paul. "Advocacy and Pluralism and Planning." *Journal of the American Institute of Planners* 31, no. 4 (1965): 331–38.

Dudley, Kathryn Marie. *The End of the Line: Lost Jobs, New Lives in Postindustrial America.* Chicago: University of Chicago Press, 1994.

Fabian, Johannes. *Time and the Other: How Anthropology Makes Its Object.* New York: Columbia University Press, 1983.

Gans, Herbert. *The Urban Villagers: Group and Class in the Life of Italian-Americans.* New York: Free Press, 1962.

Harvey, David. "Cartographic Identities: Geographical Knowledges under Globalization." In *Spaces of Capital: Towards a Critical Geography,* 208–33. Edinburgh: Edinburgh University Press, 2001.

Hayden, Dolores. *The Power of Place: Urban Landscapes as Public History.* Cambridge, Mass.: MIT Press, 1995.

Herman, Ellen. *The Romance of American Psychology: Political Culture in the Age of Experts.* Berkeley: University of California Press, 1995.

Hirsch, Arnold R. *Making the Second Ghetto: Race and Housing in Chicago, 1940–1960.* Chicago: Chicago University Press, 1998.

Hirsch, Arnold R., and Raymond M. Mohl, eds. *Urban Policy in Twentieth-Century America.* New Brunswick, N.J.: Rutgers University Press, 1993.

Jackson, J. B. *Landscape in Sight: Looking at America.* Edited by Helen Lefkowitz Horowitz. New Haven, Conn.: Yale University Press, 1997.

McAdam, Doug. *Political Process and the Development of Black Insurgency, 1930–1970.* Chicago: University of Chicago Press, 1999.

Medoff, Peter, and Holly Sklar. *Streets of Hope: The Fall and Rise of an Urban Neighborhood.* Boston: South End Press, 1994.

Miller, Zane L., and Bruce Tucker. *Changing Plans for America's Inner Cities: Cincinnati's Over-the-Rhine and Twentieth-Century Urbanism.* Columbus: Ohio State University Press, 1998.

Morris, Aldon D. *The Origins of the Civil Rights Movement: Black Communities Organizing for Change.* New York: Free Press, 1984.

Morris, Aldon D., and Carol McClurg Mueller, eds. *Frontiers in Social Movement Theory*. New Haven, Conn.: Yale University Press, 1992.

Thomson, Ross. *The Path to Mechanized Shoe Production in the United States*. Chapel Hill: University of North Carolina Press, 1989.

Tilly, Charles. *Explaining Social Processes*. Boulder, Colo.: Paradigm, 2008.

Tuttle, William M. *Race Riot: Chicago in the Red Summer of 1919*. New York: Atheneum, 1970.

Notes

Preface

1. Raymond Williams, *Marxism and Literature* (New York: Oxford University Press, 1977), 132.
2. Ibid., 212.
3. Ibid., 128.
4. Diana Taylor, *Archive and Repertoire: Performing Cultural Memory in the Americas* (Durham, N.C.: Duke University Press, 2003), xx.
5. Chuck Turner, interview by author, January 28, 2010.

Introduction

1. Christopher Klemek, *The Transatlantic Collapse of Urban Renewal: Postwar Urbanism from New York to Berlin* (Chicago: University of Chicago Press, 2011), 3.
2. Paul Rabinow, "A Modern Tour in Brazil," in Scott Lash and Jonathan Friedman, eds., *Modernity and Identity* (Oxford: Blackwell, 1992), 260. For an examination of international modernism's impact on postcolonial city planning in Brazil and North Africa, see also Paul Rabinow, "On the Archaeology of Late Modernity," in Paul Rabinow, *Essays on the Anthropology of Reason* (Princeton, N.J.: Princeton University Press, 1996), 59–79; and James Halston, *The Modernist City: An Anthropological Critique of Brasilia* (Chicago: University of Chicago Press, 1989).
3. Klemek, *Transatlantic Collapse of Urban Renewal*, 11.
4. Halston, *Modernist City*, 55; Klemek, *Transatlantic Collapse of Urban Renewal*, 49.
5. Samuel Zipp, *Manhattan Projects: The Rise and Fall of Urban Renewal in Cold War New York* (New York: Oxford University Press, 2010), 9.

6. For a consideration of the psychosocial effects of U.S. urban renewal disruptions, see Mindy Thompson Fullilove, *Rootshock: How Tearing Up City Neighborhoods Hurts America, and What We Can Do about It* (New York: One World/Ballantine Books, 2004), and Marc Friedman, "Grieving for a Lost Home: Psychological Costs of Relocation," in James Q. Wilson, ed., *Urban Renewal: The Record and the Controversy* (Cambridge, Mass.: MIT Press, 1966), 359–79.

7. Donald Craig Parson, *Making a Better World: Public Housing, the Red Scare, and the Direction of Modern Los Angeles* (Minneapolis: University of Minnesota Press, 2005).

8. Raymond M. Mohl, "Race and Space in the Modern City: Interstate-95 and the Black Community in Miami," in Arnold R. Hirsch and Raymond M. Mohl, eds., *Urban Policy in Twentieth-Century America* (New Brunswick, N.J.: Rutgers University Press, 1993), 100–158; Tom Lewis, "Revolt," in *Divided Highways: Building the Interstate Highways, Transforming American Life* (New York: Viking, 1997), 179–210; Dolores Hayden, "Edge Nodes," in *Building Suburbia: Greenfields and Urban Growth 1820–2000* (New York: Pantheon Books, 2003), 165–68. See also the documentary by Jim Klein and Martha Olson, *Taken for a Ride*, aired August 6, 1996, during *POV*, on PBS, distributed by New Day Films.

9. Mark H. Rose, *Interstate: Express Highway Politics, 1939–1989* (Knoxville: University of Tennessee Press, 1990); see especially chapter 5, "The Highway and the City, 1945–1955," 55–67, for a discussion of urban businessmen, planners, and politicians strategizing to use federal highway funds to revive central business districts.

10. Helen Leavitt, *Superhighway—Superhoax* (New York: Doubleday, 1970). See especially chapter 3, "Neither the Quick Nor the Dead Are Safe," 53–109.

11. Ibid., 231.

12. Mohl, "Race and Space in the Modern City"; Lewis, "Revolt"; Hayden, "Edge Nodes," 165–68. See also the film by Klein and Olson, *Taken for a Ride*.

13. Jane Jacobs, *The Death and Life of Great American Cities*, Modern Library Series ed. (New York: Random House, 1993), 149.

14. Ibid.

15. Ibid., 441.

16. Charles Cassell, quoted in Leavitt, *Superhighway—Superhoax*, 103.

17. Ibid.

18. Ibid.

19. A. B. C. Whipple, review of *Superhighway—Superhoax*, by Helen Leavitt, *New York Times*, May 17, 1970: "Hell hath few furies like a lady confronted with a highway through her living room." For a clear and balanced retrospective on Jacobs's contributions, see Thomas J. Campanella, "Jane Jacobs and the Life and Death of American Planning," *Design Observer Group*, April 25, 2011.

20. Barry Bluestone and Mary Huff Stevenson, eds., *The Boston Renaissance: Race, Space, and Economic Change in an American Metropolis* (New York: Russell Sage Foundation, 2000), 59; see also Thomas O'Connor, *The Hub: Boston Past and Present* (Boston: Northeastern University Press, 2001).

21. Thomas O'Connor, *Building a New Boston: Politics and Urban Renewal, 1950–1970* (Boston: Northeastern University Press, 1993); see also Marilynn S. Johnson, *The New Bostonians: How Immigrants Have Transformed the Metro Region since the 1960s* (Amherst: University of Massachusetts Press, 2015), and Jim Vrabel, *A People's History of the New Boston* (Amherst: University of Massachusetts Press, 2014).

22. Mae M. Ngai, *Impossible Subjects: Illegal Aliens and the Making of Modern America* (Princeton, N.J.: Princeton University Press, 2004); Mary Ting Yi Lui, *The Chinatown Trunk Mystery: Murder, Miscegenation, and Other Dangerous Encounters in Turn-of-the-Century New York City* (Princeton, N.J.: Princeton University Press, 2005).

23. Emily Cohen, Amy Mattlage, Matthew Reardon, and Chia-Hui Shen, "Housing in Chinatown: Yesterday, Today and Tomorrow" (Boston: Chinese Progressive Association and Tufts University Department of Urban and Environmental Planning, May 2007).

Chapter 1: People before Highways

1. Barbara Ackerman, *You the Mayor? The Education of a City Politician* (Dover, Mass.: Auburn House Publishing, 1989), 125–26.

2. Ibid., 117.

3. Chuck Turner, interview by author, January 28, 2010.

4. The South End Bypass, a local, not federal, highway project proposed by the City of Boston, encompasses a separate but related organizing history not fully considered here.

5. Boston Transportation Planning Review, "Southwest Corridor Issue Paper" (August 1971), Ken Kruckemeyer Personal Archives.

6. Alan Lupo, Frank Colcord, and Edmund P. Fowler, *Rites of Way: The Politics of Transportation in Boston and the U.S. City* (Boston: Little, Brown, 1971), 79. Lupo is attributed as author for the first eleven chapters and essentially all the content that I cite. Fowler wrote a couple of later chapters, as did Colcord.

7. Ansti Benfield, "Inner Belt Memories" (November 30, 1995), self-made video of conversation between Father McManus, Barbara Ackerman, Fred Salvucci, and Bill Cavalinni: "He [Volpe] pulled the thing back from the feds and [committed to] study the alternate route. We had a meeting with him at the State House, and I said to him, 'Well governor, how long will this take?' And he said, 'Oh about six weeks.' Which would take us just past the election [in 1964 possibly]. Well, we kept the dang thing going for six months. Meanwhile the whole city of Cambridge came together on this, the town and the gown as they say . . . We were gonna bring the [plan] down to Washington if the state went back to the original route that they wanted, which they did early in May."

8. Jamaica Plain's activists did not accept GBC's no-highway position and opted to leave the coalition at this time, though they would rejoin later.

9. "Greater Boston Committee on the Transportation Crisis" publicity materials, n.d., GBC File, Ken Kruckemeyer Personal Archives.

10. Brad Yoneoka, quoted in Lupo, Colcord, and Fowler, *Rites of Way*, 60.

11. Chuck Levenstein, interview by author, April 14, 2010. Chuck Levenstein helped organize SDS's Boston Peace Research and Education Project: "The issue we took on was conversion of defense industry to peaceful uses. So there were things like big cutbacks on Route 128, people were getting laid off. The Watertown arsenal was sitting there looking particularly vulnerable. So we were trying to do community organizing in those communities—Bedford, Lexington, Watertown—in order to get the engineers to push for peaceful uses of these facilities."

12. Lupo, Colcord, and Fowler, *Rites of Way*, 13.

13. Pamphlets, "An Introduction to the Boston Industrial Mission" and "Launching Boston Industrial Mission: The First Two Years," n.d., Boston Industrial Mission Archives, box 4, file 2, Episcopal Divinity School Library Archives. This group was formally known as the "Boston Industrial Mission" and took its cue from the England-based Sheffield Industrial Mission, itself an extension of the French worker-priests, who identified industrial capitalism as a type of illegitimate and morally destabilizing economic force in need of reform.

14. Susan Rosegrant and David R. Lampe, *Route 128: Lessons from Boston's High-Tech Community* (New York: Basic Books, 1992), 107.

15. Ibid.

16. AnnaLee Saxenian, *Regional Advantage: Culture and Competition in Silicon Valley and Route 128* (Cambridge, Mass.: Harvard University Press, 1994), 11.

17. Lupo, Colcord, and Fowler, *Rites of Way*, 13. See also Personal testimonials from Rt. 128 business owners, including Honeywell shareholder, n.d., Boston Industrial Mission Archives, box 5, folder "128 Forum," Episcopal Divinity School Library Archives.

18. *Notes of the BIM Programs*, n.d., Boston Industrial Mission Archives, box 1, folder 2 (By-laws and correspondence), Episcopal Divinity School Library Archives: "How do citizen groups play a positive role in technological decision-making? Transportation should provide us with clues that can be translated to other issues of technological planning."

19. Tom Corrigan, interview by author, November 13, 2013: "I had met him [Jim] earlier through his work at the Boston Industrial Mission. That's where I first met him, and then we met again then through the transportation stuff."

20. Tunney Lee, interview by author, April 21, 2010.

21. Ibid.: "In those days the state could just essentially send a letter to you that said, 'This property is now owned by the Turnpike Authority. And we will offer you the assessed valuation'—which was very low, maybe one-third of what the property was really worth, essentially there was no process."

22. Working in partnership with the Asian Community Development Corporation, Blockstein and Liu produced *A Chinatown Banquet* in 2006 to document the history and culture of Boston's Chinatown.

23. Lihbin Shiao, "Community Victory: Chinatown Stops the Hudson Street Ramp! DD Still on the Horizon," *Chinese Progressive Association Workers Center Newsletter*, January/December 1997, Chinese Progressive Association Records (M163), box 3, file 3, Archives & Special Collections Department, Northeastern University Libraries. On November 26, 1997, Chinatown residents and activists held a press conference celebrating the defeat of a new exit ramp proposal, again targeting Hudson Street. Resident organizers had successfully negotiated a detour of the ramp in response to local concern for pedestrian safety, noise and air pollution, and the general feeling that "Chinatown had already been sacrificed too many times for the convenience of other neighborhoods." Local activist pastor Thomas Lee offered these words: "It must be recognized that we (Chinese) are people too. Our quality of life has already bore the brunt of the highways many times for other neighborhoods. It is time to draw the line and say, 'no more.'" Pastor Lee's invocation of Chinatown's previous struggles against highway expansion highlights the ways in which Hudson Street's

history of state intrusions signify a key political narrative within Chinatown residents' activism.

24. Tunney Lee, interview by author, April 21, 2010.

25. Among other later pioneering planning projects, Lee served as the lead architect for "Resurrection City," a functioning settlement built on the Washington Mall as part of the Southern Christian Leadership Conference's 1968 Poor People's Campaign. See Jill Freedman, *Old News: Resurrection City* (New York: Grossman Publishers, 1970).

26. Tunney Lee, interview by author, April 21, 2010: "I had lived on Hudson Street, half of which was taken out by the turnpike and then he [Fred Salvucci] and I looked at the Cambridge route. We said, 'Whoa!'"

27. Ibid.

28. Fred Salvucci, interview by author, May 11, 2010. For a detailed account of urban renewal's clearance of the West End, see Herbert J. Gans, *The Urban Villagers: Group and Class in the Life of Italian-Americans* (New York: Free Press, 1962).

29. Lupo, Colcord, and Fowler, *Rites of Way*, 254.

30. Robert Goodman, interview by author, February 10, 2017.

31. "People before Highways: A UPA Critique of the Proposed Transportation Master Plan for Boston," quoted in Lupo, Colcord, and Fowler, *Rites of Way*, 255.

32. Massachusetts Advisory Committee to the U.S. Commission on Civil Rights and the Massachusetts Commission against Discrimination, *Route 128: Boston's Road to Segregation* (Washington: U.S. Commission on Civil Rights, 1975), 51. "The shift in emphasis from public transportation to private vehicles has been the result of suburban growth and decentralization of housing and employment. Transportation planning by public agencies has catered largely to middle- and upper-income groups, with highway construction decreasing the supply of housing available to minority groups." Here the commission quotes from Stephen Crosby's *Critique of the Recommended Highway and Transit Plan: A Report of Citizens for Better Transportation* (Boston: November 1969).

33. Northern Student Movement Summer Project Notes, 1965, Northern Student Movement Records, box 10, folder 1, Manuscripts, Archives and Rare Books Division, Schomburg Center for Research in Black Culture, New York Public Library. See also Jeanne Theoharis and Komozi Woodard, *Freedom North: Black Freedom Struggles Outside the South, 1940–1980* (New York: Palgrave Macmillan, 2003).

34. Chuck Turner, interview by author, January 28, 2010. Stokely Carmichael also referenced his notion of a Black United Front during a "Free Huey" Rally at Berkeley in 1968: "We need each other. We have to have each other for our survival! We *have* (emphasis added) to have each other, from the revolutionaries to the conservatives, a black united front is what we're about . . . [applause] . . . a black united front is what we're about." Radio recording, Pacifica Radio/UC Berkeley Social Activism Sound Recording Project/The Black Panther Party/Free Huey Rally/February 1968.

35. Clayborne Carson, *In Struggle: SNCC and the Black Awakening of the 1960s* (Cambridge, Mass.: Harvard University Press, 1981), 161–62: "The Alabama demonstrations illustrated the SNCC workers' ambivalence toward the use of protest tactics. Staff members were torn between their desire to encourage mass militancy among southern blacks and their desire to avoid actions that would disrupt ongoing projects and interfere with the development of long-range programs . . . The Alabama demonstrations which stimulated black militancy nation-wide, also led to

the launching of the Black Panther Party in the rural black belt county of Lowndes, situated between Selma and Montgomery."

36. "Carmichael Urges Negro Unity," *Bay State Banner*, August 27, 1966; Komozi Woodard, *A Nation within a Nation: Amiri Baraka (LeRoi Jones) and Black Power Politics* (Chapel Hill: University of North Carolina Press, 1999), 94: "In Boston, the United Front, including CORE and SNCC, rallied 10,000 black people at White Stadium in Roxbury. With a black nationalist flag flying at half-mast, the front presented twenty-one demands; one called for black control over Roxbury." Interestingly, Woodward traces the original idea for Black United Fronts to Dr. King and a surprise visit to activists Amiri and Amina Baraka in Newark on March 27, 1968.

37. Black United Front 21 Demands, Boston Black United Front, SC1, box 14, folder 1, Roxbury Community College Library Special Collections, Roxbury, Mass.

38. Floyd Hardwick, interview by author, March 10, 2010.

39. Ibid.

40. Minutes of Operation STOP Meeting, March 1969, GBC File, Ken Kruckemeyer Personal Archives.

Chapter 2: Battling Desires

1. Clay McShane, *Down the Asphalt Path: The Automobile and the American City* (New York: Columbia University Press, 1994); Tom Lewis, *Divided Highways: Building the Interstate Highways, Transforming American Life* (New York: Viking, 1997); Tom McCarthy, *Auto Mania: Cars, Consumers, and the Environment* (New Haven, Conn.: Yale University Press, 2007).

2. Karl Raitz, ed., *The National Road* (Baltimore, Md.: John Hopkins University Press, 1996). An earlier round of conversations on the necessity of building a "national road" from Maryland to West Virginia began in 1808 with Albert Gallatin, treasury secretary to Thomas Jefferson.

3. Lewis, *Divided Highways*, 8: "Thomas Harris MacDonald regarded road building as something more than a mere livelihood; it was a calling of higher moral purpose. 'Next to the education of the child,' he wrote, road building ranked as the 'greatest public responsibility.'" See "The Chief," 3–24.

4. Ibid., 14.

5. Dwight D. Eisenhower, *At Ease: Stories I Tell to Friends* (Garden City, N.Y.: Doubleday, 1967), 137.

6. Ibid., 157: "I wanted to go partly for a lark and partly to learn. The trip would dramatize the need for better main highways."

7. "Motor Truck Caravan to Cross Continent," *New York Times*, July 8, 1919.

8. Lieutenant Colonel Dwight D. Eisenhower, *Report On Trans-Continental Trip*, November 3, 1919, U.S. Department of Transportation, http://www.fhwa.dot.gov/infrastructure/convoy.cfm.

9. Eisenhower, *At Ease*, 166–67.

10. Charles A. Maguire & Associates, *The Master Highway Plan for the Boston Metropolitan Area* (1948), 43, prepared by Charles A. Maguire & Associates in cooperation with De Leuw, Cather and Company and J. E. Greiner Company, submitted to Robert F. Bradford, governor of the Commonwealth of Massachusetts,

by the Joint Board for the Metropolitan Master Highway Plan. Based upon a traffic survey by the Department of Public Works; Public Roads Administration, Federal Works Agency participating. Cited henceforth as MHP.

11. Boston Redevelopment Authority, U.S. Census Bureau. Boston's total population declined steadily from 1950 through 1980 until the numbers begin to stabilize and then reverse: 1950: 801,444; 1960: 697,197; 1970: 641,071; 1980: 562,994; 1990: 574,283.

12. MIIP, 6.

13. MHP, 12.

14. MHP, 43.

15. MHP, 60.

16. Ibid.

17. MHP, 45.

18. MHP, 44.

19. Ibid.

20. Fred Salvucci, interview by author, May 11, 2010.

21. Chester Hartman would later lead Harvard's Urban Field Service program, a pioneering effort to bring "advocacy planning" into traditional planning and design curriculum. See Chester Hartman, *Between Eminence and Notoriety: Four Decades of Radical Urban Planning* (Newark, N.J.: Center for Urban Policy Research, 2002).

22. Salvucci, interview.

23. Ibid.

24. In another twist of fate, the city councilor representing McManus's district, Daniel Hayes, grew sympathetic to the growing antihighway sentiment. Hayes would later become mayor of Cambridge and a critical advocate for the city's antihighway fight.

25. Ansti Benfield, "Inner Belt Memories" (November 30, 1995), self-made video of conversation between Father McManus, Barbara Ackerman, Fred Salvucci, and Bill Cavalinni. Notably, Jane Jacobs herself would cite Boston's West End as inspiring her to action—"I too had become outraged." Quoted in Hartman, *Between Eminence and Notoriety*, xiii.

26. "Committee Says People Have Inner Belt Voice Despite Loss of Veto," *Cambridge Chronicle*, October 7, 1965.

27. "Inner Belt Routes through Cambridge," *Cambridge Chronicle*, October 7, 1965.

28. "Three Alternative Routes Urged for Inner Belt," *Cambridge Chronicle*, October 21, 1965.

29. Salvucci, interview. See also June Manning Thomas, "Social Justice as Responsible Practice: Influence of Race, Ethnicity, and the Civil Rights Era," in Bishwapriya Sanyal, Lawrence J. Vale, and Christina D. Rosan, eds., *Planning Ideas that Matter: Livability, Territoriality, Governance, and Reflective Practice* (Cambridge, Mass.: MIT Press, 2012).

30. Robert Goodman, interview by author, February 10, 2017.

31. Ibid.

32. Urban Planning Aid Files, box 1, folder 1, University Archives and Special Collections Department, Joseph P. Healey Library, University of Massachusetts–Boston.

33. Jerry Riordan, interview by author, March 8, 2011.

34. Lily Geismer, *Don't Blame Us: Suburban Liberals and the Transformation of the Democratic Party* (Princeton, N.J.: Princeton University Press), 8.

35. Ann Hershfang, interview by author, February 9, 2010.

36. Goodman, interview.
37. Ibid.
38. Robert Goodman, *After the Planners* (New York: Simon and Schuster, 1971), 20.
39. Urban Planning Aid Files, box 1, folder 45, University Archives and Special Collections Department, Joseph P. Healey Library, University of Massachusetts–Boston.
40. Ibid., box 6, folder 26 (funding).
41. Riordan, interview.
42. Doug Rae, *City: Urbanism and Its End* (New Haven, Conn.: Yale University Press, 2003).
43. Ibid., 320.
44. Mel King, *Chain of Change: Struggles for Black Community Development* (Boston: South End Press, 1981).
45. Goodman, *After the Planners*, 20.
46. Urban Planning Aid Files, box 12, folder 5.
47. Goodman, *After the Planners*, 21.
48. Urban Planning Aid Files, box 12, folder 5.
49. Ibid.
50. Ibid.
51. Ibid.
52. Goodman, *After the Planners*, 174.
53. Alan Lupo, Frank Colcord, and Edmund P. Fowler, *Rites of Way: The Politics of Transportation in Boston and the U.S. City* (Boston: Little, Brown, 1971), 259.

Chapter 3: Groundwork

1. Some of this material first appeared in the Turn Signal issue of *ArchitectureBoston* 15, no. 4 (Winter 2012). All rights reserved.
2. Press Release, August 5, 1969, Boston Black United Front, SC1, box 14, folder 1, Roxbury Community College Library Special Collections, Roxbury, Mass.
3. "United Front Begins 'Operation Stop,'" *Bay State Banner*, August 6, 1969, Boston Black United Front, SC1, ibid.
4. Chuck Turner, interview by author, January 28, 2010.
5. Ibid.
6. "United Front Begins 'Operation Stop.'"
7. Tom Corrigan, interview by author, November 13, 2013. Corrigan also credits Fred Salvucci and Guy Rosmarin, who helped mobilize suburban constituencies, with influencing his decision to join GBC's leadership team.
8. Turner, interview.
9. Dudley Station in Roxbury once held a large head house containing several offices adjacent to the elevated train tracks.
10. Peniel Joseph, ed., *The Black Power Movement: Rethinking the Civil Rights–Black Power Era* (New York: Routledge, 2006), 25.
11. See also Jeanne Theoharis and Komozi Woodard, *Freedom North: Black Freedom Struggles Outside the South, 1940–1980* (New York: Palgrave Macmillan, 2003).
12. Komozi Woodard, *A Nation within a Nation: Amiri Baraka (LeRoi Jones) and Black Power Politics* (Chapel Hill: University of North Carolina Press, 1999), xiv.

13. Ibid., 71.
14. Stokely Carmichael and Charles Hamilton, *Black Power: The Politics of Liberation in America* (New York: Random House, 1967), 50: "One of the tragedies of the struggle against racism is that up to this point there has been no national organization, which could speak to the militancy of young black people in the urban ghettoes and the black-belt South. There has been only a 'civil rights' movement, whose tone of voice was adapted to an audience of middle class whites. It served as a sort of buffer zone between that audience and angry young blacks."
15. Ibid., 166.
16. Alan A. Altshuler, *The Black Demand for Participation in Large American Cities* (New York: Pegasus, 1970), 14.
17. Ibid., 15.
18. Ibid., 192.
19. Carmichael and Hamilton, *Black Power*, 156.
20. Ibid., 42–43.
21. Ibid., vi.
22. Operation STOP correspondence, n.d., Ken Kruckemeyer Personal Archives.
23. Mel King, interview by author, February 2, 2010.
24. Floyd Hardwick, interview by author, March 10, 2010.
25. Ronald Perry, interview by author, July 3, 2011.
26. Ibid.
27. When the federal surplus food program began in the 1930s, it was launched as an effort to stabilize prices for farmers by providing a mechanism for distributing food surplus. The program later refocused to address nutritional deficits for U.S. population following World War II on Truman's orders.
28. Perry, interview.
29. Ibid.
30. Minutes of the Executive Committee Meeting, May 19, 1970, GBC File, Ken Kruckemeyer Personal Archives.
31. GBC Flyer, 1969, Boston Black United Front, SC1, box 14, folder 1, Roxbury Community College Library Special Collections, Roxbury, Mass.
32. Steve Teichner, quoted in Alan Lupo, Frank Colcord, and Edmund P. Fowler, *Rites of Way: The Politics of Transportation in Boston and the U.S. City* (Boston: Little, Brown, 1971), 79.
33. Ibid., 83.
34. Ibid., 81.
35. "Synopsis of the Legislative Package filed by the Greater Boston Committee on the Transportation Crisis for the 1970 Session of the General Court," n.d., GBC File, Ken Kruckemeyer Personal Archives.
36. Ken Kruckemeyer, interview by author, April 7, 2010.
37. Ibid.
38. Ken Kruckemeyer, interview by author, April 28, 2010.
39. Ibid.
40. Ibid.
41. Ken Kruckemeyer, interview by author, April 21, 2010.
42. Testifier letter, March 7, 1970, GBC File, Ken Kruckemeyer Personal Archives.
43. Ibid.

224 | NOTES TO PAGES 97–109

44. Letter from Barbara Brandt to Ken Kruckemeyer, n.d., GBC File, Ken Kruckemeyer Personal Archives.
45. Ibid.
46. Ken Kruckemeyer Urban Affairs Committee Testimony, March 12, 1970, GBC File, Ken Kruckemeyer Personal Archives.
47. Ibid.
48. Ibid.
49. Fact Sheet for House Testifiers, n.d., GBC File, Ken Kruckemeyer Personal Archives.
50. Quoted in Lupo, Colcord, and Fowler, *Rites of Way*, 82.
51. Ken Kruckemeyer Urban Affairs Committee Testimony, March 12, 1970, GBC File, Ken Kruckemeyer Personal Archives.
52. Ibid.
53. Gloria Fox, interview by author, March 12, 2010.
54. Ibid.
55. Ibid.
56. Ibid.
57. Flyer, n.d., Boston Black United Front, SC1, box 14, folder 1, Roxbury Community College Library Special Collections, Roxbury, Mass.
58. Fox, interview.
59. Ibid.

Chapter 4: Planning for Tomorrow, Not Yesterday

1. Chuck Turner, interview by author, January 28, 2010. See also Richard A. Hogarty, "The Sargent Governorship: Leader and Legacy," *New England Journal of Public Policy* 15, no. 1 (1999): 124: "In his DPW role [as commissioner], Sargent was responsible for planning and design work on interstate expressway projects, and he led a successful effort to secure legislation eliminating local authority to veto state highway projects." While these actions are consistent with a prohighway position, Sargent's reputation as an outdoorsman and avid Cape Cod fisherman suggested environmental sympathies.
2. Sargent television transcript, WHDH broadcast, February 11, 1970.
3. Governor Francis W. Sargent, February 11, 1970, "Policy Statement of Transportation in the Boston Region," Ken Kruckemeyer Personal Archives.
4. Ibid.
5. In 1956 Volpe was appointed by President Eisenhower as the first administrator of the Federal Highway Administration (FHWA).
6. U.S. Department of Housing and Urban Development, Office of Policy Development and Research, "PD&R: A Historical Investigation at (Almost) 50: A HUD 50th Anniversary Publication," January 2016; John C. Boger, "Race and the American City: The Kerner Commission in Retrospect—An Introduction," *North Carolina Law Review* 71, no. 5 (1993): 1289–1349, http://scholarship.law.unc.edu/nclr/vol71/iss5/2.
7. Alexander von Hoffman, *Calling upon the Genius: Housing Policy in the Great Society, Part Three*, Joint Center for Housing Studies of Harvard University, March 2010.

8. For commentary on the Douglas Commission's recommendations regarding the relationship between state legislatures and local zoning decisions, see Carol R. Cohen, "The Equal Protection Clause and the Fair Housing Act: Judicial Alternatives for Exclusionary Zoning Challenges after Arlington Heights," *Boston College Environmental Affairs Legal Review* 6, no. 1 (1977): 63–98, http://lawdigitalcommons .bc.edu/ealr/vol6/iss1/8.

9. Ellen Herman, *The Romance of American Psychology: Political Culture in the Age of Experts* (Berkeley: University of California Press, 1995), 208.

10. National Advisory Commission on Civil Disorders, *Report of the National Advisory Commission on Civil Disorders* (New York: Bantam Books, 1968), x.

11. Ibid., 392.

12. Ibid., 393.

13. Ibid., 284–85. The commission recommends instead "scattered low rises" across multiple sites.

14. Ibid., 14.

15. Ibid., 236–39.

16. U.S. Department of Labor, Office of Policy Planning and Research, "The Negro Family: The Case for National Action," March 1965, 5.

17. Thomas Meehan, "Moynihan of the Moynihan Report," *New York Times*, July, 7, 1966: "At various forums around the country, such Negro civil-rights leaders as Bayard Rustin, Martin Luther King Jr., John Lewis and Floyd McKissick angrily spoke against the report. ('My major criticism of the report,' noted McKissick, 'is that it assumes that middle-class American values are the correct values for everyone in America . . . Moynihan thinks that everyone should have a family structure like his own. Moynihan also emphasizes the negative aspects of the Negroes and then seems to say that it's the individual's fault when it's the damn system that really needs changing.')"

18. U.S. Department of Labor, Office of Policy Planning and Research, "The Negro Family: The Case for National Action," March 1965, 17.

19. Herbert Gans, *The Urban Villagers: Group and Class in the Life of Italian-Americans* (New York: Free Press, 1962). Gans's classic work confronts class bias among urban renewal policymakers and provides insight into how the norms of white, middle-class urban reformers color local development policy at midcentury. Also see Gans's critique of Moynihan Report: Herbert J. Gans, "The Moynihan Report and Its Aftermaths: A Critical Analysis," *DuBois Review: Social Science Research on Race* 8, no. 2 (2011): 315–27.

20. See Christopher Klemek, Part II, "Converging Critiques of the Urban Renewal Order," in *The Transatlantic Collapse of Urban Renewal: Postwar Urbanism from New York to Berlin* (Chicago: University of Chicago Press, 2011), 92. Klemek tracks British, American, and German planners' self-critiques and notes a 1965 lecture by Julius Posener, architectural history professor, who asked a penetrating question: "Is the city dying from city planning?"

21. *Journal of the American Institute of Planners* 35, no. 2 (March 1969).

22. These titles also suggest that for this group of American planners, as for the authors of the Kerner and Moynihan Reports, the complex issue of race was reduced to signify black versus white.

23. H. Paul Friesema, "Black Control of Central Cities: The Hollow Prize," *Journal of the American Institute of Planners* 35, no. 2 (March 1969): 76.
24. Richard Langendorf, "Residential Desegregation Potential," *Journal of the American Institute of Planners* 35, no. 2 (March 1969): 90.
25. Walter W. Stafford and Joyce Ladner, "Comprehensive Planning and Racism," *Journal of the American Institute of Planners* 35, no. 2 (March 1969): 68.
26. Peter Marcuse, "Integration and the Planner," *Journal of the American Institute of Planners* 35, no. 2 (March 1969): 116.
27. Marshall Kaplan, "Advocacy and the Urban Poor," *Journal of the American Institute of Planners* 35, no. 2 (March 1969): 96.
28. Paul Davidoff, "Advocacy and Pluralism and Planning," *Journal of the American Institute of Planners* 31, no. 4 (November 1965): 333.
29. Ibid., 332.
30. Purpose and Title I of the National Environmental Policy Act of 1969, as amended.
31. See Helen Leavitt, *Superhighway—Superhoax* (New York: Doubleday, 1970), 178, for discussion of the Tennessee Highway Department's mishandling of I-40 hearing notification for Nashville residents living near Fisk University and Meharry Medical College. Also see Arnold R. Hirsch and Raymond M. Mohl, eds., *Making the Second Ghetto: Race and Housing in Chicago, 1940–1960* (Chicago: Chicago University Press, 1998), and June Manning Thomas, *Redevelopment and Race: Planning a Finer City in Postwar Detroit* (Baltimore, Md.: Johns Hopkins University Press, 1997).
32. Special thanks to Federal-Aid Program engineer Anthony DeSimone of the Department of Transportation for clarifying the relationship between these legislative acts. Anthony DeSimone, e-mail messages to author, September 12–13, 2012. See also Leavitt, *Superhighway—Superhoax*, for expansive coverage of the history of U.S. highway legislation, especially chap. 6, "Congress—Protectors of the Public Trust," and chap. 7, "A Road Test for Our Highway Program."
33. Ralph Gakenheimer, *Transportation Planning as Response to Controversy: The Boston Case* (Cambridge: MIT Press, 1976), 154–55.
34. Special thanks to Jack Wofford for highlighting this detail. Jack Wofford, e-mail message to author, March 7, 2017.
35. Alan Altshuler, MIT professor and later Massachusetts secretary of transportation (1971–75), recruited Wofford to provide leadership for the practice of participatory planning, an emerging field of study within which Altshuler had lectured and written. Wofford served as the BTPR's deputy director from 1970 to 1971. When Altshuler was named secretary of transportation in 1971, Wofford became his successor as BTPR's executive director (1971–73).
36. Gakenheimer, *Transportation Planning as Response to Controversy*, 147.
37. Jack Wofford, interview by author, April 23, 2010.
38. U.S. Department of Housing and Urban Development, "The Model Cities Program—Questions & Answers," booklet, 1969. Though this booklet focuses primarily on the OEO-administered Model Cities Program, it contains a helpful discussion of the importance and function of Community Action Programs. Antipoverty programs created through the Economic Opportunity Act of 1964 were designed to attack root causes of poverty. Existing poverty and social service agencies were labeled as part of the obstacles barring poor residents from economic opportunity. The

solution, broadly conceived, was to bypass older social service agencies that were deemed to be part of the problem of endemic poverty and instead create smaller, more nimble, resident-led portholes for resources. Federal money and resources would not be directed to municipal planning authorities or social service nonprofits but to community-based projects run by residents.

39. Wofford, interview.

40. Alan Altshuler, *The City Planning Process: A Political Analysis* (Ithaca, N.Y.: Cornell University Press, 1965), 6. See also Alan Altshuler, *The Politics of the Federal Bureaucracy* (New York: Dodd, Mead, 1968), and *Community Control: The Black Demand for Participation in Large American Cities* (New York: Pegasus, 1970).

41. Wofford, interview.

42. Ibid.

43. Ibid.

44. Ibid.

45. Alan Lupo, Frank Colcord, and Edmund P. Fowler, *Rites of Way: The Politics of Transportation in Boston and the U.S. City* (Boston: Little, Brown, 1971), 95.

46. Boston Transportation Planning Review, *Final Summary Report Study Element 2: Community Liaison and Technical Assistance*, February 1973, 1.

47. Ibid., 2.

48. Boston Transportation Planning Review, Massachusetts Executive Office of Transportation and Construction, Department of Public Works, Massachusetts Bay Transportation Authority, *Draft Environmental Impact Statement*, transmission letter, May 19, 1972.

49. Ibid., 27.

50. Gakenheimer, *Transportation Planning as Response to Controversy*, 1: "By the late 1960s, more perspective on the applications of these models had grown, perspective that suggested their role in the process be diminished . . . demand rose that public studies be exposed to more participation of community interests. The new point of view was partly a consequence of critique arising from accumulated experience with the use of the methods mentioned. It was partly a result of the social concerns generated by the activism of the late 1960s, and was very much affected too by the rise of the environmental movement . . . We call this new methodologic form an 'open study,' as named by Alan Altshuler following the Boston experience."

51. Ibid., 27.

52. This rising political visibility would play a decisive role in Sargent's 1970 gubernatorial election over Boston mayor Kevin White. Successful organizing by Boston's Ward 4 members had persuaded Mayor White—via his chief assistant and surrogate Barney Frank—to assume an antihighway position and reject the proposed South End Bypass. This victory as well as White's subsequent electoral defeat served to solidify the City of Boston's formal antihighway position. Herb Hershfang, interview by author, February 18, 2013; Stuart E. Weisberg, *Barney Frank: The Story of America's Only Left-Handed, Gay, Jewish Congressman* (Amherst: University of Massachusetts Press, 2009), 82: "Barney notes with pride his role in formulating White's transportation policy and persuading the mayor to strongly oppose the construction of destructive superhighways, such as the Southwest Expressway (I-95)."

53. Gakenheimer, *Transportation Planning as Response to Controversy*, 99. During its BTPR engagement, the GBC represented a broad range of organizations, including

units of the League of Women Voters, STOP of Roxbury, South End Project Area Committee, the Southern Suburban Transportation Committee, a few groups from the North Shore, and the Jamaica Plain Transportation Committee.

54. Ibid., 88.

55. Wofford, interview.

56. Department of Transportation Act, Declaration of Purpose and Section 4(f), signed October 15, 1966.

57. Wofford, interview, also notes the timeliness of the 1971 Supreme Court case *Citizens to Preserve Overton Park (Tennessee)*. This case set a legal standard for determining a "feasible alternative" to constructing a transportation facility through parkland. As Wofford observes, Justice Thurgood Marshall writes in his opinion: [Section 4(f)] "is a plain and explicit bar to the use of federal funds for the construction of highways through parks; only the most unusual situations are exempted."

58. Many state highway authorities had gingerly sidestepped the Department of Transportation's planning obligations. However, the stringent enforcement of NEPA's mandate later made these kinds of procedural evasions nearly impossible.

59. Wofford, interview.

60. See also *Robbins v. DPW* (1969), a land resolution case in which the Massachusetts Supreme Court unanimously ruled that the state's transfer of the Fowl Meadow to the Department of Public Works for I-95 was unlawful. The ruling declared that the state could not modify use of public land without explicit legislation permitting said change. This decision placed the Fowl Meadow back in the public domain and thereby subject to federal parkland protections.

61. Sargent statement on June 5, 1972: "The most important legal constraint is Section 4(f) of the federal Department of Transportation Act. This provision of federal law specifies that the choice between the Lynn Woods corridor and the new (Route 1) alternatives is not a pure policy decision for the state to make." "Governor's Statement on the North Shore" in Boston Transportation Planning Review, *Final Study Summary Report*, February 1973, 2.

62. Sargent television transcript, WCVB broadcast, November 30, 1972.

63. Governor Francis Sargent, Policy Statement on Transportation in the Boston Region, Nov 20, 1972, 8.

64. Gakenheimer, *Transportation Planning as Response to Controversy*, 169.

65. Fred Salvucci has commented that the movement was "more of an anti-highway than pro-transit fight." Cambridge Historical Society's "Inner Belt Symposium," April 4, 2012, Cambridge, Mass.

66. Wofford, interview.

67. Boston Transportation Planning Review, *BTPR Final Study Summary Report*, February 1973, 39.

68. Department of Transportation, "Highway History, Part V: Interstate Withdrawal-Substitution Program," http://www.fhwa.dot.gov/highwayhistory/data/page05.cfm.

69. Wofford, interview.

70. Edward Weiner, "Urban Transportation Planning in the U.S.—A Historical Overview," rev. ed. (November 1992), U.S. Department of Transportation, National Transportation Library, 42.

71. A future research study might examine the 20-plus cities that received highway substitution funds for mass transit and map their route changes against areas of

"civil disorder" as reported by the Kerner Commission. It would be interesting to note any potential correlations between urban uprisings and changes to post-1960s local and transportation planning agendas.

72. Anthony DeSimone, Department of Transportation, e-mail message to author, September 12, 2012.

Chapter 5: New Territory

1. "Sargent expected to reject Moratorium on Highways," *Boston Globe*, February 11, 1970. A reporter described Sargent's statement as a "climax to lengthy soul searching," yet, as this headline suggests, the press was unprepared for Sargent's surprise decision.

2. Governor Francis Sargent, Policy Statement on Transportation in the Boston Region, February 11, 1970, in Boston Transportation Planning Review, *BTPR Final Study Summary Report*, February 1973.

3. Governor Francis Sargent, Policy Statement on Transportation in the Boston Region, November 30, 1972, in ibid., 14.

4. Chaim M. Rosenberg, *The Great Workshop: Boston's Victorian Age* (Charleston, S.C.: Arcadia Publishing, 2004); Orra Stone, *History of Massachusetts Industries— Their Inception, Growth, and Success* (Boston: S. J. Clarke Publishing, 1930).

5. Orra Stone, *History of Massachusetts Industries—Their Inception, Growth, and Success*.

6. Barry Hadfield Rodrigue, *Tom Plant: The Making of a Franco-American Entrepreneur, 1859–1941* (New York: Garland Publishing, 1994).

7. Bromley Heath Facebook Group Thread, February 1, 2010.

8. Sam Bass Warner Jr., *Streetcar Suburbs: The Process of Growth in Boston, 1870– 1900* (Cambridge, Mass.: Harvard University Press, 1962). See chap. 4, "Selective Melting Pot," 44–66, where Warner presents an insightful discussion on how both the growth and placement of Boston's railroads had a determinative effect on the "building potential of land."

9. "$2,721,000 Jamaica Plain Housing Plan," *Boston Globe*, April 30, 1940; "Housing Board Takes Final Parcels of Land," *Boston Globe*, July 31, 1940.

10. "Badly Burned Vet Saved by 3 Men from Flaming Bed," *Boston Globe*, July 10, 1948. The article lists names and military affiliations of men who saved a fellow Bromley Heath tenant, revealing a community full of skilled neighbors.

11. The rapid outmigration of Boston's white residents between 1950 and 1990 led to a population decline of over 100,000 people, more than a 10 percent loss of the city's entire population (U.S. Census Bureau).

12. Lawrence J. Vale, "Building Selective Collectives, 1934–1954," in *From the Puritans to the Projects: Public Housing and Public Neighbors* (Cambridge, Mass.: Harvard University Press, 2000), 161–266.

13. Richard Broadman, Director, *Mission Hill and the Miracle of Boston*, 1978 (Boston: Documentary Educational Resources). This film by the legendary independent filmmaker documents Boston's early urban renewal and public housing history from the perspectives of city residents.

14. Vale, "Building Selective Collectives," 252: "By 1956, 115 nonwhite families had moved into Bromley Park, while only six such families lived next to them in Heath Street."

15. Vale, "Building Selective Collectives"; see chap. 4, "Managing Poverty and Race, 1955–1980." Vale further discusses how public housing options become ordered by race and class in the postwar period.
16. Broadman, *Mission Hill and the Miracle of Boston.*
17. Ibid.
18. Ibid. Jarrell stated, "My mother just said she had to get up and go because it's like her children had been harassed and she had herself and through this thing that was like the change, the holocaust or whatever she just said she had to do it. I know now myself that my mother could not financially do it. She did—she just got up and left."
19. Ibid.
20. Mildred Hailey's typed testimony to the Congressional Housing Subcommittee on Housing and Community Development, March 24, 1986, Bromley Heath Vertical File, Tenant Management Corporation Institutional Archives, Boston, Mass.
21. TMC "Scrapbook 1984–1988," unsigned article, Tenant Management Corporation Institutional Archives, Boston, Mass.
22. "Bromley Heath Tenant Management Corporation: A Brief History," n.d., Bromley Heath Vertical File, Tenant Management Corporation Institutional Archives. Boston, Mass.
23. David Worrell, interview by author, March 16, 2010.
24. Chuck Turner, interview by author, January 28, 2010.
25. Ibid.
26. *Southwest Corridor Land Development Coalition, Inc. Newsletter*, Summer 1976, SC1, Boston Black United Front, box 14, folder 1, Roxbury Community College Library Special Collections, Roxbury, Mass.
27. *Southwest Corridor Land Development Coalition Preliminary Report* (preface), March 27, 1972, Corridor File, Ken Kruckemeyer Personal Archives.
28. Mel King, interview by author, May 10, 2010.
29. Yawu Miller, "Luxury Condos Planned on 'New York Street,'" *Bay State Banner*, June 16, 2011.
30. Ibid.
31. Femke and Peter Rosenbaum, interview by author, March 1, 2010.
32. Ibid.
33. Leroy Stoddard, interview by author, March 2, 2011.
34. Ibid.
35. Ibid.
36. *Wake Up the Earth: Festival Views, 1979–1987*, May 1987, "What Happened This Year," Femke and Peter Rosenbaum Personal Archives.
37. Stoddard, interview.
38. Willard Johnson, interview by author, November 26, 2012.
39. Ibid. When the group learned that Boston's Urban League chapter was looking for a new executive director, CIRCLE's membership decided collectively to support Mel King as a candidate for the position. Members met with King to craft a city-wide agenda and then mobilized their professional networks to raise the visibility around his candidacy. It worked. In Johnson's words, "We got the first Black Power-oriented chapter of the Urban League in the country, but by stealth."
40. Ibid.
41. Martin Atangana, *French Investment in Colonial Cameroon: The FIDES Era, 1946–1957* (New York: Peter Lang Publishing), 2009.

42. Johnson, interview.
43. Ibid.
44. Ibid.
45. Ibid.
46. CIRCLE Inc., "Southwest Corridor Special Mobility Study," prepared for the Boston Transportation Planning Review, April 6, 1973.
47. Johnson, interview.
48. The CIRCLE study identified the mobility needs of elderly and young residents as a critical, if potentially overlooked, set of Corridor user needs to consider. The study also prioritized the area's redevelopment as an opportunity to connect the Corridor's residents with a growing concentration of well-paying employment opportunities outside Boston.
49. Johnson, interview.
50. The Commonwealth of Massachusetts Acts & Resolves 1968 (7507-0001), A01: College History, Documents Related to the founding of RCC, Roxbury Community College Archives & Special Collection College Archives, box 1, folder 1, Roxbury Community College Library Special Collections, Roxbury, Mass.
51. Letter to Roxbury Community College Advisory Board, March 1969, A01: College History, Documents Related to the founding of RCC, Roxbury Community College Archives & Special Collection College Archives, box 1, folder 2, ibid.
52. The Boston Association of Afro-American Educators, Position Paper in Regard to Community Control of Educational Institutions, March 26, 1969, ibid.
53. Letter to Kenneth Hubbard from Roger Putnam, May 27, 1969, ibid.
54. Ibid.
55. Letter to Kenneth Hubbard from Daniel H. O'Leary, June 16, 1969, ibid.
56. Letter to Theodore Chase from Kenneth Hubbard, June 18, 1969, ibid.

Chapter 6: Making Victory Stick

1. Anthony Pangaro, interview by author, April 22, 2010.
2. David Lee, interview by author, March 16, 2010.
3. Ibid.
4. Lee credits Ann Hershfang and Ken Kruckemeyer in particular for helping convince area residents to see an urban park as an appropriate land use option for the Southwest Corridor.
5. Ken Kruckemeyer, interview by author, April 28, 2010.
6. Boston's park was, however, largely modeled on Olmsted's previous work on the park system of Buffalo, New York. See Cynthia Zaitzevsky, *Frederick Law Olmsted and the Boston Park System* (Cambridge, Mass.: Belknap Press of Harvard University Press, 1982).
7. Dolores Hayden, *Redesigning the American Dream: The Future of Housing, Work, and Family Life*, 2nd ed. (New York: W. W. Norton, 2002), 43.
8. Frederick Law Olmsted, "Public Parks and the Enlargement of Towns" (address, American Social Science Association, Boston, Mass., 1870). Also quoted in Hayden, *Redesigning the American Dream*, 43.
9. Hayden, *Redesigning the American Dream*, 222.
10. Kruckemeyer, interview.

11. Ibid.

12. Michael Dukakis, interview by author, May 20, 2010. When Governor Michael Dukakis tapped Fred Salvucci as Massachusetts secretary of transportation in 1975, Salvucci moved the administration of the Southwest Corridor Project and Tony Pangaro, as its coordinator, to the Massachusetts Bay Transportation Authority to strengthen Pangaro's authority and build intra-agency ownership of the Corridor's completion.

13. Fred Salvucci, interview by author, May 11, 2010.

14. The Office of the Southwest Corridor, Executive Department, Commonwealth of Massachusetts, Southwest Corridor Development Report, Summer 1976, "Southwest Corridor Project" File, Ken Kruckemeyer Personal Archives.

15. Ibid., 1.

16. Roy Mann Associates, Inc., "New Parkland for the Southwest Corridor: An Overview," report prepared for Massachusetts Bay Transportation Authority, Southwest Corridor Project, January 1978, 1.

17. Governor Francis W. Sargent, November 30, 1972, "Policy Statement on Transportation in the Boston Region," Boston Transportation Planning Review, *Final Study Summary Report*, February 1973, 33, Ken Kruckemeyer Personal Archives.

18. Before a subsequent public project to depress Boston's Central Artery roadway (also known as "the Big Dig") would steal the distinction, the development of the Southwest Corridor stood as the largest single construction project in Boston's history. Massachusetts Bay Transportation Authority, Southwest Corridor Development Plan, Southwest Corridor Project, Fall 1979, "Southwest Corridor Project" File, Ken Kruckemeyer Personal Archives.

19. The Office of the Southwest Corridor, Executive Department, Commonwealth of Massachusetts, Southwest Corridor Development Report, Summer 1976, ibid.

20. Massachusetts Bay Transportation Authority, Southwest Corridor Development Plan, Southwest Corridor Project, Fall 1979, ibid., 5.

21. Ibid.

22. David Lee, interview.

23. Ibid.

24. Massachusetts Bay Transportation Authority, Southwest Corridor Development Plan, Southwest Corridor Project, Fall 1979, "Southwest Corridor Project" File, Ken Kruckemeyer Personal Archives.

25. The Office of the Southwest Corridor, Executive Department, Commonwealth of Massachusetts, Southwest Corridor Development Report, Summer 1976, 13, ibid.

26. Pangaro, interview.

27. Pangaro, interview.

28. Janet Hunkel, interview by author, March 25, 2011.

29. Neighborhood Committee Meeting Minutes—Section III, December 13, 1978, "Southwest Corridor Project" File, Ken Kruckemeyer Personal Archives.

30. Pangaro, interview.

31. Stull and Lee Vertical File, Stull and Lee Corporate Archives; Catherine Foster, "Subway with a Park on Top," *Christian Science Monitor*, February 24, 1989.

32. Hunkel, interview.

33. Ann Hershfang had been a prominent antihighway activist in the South End, working with her husband, Herb Hershfang, to defeat the proposed South End Bypass. She later served as Massachusetts transportation undersecretary, 1983–88.

34. Fred Salvucci, Tony Pangaro, Ken Kruckemeyer, and Tunney Lee, private Southwest Corridor walk with author, April 21, 2010.

35. Ibid.

36. David Lee, interview.

37. Salvucci, Pangaro, Kruckemeyer, and Lee, Southwest Corridor walk. Marvin Gilmore would become general manager of the Community Development Corporation of Boston, an organization whose roots were based in Willard Johnson's early conception of CIRCLE but had adopted an alternative business model. Willard Johnson, interview by author, November 26, 2012.

38. Salvucci, interview. Center for Community Economic Development Newsletter, October–November 1976, 8, Ken Kruckemeyer Personal Archives: "Last year a meeting was arranged by Senator Ed Brooke between Secretary Coleman, the [Southwest Corridor] Coalition, and representatives of the many involved federal and state agencies to discuss the problem of land cost and its effect on Corridor development plans. A major hurdle was cleared when Coleman agreed to lower the reimbursement payment for Corridor land; he was impressed by the way the state has actively tried to consider the wishes of its people in developing the Corridor."

39. William T. Coleman obituary, *New York Times,* March 31, 2017. Prior to his government service, Coleman led a prominent legal career and assisted Thurgood Marshall in the preparation of briefs for *Brown v. Board of Education.*

40. David Lee, interview.

41. Ibid.

42. Stull and Lee Vertical Files, unsigned report, "Southwest Corridor Project," Stull and Lee Corporate Archives.

43. Ibid.

44. Ibid.

45. Ibid.

46. Salvucci, Pangaro, Kruckemeyer, and Lee, Southwest Corridor walk.

47. Ibid.

48. Ibid.

49. David Lee, interview.

50. Press release from the Office of Governor Michael S. Dukakis, "Dukakis, City Enter Agreement on Southwest Corridor Development," July 31, 1985, Ken Kruckemeyer Personal Archives.

51. Ibid.

52. Pangaro, interview.

53. Ibid.

54. Antoinette Frederick, *Northeastern University, Coming of Age: The Ryder Years, 1975–1989* (Boston: Northeastern University, 1995), 198–207. Frederick acknowledges Northeastern's ambivalent and often turbulent relationship with its Mission Hill, Roxbury, and Fenway neighbors and attempts to contrast the presidency of Asa S. Knowles (1959–75) with that of her subject, Kenneth G. Ryder (1975–89). Ryder is characterized by Frederick as more conciliatory and collaborative than some Southwest Corridor meeting minutes otherwise suggest. However, the personal relationship between Ryder and Alice Taylor, which was critical to the successful development of Ruggles Station, is well documented by the author. At Taylor's request, Ryder took a tour of the Mission Extension housing development and began a lasting partnership that would result in several victories for Taylor and

| NOTES TO PAGES 191-204

her neighbors, including the later naming of the Alice Taylor Grant Program of five-year full-tuition scholarships to Northeastern for Mission Extension residents.
55. Ibid.
56. Daniel Hiram Perlstein's *Justice, Justice: School Politics and the Eclipse of Liberalism* (New York: Peter Lang, 2004) provides a compelling account of mid-1960s debates among veteran civil rights leaders struggling to identify the movement's strategic direction in the face of mounting evidence that non-violent civil disobedience, litigation, and direct action were failing to make "the system" work for black Americans. For many activists, including former SNCC chairman John Lewis, a deepening sense that the system might never heed their appeals produced a storm cloud of discussion. Bayard Rustin emerged as vocal opponent of the notion of local community control, which he dismissed as "politics of frustration" (83). Rustin reasoned that without the backing of a white progressive majority, there could be no black liberation in the United States.

Epilogue

1. A casual term of endearment for good friends.
2. Walter Lewis, interview by Maleik Tarrant, May 11, 2010.
3. David Worrell, interview by author, March 16, 2010.
4. Maria Cramer and Brian R. Ballou, "Playing Scared, a Neighborhood Reflects as Teen Killed on Court Is Mourned," *Boston Globe,* May 12, 2010.
5. Rebeca Oliveira, "Boy Shot to Death in Park," *Jamaica Plain Gazette,* May 14, 2010.
6. Dave Goodman, "Residents of Jamaica Plain Meet following Homicide in Southwest Corridor Park," *Open Media Boston,* May 2, 2008; Andy Zagastizabal, "Killing Shakes Neighborhood," *Jamaica Plain Gazette*, May 2, 2008.
7. Janet Hunkel, interview by author, March 25, 2011.
8. Ibid.
9. PMAC meeting at St. Botolph Street Housing, attended by author, July 6, 2010.
10. Ibid.
11. Ibid.
12. Boston Housing Authority Police use the Corridor as a connecting pathway to patrol Bromley Heath, Alice Taylor, Whittier Street, and Lenox Camden Housing Developments. Campus police for Northeastern University and Wentworth Institute of Technology also patrol the Corridor's edge lines.
13. PMAC meeting at Ruggles Police Headquarters, attended by author, September 7, 2011.
14. Ibid.
15. Ibid.

Index